CHEVROLET PICKUPS
1946–1972

John Gunnell

MBI Publishing Company

To my father, Albert A. Gunnell, Jr., who fostered in me, many years ago, a deep appreciation of postwar cars and trucks. Thank you, Dad, for making me an old-car lover.

First published in 1988 by MBI Publishing Company, PO Box 1, 729 Prospect Avenue, Osceola, WI 54020-0001 USA

MBI Publishing Company books are also available at discounts in bulk quantity for industrial or sales-promotional use. For details write to Special Sales Manager at Motorbooks International Wholesalers & Distributors, 729 Prospect Avenue, PO Box 1, Osceola, WI 54020-0001 USA.

Library of Congress Cataloging-in-Publication Data

Gunnell, John.
    Chevrolet pickups, 1946–1972.

        1. Chevrolet trucks—Collectors and collecting.
I. Title.
TL230.5.C45G86   1988   629.2'23   87-28335
ISBN 0-87938-282-1 (soft)

On the front cover: The classic Chevrolet pickup, a 1957 Cameo Carrier. *Jerry Heasley*

On the back cover: A shiny 1954 Chevrolet half-ton pickup, Dynasty Motors, La Habra, California. *Tim Parker*

Printed in the United States of America

Contents

Acknowledgments

One cannot put this type of book together without direct or indirect help from many people and sources. Among those that have contributed are Applegate & Applegate Photographs; Robert Hensel of All Chevy Acres; *Old Cars Weekly, Old Cars Price Guide* and *Standard Catalog of American Light-Duty Trucks 1896–1986* (Krause Publications); Elliott Kahn; Hope Emerich; The Light Commercial Vehicle Association; *Collectible Automobiles* magazine; *Special-Interest Autos* magazine; Terry V. Boyce; Jack L. Martin; The Rearview Mirror Museum; U.S. Department of Interior, Bureau of Reclamation; Chevrolet Motor Division, General Motors Corporation; Antique Truck Club of America; The American Truck Historical Society; Motors Repair Manuals; *The Pickup and Vans Spotters Guide,* by Tad Burness; George H. Dammann of Crestline Publishing Company; The Vintage Chevrolet Club of America. The author would like to thank these and others who helped make this book a reality.

Many of the photos of original or restored Chevrolet trucks in this book were taken by the author at antique car shows where the trucks were put on public display by their owners. Some trucks were identified by a window placard providing the owner's name. In other cases, no owner identification was provided. The following list gives the year, model and license plate number (if available) of pictured vehicles for which owners are identifiable. The author would like to thank these owners, and those who must remain unnamed, for putting their vintage vehicles on public display.

1946 half-ton pickup, A. Kaylor; 1946 half-ton pickup, P. George; 1947 panel delivery, August Tiedje, plate no. 21218; 1947 three-quarter-ton pickup, Ken Kutz, plate no. 38581; 1949 half-ton pickup, Bill Wendelgar, plate no. QQZ352; 1949 half-ton canopy delivery, Larry Taylor, plate no. QQ-U106; 1950 half-ton pickup, P. Bachman, plate no. R2J6E; 1950 half-ton pickup, Roland Kowalke, plate no. 6138; 1950 customized pickup, D. Beerens; 1952 half-ton panel delivery, Bob Trueax, Navy survey truck; 1953 half-ton pickup, G. Landry, plate no. B35594; 1953 half-ton pickup, Dave Tesch, plate no. 21013; 1955 customized Cameo, Art and Vivian Lenz, plate no. 41187; 1957 Cameo pickup, Del and Donna Hansen, plate no. 8762-DL; 1957 half-ton long-box pickup, Pete Scovronski, plate no. 417; 1957 sedan delivery, H. Fries; 1957 Cameo pickup, Marshall Whitt, plate no. 37966; 1954 half-ton customized pickup, Kenneth Furbur, plate no. LRN-648; 1956 half-ton panel, Clyde Horst; 1958 Apache pickup, George Crocker/Rearview Mirror Museum, plate no. VE-1058; 1963 Corvair 95 Rampside pickup, Bill Fuss, plate no. 948-796; 1966 C10 Fleetside, Scott Andrews, plate no. 2888-SA; 1971 Cheyenne Super 10 Fleetside, Bob Peer, plate no. BA12-127; 1972 Cheyenne Super 10, Ken Buttolph, plate no. AC18-106.

Introduction

Chevrolet has built light-duty trucks since 1918 although only 879 trucks of all types were made that first year. By the end of 1919, sales were up to 8,179, and the 500,000th Chevrolet truck was manufactured in 1929. By 1933, the company was America's largest truck maker and held a fifty-percent share of the market.

Chevrolet continued to lead the industry in sales after World War II. Trade magazines described 1947 as a "banner year," based on sales of 259,533 units. All records were broken in 1950, when 323,648 Chevy trucks were retailed, and this was only the beginning of the postwar boom. By 1956, cumulative sales exceeded six million. The ten-million level was achieved in 1966. Seven years later, the fifteen-millionth Chevrolet truck was assembled.

About eighty percent of the Chevrolet trucks produced through 1973—close to twelve million vehicles—were manufactured during the twenty-five or so years covered by this book. The great majority of them were light-duty pickups in the half-ton or three-quarter-ton categories. These will be the main focus here.

Several other types of light-duty trucks, such as El Caminos, Corvairs and Blazers, will also be covered in some detail. In addition, Chevy Vans, panel deliveries and Suburbans will be discussed to round out the overall picture of the Chevrolet truck collecting hobby.

Interest in older light-duty Chevrolet trucks is growing. In fact, America has generally become a nation of pickup truck lovers. New trucks outsell new cars in about sixteen states today, and this trend is growing, too. Chevrolet and Ford annually retail about one million trucks each, and most are pickups. Chevy has even predicted that its all-new, 1988 full-size pickup will see 500,000 deliveries in the model's first year. All in all, the market for light-duty trucks, old or new, is a strong one.

Interest in older pickups has followed the new-truck sales trend. Collectors—who always enjoy driving something a little bit out of the ordinary—are buying vintage trucks and getting from them much the same kind of utility value offered in new ones. In addition, certain older pickups—particularly postwar Chevys—have become (at least in the short term) excellent investments.

Two years ago, I went to the large Carlisle, Pennsylvania, swap meet and saw trailerloads of postwar Chevy trucks being brought to the cars-for-sale corral. At the time, asking prices ranging up to $7,000 seemed startling, especially for the newer 1969–72 models. Such figures no longer shock me. At an auction in Tulsa during June 1986, I watched a '72 Custom Deluxe Fleetside pickup sell for $14,250 in "real money."

This particular truck was purchased for show only. But it seems as though all postwar Chevys—even those driven everyday—are skyrocketing in value.

While the value and investment picture looks good, many light-duty truckers don't give a hoot about auction prices. They prefer buying worn-out trucks at cheap prices, and doing the restoration themselves. Some stick to 100-percent original features, while others go the modified route. In either case, they find pickups simpler to fix and easier on the pocketbook than old cars. Trucks have fewer components, and those they have are more basic. They require far less of the expensive chrome plating, and interior repairs can often be done without farming work out to professionals with $35-per-hour shop rates.

Availability of parts for older trucks is quite good. Original new-old-stock (NOS) components can still be found. Even more important, since trucks tended to have long production runs without major mechanical design changes, reproduction parts makers have found it economically feasible to remanufacture many parts. On the other hand, lots of old pickups can be found in wrecking yards picked clean of car parts years ago.

Postwar Chevrolet trucks have grown in appeal with both investment-conscious collectors and restore-and-drive-'em hobbyists. This probably has much to do with their popularity when new. The pickups, especially, were always considered good-looking and reliable vehicles. Their reputation for being well-engineered and sturdily built trucks made them the country's number-one-selling brand. When these vehicles are brought back to like-new condition, it's easy to understand why Chevrolet sold so many units for so many years.

This book has several goals. The first is to trace details on how these truck lines evolved. Another is to provide how-to information for restorers. Along the way, such things as values, clubs, parts sources, hobby activities and the modified-vehicle sport will also be discussed. In the end, what I hope to do is provide a product history, present some useful restoration tips and give you a lot of solid information about collecting older trucks.

John Gunnell, 1987

Chapter 1

Historical perspective

Before leaping into Chevrolet's postwar truck story, let's examine the overall commercial vehicle market in the era covered by this book. Understanding how the industry grew will help explain the edge that Chevrolet enjoyed over its competition in most years between 1946 and 1972.

The postwar light truck market

Following World War II, the truck industry as a whole grew into a booming business. Much of the growth was in the light-duty market segment, including trucks with payload ratings up to three-quarter-ton. In 1946, in spite of factories operating at partial capacity

The styling introduced on 1941 Chevrolet trucks, like this half-ton pickup, survived until 1947.

and labor strikes in progress at many plants, truck output in the United States hit 942,306 units, the second highest production total in history. The following year, this climbed to 1,236,703 units, an all-time record that would lead the truck makers to view their combined market as a million-unit-a-year business.

In 1947, *Automotive News* reported statistics indicating that one postwar truck was being manufactured for every two-and-a-half automobiles. Before the war, the ratio had been one truck for every four cars. This sales statistic explains why companies like Chevrolet, Ford and Dodge pulled out all stops in their efforts to rush their all-new postwar trucks to showrooms before new cars.

One reason for the bulge in the demand curve was a truck shortage caused by the war. While this shortage was being filled between 1948 and 1951, annual output of trucks from domestic factories soared to an average 1,324,000 units. In the early fifties, production tapered off, but the market still represented over one million trucks per year.

After 1947, this level could almost be taken for granted. In fact, for the era covered by this book, only 1946 (a half-year due to postwar retooling) and 1958 (a recession year) failed to achieve that magic number. By 1963, the 1.5-million-unit barrier had nearly been hit, and two million became the next goal. This was modestly surpassed in 1971, and by 1972 the annual total production for the entire industry was 2,446,807 trucks.

Strong economic conditions in the mid-fifties and throughout the sixties are one reason the truck market grew. The good times gave birth to many new, small businesses run by tradesmen who needed trucks. There was also a great increase in the number of multi-vehicle American families, with many using pickups or carryalls as their second car. In addition, new models such as luxury pickups, sport trucks, compact vans and four-wheel-drives had appeal to a wider audience. GIs serving in World War II and Korea probably used or rode in trucks overseas and became familiar with their advantages.

As the truck business grew, Chevrolet benefited more than any other manufacturer. The company was the largest truck maker in all calendar years covered by this book except 1959, 1970 and 1972. Stated another way, the first twenty-seven years of the postwar truck industry was truly Chevrolet's bow tie era.

Chevy's competition

Although Chevrolet has dominated the postwar truck market, it didn't win the battle for sales and production due to a lack of competition. In fact, the challenge from companies such as Ford, Dodge and Interna-

tional Harvester has been sharp at times. In addition, Chevrolet's own cousin—GMC—has always managed to tempt a few bow tie buyers away. Let's take a quick look at the product history of these four companies from 1946 to 1972.

Ford

In terms of calendar-year output, Ford typically ran second during this period, managing to grab the number-one rank in 1959, 1970 and 1972. Sometimes the difference in annual output has exceeded 100,000 in Chevrolet's favor. In other cases, it has been less than 4,000 trucks.

Chevy's Advance-Design postwar models beat the handsome Ford F-1 to the market by six months. Ford stressed V-8 power when buyers preferred a six, and the F-1 never became a true threat in the marketplace.

The Ford F-100 series, introduced in 1953 and now considered a classic truck line, was a stronger challenger to bow tie supremacy. After its arrival, Ford immediately climbed to within 20,000 units of Chevy's calendar-year output.

During the late-fifties, Ford made two exciting product improvements. The first was the car-based Ranchero sport pickup, an image machine that had no competition at first. The second was an all-steel fenderless pickup called the Styleside. It looked like Chevy's fancy Cameo Carrier but sold for the same price as a regular pickup, not hundreds of dollars more. Ford also gained extra sales with long-bed pickups, models that Chevrolet lacked. By the time Chevy caught up, Ford had taken first place in production.

In 1960, Chevrolet moved back to the top, but Ford was still hot on its heels. The Ford Econoline compact van was one reason that the two firms stayed neck-and-neck for a while. A good-looking line of regular Ford pickups didn't hurt either; they included the second-generation Ranchero, now on the compact Falcon platform. An I-beam front suspension, for full-size light-duties, was added in 1962.

By the mid-sixties, Chevrolet replaced its radical Corvan with a conventional-type van and reintroduced the El Camino as a mid-size truck. As a result, the production spread between the two rivals again grew in Chevrolet's favor. Chevy simply had more dealers to sell and service its products.

In 1967, the Ranchero was switched to the Fairlane chassis and became sportier and hotter. All Ford trucks gained new sports options, bigger engines and fancier interiors. To gain a bigger share of the booming RV (recreational vehicle) market, Ford introduced Camper Specials. Equally important was the 1966 Bronco, a sport utility model aimed at the off-road market pioneered by the Willys Jeep and International Scout.

With its widened market and fancy options, Ford began knocking at Chevrolet's door again by the late-sixties. Ford retook the top slot in calendar-year production during 1970, lost it in 1971 and regained first place in 1972. From that point on, the annual honors would swing back and forth much more than ever before. For the first twenty-seven years of the postwar era, however, Chevy was king and Ford was runner-up in the light-duty truck field.

Dodge

This Chrysler Corporation branch was long recognized as a builder of reliable, well-engineered commercial vehicles that held up extremely well under tough conditions. During the 1946–1972 era, the company's strongest periods were the first few and the last few years.

From 1946 to 1952, Dodge was the third largest truck maker. Between 1954 and 1967, International Harvester (and sometimes GMC) out-produced Dodge by a noticeable margin. The tides turned again in mid-1967, and Dodge soon found itself back in the truck industry's number-three slot.

Dodge's immediate postwar popularity came from its B series combined with civilian versions of the four-wheel-drive Power Wagon. But, like other Chrysler divisions, the company failed to modernize styling as quickly as larger manufacturers. When changes were made, they often amounted to little more than a facelift, or included models like the 1957 Sweptside, with its passenger-car fenders grafted on to the cargo box to make a fenderless pickup.

Collectors love these unusual models, but the public did not eat them up at the time. Nor did the public buy many trucks with Fluid Drive when other companies offered automatics. In addition, the Town Wagon of the early-sixties bore a strong resemblance to the Town Panel of the fifties. Chrysler—the number-three auto maker—simply did not have the resources or the large dealer network necessary to challenge the lead of Chevrolet and Ford.

By the mid-sixties, however, positive changes were being planned. The A-100 compact van, introduced in 1964, was the first step. It was followed in mid-1967 by the A-108 king-size van. Then came the venerable 383 cubic inch V-8 and the new-for-1968 high-styled Adventurer pickup. Before long, the company found itself back in third place for the first time in fourteen years.

From this point on, Dodge was intent on firming up its revitalization program. An all-new generation of vans

Chrome grille and bumper appear on this 1942 BK model. After World War II began, blackout style (painted) trim parts were used.

with new looks, suspension improvements and easy-to-access engine compartments was a 1970 innovation that made Dodge the nation's largest van producer. During 1972, lower and wider cabs, an independent front suspension and electronic ignition were introduced. Dodge was simply doing the things it had failed to accomplish in 1953, modernizing its products to keep abreast of the competition.

International Harvester

International Harvester trucks were known as "corn binders"; the company was among the earliest of truck makers and also manufactured farm implements. During the twenties, the popular Red Baby model was marketed through farm equipment dealers blanketing both the United States and Canada. Farmers, being big users of trucks, enjoyed buying them from their farm implement dealers. As a result, sales started climbing. For years, only Chevy and Ford out-produced IH.

After the war, the all-new 1949 KB model introduced column gearshifting and an 82 hp Green Diamond six. The Travelall, a type of heavy-duty station wagon, was also introduced. IH soon found itself competing nearly neck-and-neck with Dodge and GMC.

Unlike Dodge, the Fort Wayne, Indiana-based IH adopted new ideas rather quickly, although styling changed little. Features like wraparound windshields, 12-volt electrical systems, automatic transmissions and two-tone paint jobs were introduced in the early 1950s.

Through 1953, IH production trailed that of Dodge, while leaping back and forth with GMC for the fourth rank in the industry. But at the end of 1953 the company came in third, and was able to maintain this position in most years through 1968 (Jeep was number three in 1958 and 1960, however). Much of IH's strength was based on its heavy-duty truck line, a market segment in which it had a large impact.

In the light-duty field, stylish new Fiftieth Anniversary models were brought out in mid-1957. Added for 1959 were fenderless Bonus Load pickups with their all-steel double-wall cargo boxes offering twenty-five percent more load room. The following season saw introduction of an independent front suspension and hydraulic clutch. Also, the company's popular Metro walk-in delivery van was given a modernized boxlike appearance; and a smaller version, called the Metro-Mite, arrived with similarly modernized styling.

Coming on stream in 1961 was the Universal Scout. This was a stylized four-wheel-drive utility vehicle that sold over 28,000 units the first year. With the Scout on the market, IH no longer had to worry about losing sales to Jeep. In fact, there are hints that the company started to take its success for granted, bragging in advertisements that it didn't believe in annual model year changes.

In 1968, Dodge slipped by IH on the strength of its new king-size vans, and the corn-binder company found itself in trouble. Its response was a new 1969 pickup styled to resemble a large Scout, plus sportier options for the original Scout.

A larger, longer, lower, more luxurious Scout II made 1971 a particularly good calendar year for IH. The company built a record 185,859 trucks. By 1972, this figure climbed again, breaking the 200,000 barrier by close to 13,000 units. In addition to being IH's top year ever, however, this was also to be the firm's all-time peak season. The OPEC oil embargo would have a devastating effect on both the farm equipment and the heavy-duty truck divisions, as well as the entire four-wheel-drive industry. It was to prove a blow from which IH would never recover.

GMC

From 1927 on, GMC (General Motors Truck & Coach) was basically an assembler of trucks made of parts sourced from other General Motors divisions. These models were styled, trimmed and engineered to give a character to the products that were slightly up-market from the comparable Chevrolet offerings.

Postwar GMC models looked much like Chevrolets and used many body panels that were interchangeable with Chevys'. The GMC grille was distinctive, however, and mechanical components were of heavier-duty construction.

Since the styling of postwar Chevy trucks was well-received, the GMC trucks rode on Chevy's shirttail and became popular, too. In addition, the company was more of a force in the heavy truck market, where things sometimes worked the opposite way. That is, GMC engineered the corporation's "heavies," and a portion of those were then sold under the Chevrolet nameplate.

GMC was a smaller producer than Dodge or IH in most years before World War II. Its output nearly doubled during 1941, however, and the following season it passed Dodge and built more than three times as many trucks as IH. It enjoyed third place in calendar-year production again in 1945, then built less than one-third as many units in 1946, when both Willys and Studebaker did better.

In 1948 GMC overtook Studebaker, coming in sixth behind Chevy, Ford, Dodge, IH and Willys. The next year, it was fifth, then fourth in 1950, then fifth again in 1951 and 1952, beating Willys by just ninety-eight units in the latter season. In 1953 GMC introduced Hydra-matic transmission in light-duty models, which resulted in its passing Dodge and regaining fourth slot in calendar-year output for the season. In 1954 it dropped behind Dodge, but then moved ahead again in 1955, when the Cameo-like Suburban pickup arrived. GMC was fourth once more in 1956, this time beating Dodge by an edge of only ninety-eight trucks.

The seesawing continued, Dodge regaining fourth rank in 1957 and everything changing in 1958, when the finish order was Chevrolet, Ford, Willys, IH, GMC and Dodge.

At this time, the GMC light-duties resembled Chevrolet Task Force trucks, but used larger sixes or optional Pontiac-built V-8s. Grilles and trim were also different than those of the corresponding Chevrolets.

For 1959 the production race went to Ford, with Chevy second, IH third, Jeep fourth and GMC fifth. In 1960 a new body pushed Chevy ahead of Ford again, but could not change GMC's ranking, although total sales increased by 37,000 units. The 1961 finish order was the same, but in 1962 GMC beat Jeep, while Dodge moved ahead, making GMC fifth again. This changed to sixth in 1963 and 1964, although a new Handi-Van boosted overall production significantly. When Jeep began to falter in 1965, GMC was still going strong and took fifth rank again. Moving temporarily ahead of IH in 1968, the company dropped down to fifth the next two seasons.

Beginning in 1967, GMCs adopted the same all-new body that Chevrolet offered. In 1970 the Jimmy sport utility was introduced in two- and four-wheel-drive models. A badge-engineered El Camino-type pickup named the Sprint was new for 1971. GMC wound up fifth in the 1972 market, behind Ford, Chevy, Dodge and IH, respectively.

Some people feel that GMC hurt Chevrolet sales, and that those who preferred the General Motors styling would have purchased more Chevys if GMCs were not available. This may be true to some degree. Still, the practice of "dualing" truck lines was an overall benefit to the corporation, as it increased the number of dealers and production line capacity. In addition, this technique of marketing Chevy-like trucks with richer trim provided a product line that was just different enough to attract certain buyers who wanted to step up from Chevrolet. In addition, GMC had the big-truck reputation that Chevrolet lacked because of its strong light-duty image. Eventually, Chevrolet would totally abandon the heavy-duty market, leaving its share to GMC.

Interim models

To finish setting the stage for the story of Chevrolet's postwar years, it's necessary to touch upon what was happening in the company's factories as the fighting in Europe and Asia began to wind down. As mentioned earlier, an acute shortage of trucks had developed in the civilian sector as older models wore out and couldn't be repaired or replaced with new vehicles.

As a result, in 1945, the government permitted Chevrolet to build a limited number of certain models as a continuation of the company's 1942 line. These trucks were probably intended for sale to people in crucial occupations such as munition plant workers, doctors and civilian defense personnel.

These were called interim models; details about them will be found in the next chapter. From a historical perspective, they played an important role in keeping the manufacturing and assembly plants on "active duty" during the war years. In other words, since production was able to continue, the equipment used to make civilian trucks was kept in service.

Because of this, the return to volume production after World War II was accomplished faster for trucks than for cars. By the end of 1946, Chevrolet had already out-produced Ford by 409,880 units to 407,356 units in the 1945–1946 period. This continued in 1947, when the totals were 695,986 to 601,665 in Chevy's favor.

The momentum gained by early release of the interim models helped push Chevrolet right to the top of the sales charts. This gave the company nearly a five-percent average advantage in the market share, clear through 1951. Simply stated, Chevrolet's truck division got off on the right foot immediately after the war. It would stay in that position for nearly three decades.

Note that chapters two through six are concerned primarily with the developmental history of *conventional* Chevrolet pickups, including all full-size models and the 1972 LUV mini-pickup. Chapter seven covers other types of Chevrolet light-duty trucks, including three pickup styles—El Camino, Corvair and Blazer—and three closed-body styles—panel delivery, Suburban Carryall and foward control vans. For the sake of convenience and greater clarity, however, the specifications charts for *all* of these models appear at the back of the book.

Chapter 2

Wurlitzer Juke Boxes: 1944-1946

Even before World War II ended, Chevrolet was back selling pickups to farmers and tradesmen who'd worn out their working wheels. Because of the acute shortage of commercial vehicles that had developed by 1944, the government permitted Chevy to start offering a small line of trucks beginning in 1945.

This 1946 Chevy half-ton pickup was displayed at Hershey (the big show/swap meet in Hershey, Pennsylvania). These trucks had cab and box painted in one color and fenders in black. Plated grille and bumper were standard; chrome hubcaps were options. Right-hand windshield wiper and mirrors cost extra, too.

These included half-ton BK series pickups, those "Wurlitzer Juke Boxes" with art deco grilles that Chevrolet had brought out in 1941. These were not postwar models but a continuation of the 1942 line, with similar coding and serial numbers.

It wasn't long before the supply of these prewar trucks was also depleted, but the demand still wasn't satisfied. The American home front needed more trucks, and before long it got them.

Chevrolet's 1947 *Engineering Features Book* tells the story: "Long before the war ended, the government permitted Chevrolet to begin production of trucks for civilians on the same lines on which military vehicles were being built," wrote chief engineer John G. Wood. "Hence, when the war was won, it was not necessary to reconvert lines and continued production averted an acute truck shortage."

The light-duty trucks built with special permission of the War Production Board were known as interim models and carried CK prefixes. These, again, had the Wurlitzer appearance, along with a few minor detail changes phased in between 1942 and early 1946.

Used-car books specifically noted "they are not to be considered postwar models," but enthusiasts view them as such today. Many were originally titled as 1946 or 1947 trucks and, since the production starting date was September 1, 1945, the majority were made after Japan's formal surrender the following day. Don't you agree that this makes them postwar vehicles?

With this return to regular production, there was still no letup in the demand for postwar trucks. Buyers, in fact, were lining up at Chevrolet dealerships to place their orders. Sales and production weren't everything, however. The postwar period also brought material shortages and labor problems. Such factors teamed up to slow the release of all-new models.

The aftermarket bumper guard and grille guard arrangement of this 1946 half-ton is quite elaborate. Truck was for sale at Hershey in 1986 with an $8,000 pricetag. A sign on the truck said that it originally belonged to the owner's grandfather.

In late 1945, a United Auto Workers strike closed nearly all GM factories. The walkout lasted until March 13, 1946, and wildcat actions kept some plants from hitting full stride for up to sixty days longer. When the assembly lines got rolling again, a new series of late-1946 trucks was announced.

These were, again, characterized by the prewar Wurlitzer styling. The prefixes DP and DR identified the half- and three-quarter-ton models respectively. They remained in production until the summer of 1947.

This 1946 Series PA pickup with single windshield wiper was exhibited at Hershey. These trucks originally came with synthetic rubber blackwall tires.

Factory photo from 1946 shows clearly the location of the gas filler on the lower rear of cab. Also seen here is another factory bumper guard treatment.

General description

Chevrolet's 1941–1946 Wurlitzer Juke Box-style pickups all had the same basic styling. All of the other body styles, excluding the sedan delivery, had similar appearances. An upper grille section decorated the ship's prow nose on these trucks. It had four U-shaped horizontal moldings with the bottom bar slightly flared and stamped with the company name.

Below this was a lower grille with seventeen vertical moldings of varying size arranged to create a curving top border. An emblem on the center vertical bar carried a shield-shaped badge. Hood sides were decorated with a louver-bar arrangement along most of their length. When the trim was chrome-plated (as on all 1941 and most postwar trucks) or painted, the upper grille and hood moldings featured red accent stripes.

Cab styling came from the "turret top" school of design and featured all-steel construction. This cab first appeared with 1939 models. A year later, the dashboard was restyled, and this new cab-and-dash combination was continued from 1941 to 1946. The 1941 cab was promoted as being 1.5 inches longer to give extra legroom and permit seatbacks to be sloped at an easier riding angle.

The early postwar trucks continued the fat-fendered look of the postwar era. Headlamps were set into pods, mounted on the fenders, which blended into the sheet metal. Headlights were of the sealed-beam type, with parking lamps forming little fins on top of the pods. Bumpers, except during the 1942–1945 period, were chrome-plated. Fenders were finished in black.

Double-unit construction of heavy-gauge steel was featured for cargo boxes. They had wooden floors reinforced and protected with steel skid strips. At the rear was a tailgate heavily reinforced with boxlike girders and channels, which was welded to form a strong, all-steel unit. It was fitted with an antirattling fastener. Full running boards ran between the front and the pontoon-style rear fenders.

Only one engine, a 216.5 ci overhead valve, inline six-cylinder was offered in the 3100 half-ton and 3600 three-quarter-ton series. For the larger trucks, a special 10¾ inch clutch disc was used. The powerplant had a 6.5:1 compression ratio and single-barrel carburetor. It produced 90 bhp at 3300 rpm and 174 pounds-feet of torque at 1200–2000 rpm. The standard three-speed manual gearbox was a synchromesh type with helical cut gears. A four-speed manual transmission was optional.

Semi-floating rear axles were used on all half-ton models, while three-quarter-tons (and others) employed a full-floating type. Standard equipment tires varied according to series, as follows: BK models used 6.50x16 six-ply tires; CKs used 6.00x16 six-ply; DP used 6.00x16 six-ply and DR used 6.00x15 six-ply. They were mounted on pressed steel disc wheels. Synthetic rubber tires were first adopted in January 1944 as part of standard equipment.

Details for collectors

Chevrolet expert Robert Hensel, of Brillion, Wisconsin, helped research some details about the Wurlitzer pickups that collectors might be interested in. Most of these will come in handy for those who expect to have their trucks judged in shows. They are based on Chevrolet factory service bulletins or Hensel's personal experience in collecting and judging for the Vintage Chevrolet Club of America (VCCA).

Blackout trim

During 1942, painted ("blackout") trim was adopted, and a number of other changes were made in Chevrolet trucks. Nearly all trucks sold in 1944 and the early 1945–1946 interim model came with the trim painted. Most were finished in Turret Gray, although white, cream, yellow and orange trucks were also manufactured and had their grilles painted the same color as the body.

Grille emblem

A shield-shaped badge was located on the vertical center bar of the lower grille. Some sources say this was eliminated during the war and returned on postwar models. "I don't know of the grille emblem ever being deleted," says Hensel, "as all the trucks that I have [owned] have them." Bob adds that the emblems were chrome-plated on trucks with chrome grilles and painted on those with painted grilles.

Wurlitzer-style production dates

Series	Beginning	Closing	Model years	Titled as
BK	Jan. 1, 1944	Aug. 31, 1945	1944–1945	1944, 1945, 1946
CK, CL	Sept. 1, 1945	Sept. 1, 1946	1946 (interim)	1945–1946
DP, DR	May 1, 1946	May 31, 1947	1946 (2nd series)	1946, 1947

Note: The production of CK/CL and DP/DR models overlapped between May 1946 and September 1946. The production of DP/DK models also overlapped that of Advance-Design models for two months.

Technical changes 1942

Numerous small changes were made in commercial vehicles between 1941 and 1942. These are described in the 1942 Chevrolet *Engineering Features Book.* They are listed again in Technical Service Bulletin number WPR 29 issued by H. W. Page, of Chevrolet's War Products Field Organization, on November 5, 1945. Page explains that he was including these in the postwar bulletin because the 1942–1946 models would be new to a high percentage of the motoring public because of low 1942 sales.

There were five basic changes outlined, but one applied only to large car-over-engine (COE) models. The other four included: changes to the truck fender attachment to provide a right-angle bracket riveted to the cowl, minimizing the possibility of fender cracking; the 1942 models adopted Army design shocks, which were more durable than the civilian type formerly used; engine flywheel bolts were increased in diameter providing better flywheel attachment to the crankshaft on all engines, and standardized flywheel bolt diameter on 235 and 216 ci engines; a heavy duty single-speed axle was now available, providing an axle housing with the same carrying capacity as the two-speed and heavy axle shafts.

Technical changes 1942–1945

Bulletin number WPR 29 listed two other changes that were made to half- and three-quarter-ton trucks during the war years. First, the universal joint yoke was changed with a heavier rear universal joint yoke used on all half-ton trucks with four-speed transmissions, providing additional strength for increased torque in the low ratio. Second, the pickups' rear fender mounting was redesigned, featuring additional reinforcements and bracing to prevent flexing of the rear fender and consequent breakage.

In addition, during the same years six other changes occurred in both Chevrolet cars and trucks. These included: new synthetic rubber engine mounts; added exhaust valve umbrellas; an increased size opening in timing gear plate; improved polarity-reversing switch (with wider base and better sealing); an improved vacuum advance mechanism, with cyanide hardened arm and pivot screws to reduce wear; and use of cast-iron—instead of diecast—transmission main drive gear bearing retainer, with a relocated hole for better draining.

Technical Service Bulletin number TSB 19; Dealer 15, issued August 31, 1945, makes it clear that all of the above were carried over for 1945–1946 models with prefex CK. It states, "Note: No change is being

This 1946 pickup illustrates the appearance of the standard models with painted grille, bumper and hubcaps. This sidemount spare-tire carrier may have been homemade. Chevrolet introduced a factory version in 1953.

made in any of the specifications of either commercial cars or trucks at this time." Chevy used the term commercial car for sedan deliveries. The half-ton and three-quarter-ton pickups and other body styles are listed under a series of different names in various types of factory literature: light-delivery, utility or commercial.

Door handles

Bob Hensel also advises that the CK trucks had several other changes, such as plastic inside door handles and knobs.

The prewar styling was carried over until late May 1947, and trucks like this one were sold as 1947 models. The running board step plate is aftermarket, and the flareboards on the cargo box are handmade. Elliott Kahn

Production problem

"Another interesting fact is that the trucks made in 1945, and some early 1946s, still had body welds on them," Hensel pointed out. "The story goes that they (Chevrolet) could not get enough grinding wheels to clean them up."

Production totals

Only calendar-year production totals are available for the 1941–1946 Chevrolet trucks, with no breakouts given for model year, body type, series, and so on. Also, the Wurlitzer Juke Boxes continued to be built through July 31, 1947, and many were registered as 1947s.

"There were a lot of 1946-style trucks sold as 1947 models," said Bob Hensel. "We have come across this in VCCA judging. I think this is because of the late introduction of 1947s and I've heard that some states used a date that a title was issued to determine model-year."

Calendar year	Production total	Market share
1940	247,689	31.53%
1941	321,804	29.41%
1942*	119,077	13.58%
1945	94,634	13.50%
1946	270,140	28.67%
1947**	335,343	27.12%

*May include early 1945 trucks.
**Includes late-1946 trucks.

Chapter 3

Advance-Design era: 1947-1955

Advance-Design trucks entered production May 1, 1947, bringing with them Chevrolet's most dramatic styling and engineering features in seven years. Competing companies like Ford and Dodge did not introduce all-new models until 1948 or 1949. This gave Chevy a marketing edge that restored it to top-rank in the truck industry. The success of this series was also long-lived, since no major redesign would occur until mid-1955.

1947

In terms of appearance, the 1947 trucks were heavily modernized. A cleaner look, with rounder lines and larger proportions, characterized the Advance-Design series. Bodies were widened, wheelbases were lengthened and hoodlines were lowered. The cab height was reduced, but the front fenders looked higher and humpier.

Chevrolet's Advance-Design trucks entered production on May 1, 1947. They were wider, longer and lower than the previous models. This half-ton could be either a 1947 or 1948.

Advance-Design styling was very similar between 1947 and 1953. This can be identified as a 1947–1948 model because it has no vent windows and because there is no 3600 call-out under the hoodside nameplate. Vent door on left-hand side of cowl is open for fresh air intake. It is a three-quarter-ton model and titled as a 1947 truck.

Among major updates was an alligator-jaw hood that was hinged at the cowl. It was smooth, broad and round-nosed. Two panels forming the hood were bolted together at the center, with the seam hidden by a body-color trim molding. At the front was a chrome nameplate having a bow tie above the word Chevrolet. Near the cowl, on both sides of the hood, were chrome call-outs with the Chevrolet name.

Series designations included 3100 for half-tons and 3600 for three-quarter-tons. There were seventeen other truck lines and a total of 107 models. For now, we'll stick mainly to the pickups in the 3100/3600 series. The half-ton was also identified by an EP prefix, the three-quarter-ton by an ER prefix. These prefixes were part of the serial number.

A modern touch was the use of integral headlights. The housings for these were no more than holes in the fenders, trimmed with circular chrome doors. Six-volt sealed-beam headlamps were used. Parking lamps were rectangular units attached to the outer ends of the next-to-highest grille members.

Five horizontal bars, which bulged outward at the center, made up the grille. They were stacked between upper and lower baffles. The top bar had double bevels running end-to-end and the rest had three bevels, with the ribs on each bar getting slightly thicker and wider toward the bottom. Painted finish was used for grilles on standard trucks, while deluxe models had chrome plating. The bumper was sturdy and slightly bowed of single-bar design. It was also painted or chromed. A flat body-colored gravel pan was mounted between it and the grille. This same grille was used from 1947 to 1953.

Cab styling was again basically turret-topped. Chevrolet called the design a Unisteel cab. Construction was of four major panels: cowl, back, top and floor, with numerous reinforcing panels and braces welded into one unit. Newly available were rear corner cab windows, measuring 7¼x13¾ inches, which provided better rear vision. The parts involved originally cost less than $20, but this Deluxe Cab option adds considerably to collector values today.

A larger, more slanted two-piece windshield was used. Total glass area was up fifteen percent. Door openings were four inches wider, legroom increased seven inches and one additional inch of headroom was provided. The bench seat was fifty-six inches wide. It had nearly twice as many coil springs, which were all individually wrapped, as on a fine mattress. Also new was the use of concealed door hinges, a step-on parking brake and an attractive one-piece dash.

On the right-hand exterior side of the cowl on trucks with a heater-defroster, there was a stack of

Early Advance-Designs had gas filler on right side of box. This 3600 has Deluxe Cab with bright window moldings and Nu-Vue rear quarter windows. Chrome grille and bumpers were options. Louvers on cowl indicate that a heater-defroster unit was installed at the factory.

The 1949 models were the first to wear numerical series call-outs under the Chevrolet name on hoodsides. This '49 has all the Deluxe features, plus accessory hood ornament. It's a 3100 half-ton. Hope Emerich

eleven short horizontal louvers. On the left-hand side was a vertical vent door. The integral cowl ventilation system could be mated with an optional thermostatically controlled heater-defroster. Windshield wipers were now mounted below, instead of above, the windshield. The wiper motor and mechanism was below the cowl.

Frames for these trucks were promoted as being stronger than in the past. The side-members were formed in deep channel sections and cross-members were of flanged U-design with box-sectional construction. Most measurements for the half-ton and three-quarter-ton trucks were identical, but the lighter-duty models had a wider spread at the rear side-members and longer distance between the spring perches. Maximum gross vehicle weight ratings were 4,600 pounds for half-tons and 5,800 pounds for three-quarter-tons.

Wheelbases were 116 inches for the 3100 series and 125¼ inches for the 3600 series. The cargo box, or dispatch box, consisted of side assemblies and an endgate. With the wider Advance-Design cabs came a two-inch-wider box. It had the same seventy-eight-inch load space as prewar trucks, but measured fifty inches across. All 1941–1953 Chevy trucks used the same cargo box side assemblies, while endgates were the same for all 1941–1946 models and of a different design on all 1947–1953 models. A different side assembly was adopted in 1954 and used for early 1955 models, too. Security chains were first added in 1947, with the same parts employed through 1953. The chains used in 1954 and early-1955 were changed.

Only one engine was used in all 1947 Chevrolet trucks below one-and-one-half-ton capacity. It was the 216.5 ci overhead valve, inline six having a 3½-inch bore and 3¾-inch stroke. This powerplant had a 6.6:1 compression ratio and developed 29.4 SAE hp or 90 gross hp at 3400 rpm. A Carter downdraft carburetor with three venturis was employed.

Standard transmission for half-ton and three-quarter-ton trucks was a three-speed manual synchromesh type with all-helical gears. Gear shifting was manual through the steering column. A four-speed gearbox with non-synchromesh first was a heavy-duty option. It had straight-cut gears for first and reverse.

Front axles were of the reverse Elliott type, with king pins and 38x1¾-inch eight-leaf front springs. The half-ton used a semi-floating rear axle with hypoid gears, while all three-quarter-ton and heavier trucks had a full-floating axle with hypoid ring gear and pinion. Axle ratios were 4.11:1 for the 3100s and 4.57:1 for 3600s. The lighter-duty models used 1¾x54-inch rubber-bushed, semi-elliptic rear springs, while the three-quarter-ton had 2x46-inch two-stage semi-elliptics with fixed bushings.

Factory documents indicate that all these early Advance-Design trucks entered production the first day of May, while late-1946 Wurlitzer-style models were still being built. Assembly of the prewar-styled units ceased on May 31, 1947. Remember that both types of vehicles were sometimes titled according to the calendar year in which final assembly took place, regardless of Chevrolet's model-year designations.

Trucks with the serial number prefixes EP or ER are clearly indicated to be 1947 models in all Chevrolet technical literature. "The 1947 trucks were introduced

Fuel filler was relocated behind right-hand door handle in 1949. This 3100 has standard cab, but optional chrome extras including hood ornament and step plates. Grille guard features double crossbars. Note half-open cowl vent.

Chevy 1949 and 1950 models are virtually identical. Note extra bracing on box on this 3600 three-quarter-ton. Wheel trim rings were a popular extra. All 1947–1953 trucks had similar hubcap design, but three-quarter-ton caps were larger sized.

The 1950 models looked just like 1949s. Series designation changed to HP for half-ton 3100s. This one is a basically plain truck with chrome grille and hubcaps. Cowls had vent door on left-hand side until 1951.

in May 1947, and were, indeed, 1947 models and not 1948 models," Bob Hensel says. This is supported by listings in factory shop manuals, Chevrolet master parts catalogs, technical service bulletins and other company documents.

For example, Technical Service Bulletin DR number 13, issued by E. L. Harrig on July 3, 1947, reads: "The information in this bulletin applies to the 1947 trucks." Harrig was manager of the service and mechanical department and his bulletin shows the complete list of serial letters (prefixes) "assigned to the new 1947 trucks."

Chief Engineer John G. Wood also explained Chevrolet's thinking in the front of the 1947 *Engineering Features Book.* "In most years, the new features of passenger cars are predominent and the *Features Book*

is issued ahead of their introduction so that sales programs may be expedited," he wrote. "This year, however, the new features of trucks are more important. For this reason, we provided advance information of the cars to the interested departments by other media and purposely delayed issuance of this book until shortly before truck announcement. Because the truck information is so important, we ask that it be kept confidential until the official introduction of the trucks to the public. Information in this book is correct as of May 10, 1947 and no subsequent changes are contemplated."

In passing, it should be noted that sources like the National Automobile Dealers Association and *Red Book* identified these trucks correctly, as to their intended model year, although a seemingly incorrect starting date of January 1947 is indicated. It is my contention that this is probably the correct starting date for the sedan delivery, which is listed first, but not for the other truck lines. (The sedan deliveries were based on passenger cars and did not change design when the trucks did.)

A surprising number of history books refer to the first Advance-Design trucks as 1948 models. This happens mainly because series production continued through March 31, 1948. Therefore, advertising and promotions issued in the later calendar year carry 1948 dates, as do many state title certificates. It's all academic, of course. Still, when you're looking for certain parts, following technical literature is the best practice.

Rear view of 1950 Deluxe Cab half-ton shows the wood floor construction of the box and Chevrolet name across tailgate. Rear bumper was extra. Note single taillight in chrome housing.

Half-ton models were distinguished by 3100 emblems on sides of hood in 1950 and 1951, but the '51s also had vent windows. That means this is a 1950 model, with one-piece side glass. Chrome grille and bumper were separate options; this truck has painted grille.

Early Advance-Design pickup trucks had the gasoline filler on the side of the cargo box, instead of the side of the cab. This probably was related to having the gas tank relocated from inside the cab to under the frame, a safety feature of most postwar trucks.

Due to the early release of the new postwar models, Chevrolet was able to boost production in calendar year 1947 up to 335,343 units, which gave the company a 27.12 percent market share. This compared to 247,832 and 20.04 percent for second place Ford, and 166,432 units and 13.46 percent for number-three Dodge. Since the model year and the calendar year overlapped, it's impossible to determine exactly how many 1947 Advance-Design trucks were made. Nevertheless, the total was substantial and brought a fifty-percent expan-

A 1950 standard 3100 was exhibited at Hershey 1986. It has painted grille, but chrome bumper, hubcaps and wheel rings. Also notice radio antenna and fender clearance lamps. The absence of louver vents on the right-hand cowl indicates this truck was delivered without heater-defroster.

The addition of vent windows in 1951 eliminated the cowl vent door on left-hand side of cowl. As you can see on the Deluxe 1951, the vent on top of the cowl remained. Vent windows made door window glass smaller.

Push-button door handles were introduced in 1952, the year this truck was sold. Note the absence of series number below

Chevrolet nameplate on side of hood. The 3600 three-quarter-tons still had them.

This half-ton was displayed at Hershey as a '53, but hood nameplate appears to be 1952 design. State titling procedures caused this type of confusion in the fifties. Hood ornament was a 1954 dealer accessory. Also seen are window vent shades and windshield spotlight. G. Landry owned this truck.

sion to the company's commercial body plant at Indianapolis.

1948

The 1948 Chevrolet trucks used the Advance-Design Unisteel cab and sheet metal of the 1947 models. The gas filler was still not standardized in the cab-side location but this was the final year for having the gas tank on cab models mounted on the frame side rail, between the cab location and rear axle. Gaining increased popularity was the deluxe cab treatment with rear quarter windows added.

Several changes and improvements were made in the 1948 Chevrolet engine. The main bearings were now of the precision type, replacing the former rough bearings that required line reaming. The new rods had thinner babbitt for better heat dissipation and longer bearing life. A running production change, taking place in mid-season, was elimination of the polarity-reversing switch. Points were changed back to the same type used on 1937–1940 models.

Gross vehicle weight ratings now varied according to the types of tires used. For half-ton and three-quarter-ton models, the available options were:

Nominal rating	Gross vehicle weight	Tires
½-ton	4,200 lb.	6.00x16 six-ply
½	4,200	6.70x15 six-ply
½	4,500	6.50x16 six-ply
½	4,600	15-6 or -8
¾	5,200	15-6
¾	5,200	7.00x17 six-ply
¾	5,400	15-8
¾	5,800	7.00x17 eight-ply
¾	5,800	7.50x17 eight-ply

These trucks were probably released after March 31, 1948, when the 1947 series went out of production. Chevrolet Truck and Car Identification sheets do not show the exact starting date and there may, again, have been some overlap. They appear to have been manufactured through the end of the calendar year, as coding given for 1949 models begins with the month code A, for January.

Prices were raised slightly, despite the fact that the postwar seller's market was beginning to evaporate. The overall Chevrolet truck line-up now consisted of twenty-one series of half-, three-quarter-, one-, one-and-one-

Here's a good look at the optional Nu-Vue windows on 1952 cab. This is a Deluxe Cab model, judging by chrome window moldings. Bright gas filler cap was an extra.

This 1953 3100 pickup is a standard cab model with Nu-Vue windows. The Deluxe Cab version would have bright moldings around windows like the 1952 pictured earlier. Vent windows and push-button door handles were seen again in 1953.

24

half- and two-ton trucks and school buses. There were well over eighty models and probably over 100 variations when chassis options like dual rear wheels were considered. Not counting sedan deliveries, the half- and three-quarter-ton models were the same as before, except that new job number codes were used for half-ton panels, Suburbans and canopy express trucks.

Production and market penetration levels for Chevrolet trucks in calendar year 1948 both increased. Chevrolet built 389,690 units in the calendar year and posted a 28.46 percent market share. Since the model year and calendar year overlapped, these figures include 1947 models built in the first three months of 1948.

1949

By model year 1949, the Advance-Design Chevrolet trucks were out long enough that the company saw the need to start making refinements and improvements of a substantial nature. The overall appearance and mechanical makeup were largely the same, but the changes were the most dramatic yet seen in the series.

One difference was in the attachment of cabs to the chassis. They were now flexibly mounted at four points, which had a pentagon layout when viewed from above. At each rear corner, the cab was supported by shackle-type mounts. Eye-shaped brackets were bolted to both the frame and the cab underbody, near the door pillars. Shackles, similar to those used in spring suspensions, connected the eye brackets. The shackle studs were mounted in rubber bushings at the eyes.

The front corners of the cab just ahead of the door-hinge pillars were bolted, through rubber shims, to mounting brackets projecting outward from the frame side rails. At a fifth point, at the center of the front frame cross-member, was a nonflexible, stabilized front end mounting.

The method of retaining door-opening weatherstrips was also changed in 1949. Grooved retainers spot-welded along the front, top and rear of the opening were used in conjunction with a doorsill weatherstrip held in place by retainers and screws. Previous models had a flat retainer held in place by sheet metal screws.

A change in the 216 ci engine, adopted for 1949, was provision for pressure lubrication of the timing gears via an oil passage from the front camshaft bearing. It ran through a milled slot in the rear of the engine front plate to a nozzle extending out from the front plate and aimed so that all oil entering the passage was delivered to the timing gears for effective lubrication.

New 14 mm AC spark plugs (Model 44-5 Com.) replaced the 10 mm type (AC-104) used for 1948 models. Chevrolet also changed the recommended torque rating for installation of 1949 spark plugs to 20–25 pounds-feet. When a torque wrench was not available, the plugs were to be installed finger tight and wrenched an additional one-half turn. The recommended plug gap was also changed from 0.040 inch (1948) to 0.035 inch.

Used this year for the final time was a Carter downdraft carburetor. The accelerating pump arrangement was slightly different than in 1948, however, in that the plunger coil spring was relocated above the piston instead of below it. This lowered the piston in the cylinder and kept it below the fluid level at all times. On 1949 models only, the carburetor inner choke lever also incorporated a pin that engaged a slot in the fast-idle link to control choke-valve operation and prevent unnecessary flooding.

Some 1949 models with the optional heavy-duty four-speed transmission will show a design difference

Here's a close-up of the 1953-style hood nameplates on the right side of truck. Louver vents continued to appear on trucks with heater-defroster option. This is another standard cab with black rubber windshield moldings.

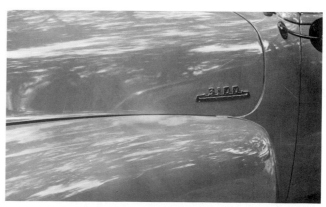

Detail of left-hand side of 1953 pickup shows the styling that was in effect since 1951, without cowl vent door. This type of hoodside nameplate was used for 1953, 1954 and first series 1955 models.

25

introduced as a running change. The skip tooth design provides a closer fit between the reverse sliding gear and mainshaft at the spline location. A change was also made in the machining of the key slots in the third- and fourth-speed clutch hub attachments at the same time.

Slight changes were accomplished in the steering column gearshift mechanism for 1949, demanding minor differences in service operations. For example, clearance between the end of the gearshift lever and lower edge of the steering wheel rim was one-quarter inch greater and control rod adjustment procedures varied.

All 1949 cab models had the gasoline tank relocated behind the driver's seat. The tank, of 17½-gallon capacity, was made with two steel sections seam-welded together. The filler neck came through the right side of the cab, at a convenient height from the ground. The tank was mounted on two supports and secured with a pair of adjustable steel straps attached to the supports with antisqueak material that prevented metal-to-metal contact.

The 1949 models continued to offer the same GVW ratings as the 1948s with the same tire options. As before, the ratings decreased when tires of lesser capacity were used, as per the chart previously shown. Eight-leaf rear springs were carried over as required equipment on half-tons, as was a 4.11:1 rear axle ratio. Buyers of three-quarter-tons had a choice between two-stage seven-leaf springs (with 15-6 or 15-8 tires) or two-stage eight-leaf rear springs (with all 17-inch tires).

This photo shows the overall similarity of 1953 model on left and 1950 model on right. Small details like vent windows and push-button door handles distinguish the later truck, however. Still, many parts are interchangeable.

A 1953 pickup on display at a car show in Appleton, Wisconsin. Trucks of this model year still used the original

Advance-Design grille and hubcaps. Black paint on bumper appears to be a personal touch.

A 4.57:1 rear axle was still standard for the larger trucks, but a new option was 5.14:1. Model year 1949 was the last in which lever-action shock absorbers were used.

An external trim feature first seen on 1949 models was the addition of a hood-side plate bearing the series designations 3100 for half-tons and 3600 for three-quarter-tons. It was placed below the Chevrolet nameplate that was used on all 1947 to 1952 commercial and utility trucks. The half-tons had this extra trim only through 1951, while the three-quarter-tons kept it until 1954. The 1952 half-tons nameplate said only Chevrolet, while the 1953–1954 versions used a different 3100 plate (part no. 370020 instead of 3692106). Another ornament with a Chevrolet emblem was used on the front of the hood on all 1947–1953 models.

Models available in the 1949 half-ton and three-quarter-ton lines continued to be the same ones previously offered, although *all* job number designations were new.

Calendar-year statistics show production of 383,543 units in all 1949 Chevrolet truck lines, which equates to a 33.88 percent share of total industry output. Of the total, 201,537 units were half-tons (under 5,000 lb. GVW) and 97,678 units were built in the next higher weight class (5,001-10,000 lb. GVW), which included three-quarter-tons as well as some heavier models.

1950

Production and sales of Chevrolet trucks set an all-time record in 1950, a record that would stand for years. There were no drastic product changes to explain the boom in demand. Instead, it was spurred on by very positive marketing conditions. The trend in America was toward more multi-vehicle families, and pickup trucks were seeing greater use as second cars.

Improvements to the trucks were, again, not obvious, although several refinements were made. The most important ones involved the engine, but other mechanical systems also had minor enhancements.

Shock absorbers were changed from the old knee-action type to more modern airplane-type shocks. In the rear, they were now connected to the anchor plate by eyes rather than links. Early-1950 trucks continued to hold propeller shaft bushings in place with peened dowels. Later in the year, these bushings were press-fitted into the torque tube. This required the use of a special tool for installation or removal operations.

A change made in the Loadmaster 235 ci engine (used in larger trucks) could affect restorers of half- and three-quarter-ton models with the Thriftmaster 216 ci powerplant. Previously, the exhaust manifolds of the two engines had been interchangeable, but the 1950 version of the 235 had a proportionately larger manifold.

The small engine had other improvements that combined to raise its maximum brake horsepower rating of 92 at 3400 rpm. Maximum torque also increased to 176 pounds-feet at 1500 rpm. In addition, the exhaust valve seat angle was changed from thirty to forty-five degrees. Exhaust valves also had longer overall lengths, changed from 4.902 to 4.932 inches. The muffler used on all trucks this season was of straight-through construction with 1¾-inch central tubing. This provided a low back pressure exhaust system with satisfactory sound absorption qualities.

A GM model B downdraft carburetor was adopted for 1950 Chevrolet trucks. Features of this Power-Jet

This 1953 half-ton was in the 1986 Tulsa auction. Paint stripe on upper beltline is not correct; it's too heavy. Running boards were finished in black. The 3100 hood call-outs returned this year, but the Chevrolet nameplate was gone.

Factory photo shows the correct appearance of standard painted bumper on the 1953 pickups. This is a 3600 three-quarter-ton model according to the hoodside nameplate. It has Deluxe moldings around the window opening and Nu-Vue cab windows. Tinted glass was introduced for 1953.

carburetor included a concentric fuel bowl, centrally located main discharge nozzle, easy-to-service main well and support assembly and improved fast-idle/choke mechanism for better cold weather starts. The carburetor used on 216 ci engines was slightly smaller than a similar one for 235 ci engines and had a 1.5-inch throttle bore and 1.218-inch main venturi inside diameter. This carb was simplified and had provisions for only two external and one internal adjustments.

The electrical system was simplified this year, too. In 1948–1949 trucks, the fuse box on the engine side of the dash had individually fused circuits for upper and lower headlamp beams, parking lamps, taillights and stop lights. The 1950–1951 fuse box was in the same place, but it contained fuses for the taillights and stop lights only.

Another change was in the location of the voltage regulator, which was moved to the left-hand side of the cowl instead of the left fender skirt. A 42-amp thermal circuit breaker was now used in the lighting system in place of the 30-amp type previously employed.

On the exterior, 1950 pickups in the half-ton and three-quarter-ton series continued to look the same as the 1949 models in all regards, including hood trim and hubcaps. The hubcap used from 1947–1953 on half-tons was a chrome wheel hub (bottle cap type) cover with a 9⅞-inch outside diameter and the name Chevrolet stamped across it. Larger chrome hubcaps, with an 11 1/16-inch outside diameter, were used on three-quarter- and one-ton trucks during the same years.

Chrome-plated grilles and bumpers were again optional equipment. One history of Chevrolet states that the accessory fender moldings (four on front fenders and three on rears) offered for panel trucks was made available for other half-ton models this year. The *1958 Chevrolet Master Parts Catalog* does not agree with this. It lists this combination of triple lower fender speed-lines and one upper front fender bar for the panel truck model only. Some dealers could easily have bolted these parts on pickups to make them look fancier, however.

Numerous other factory accessories like wheel trim rings, grille guards, fog lamps, spotlights, dual taillamps, rear bumpers, external sun visors and clearance marker lamps were regularly available for dress-up purposes.

Despite the fact that there were few product changes, 1950 turned out to be a banner season. In August alone, 45,779 Chevrolet trucks were manufactured, making it the peak month in the company's history. Calendar-year output of 494,573 units was somewhat incredible, with Chevrolet posting a 36.79 percent market share. Chevy outsold Ford by 148,773 trucks, and Dodge was 368,800 units behind. Cousin brand GMC—using the same bodies with different trim and engines—broke the 100,000-unit barrier for the first time. By weight class, Chevrolet's calendar-year production was as follows:

5,000 lb. and less (sedan delivery and 3100 series) 265,515

5,001 to 10,000 lb. (3600-3800 series and small school bus) 102,669

This 1953 billboard artwork shows the one-ton 3800, the three-quarter-ton 3600 and half-ton 3100 trucks from left to right. It also stresses Chevy's Number 1 sales rank. Institute of Outdoor Advertising

10,001 to 14,000 lb. (one-and-one-half-ton and large school bus) 27,848

14,001 to 16,000 lb. (two-ton and 48-54 passenger bus) 98,591

1951

The Advance-Design trucks were continued for 1951. A noticeable difference on the exteriors was the disappearance of the hinged side vent (door) on the left-hand side of the cowl. Side door ventilators (vent windows) were now relied on for fresh-air intake on both sides of the cab. These had friction-type mechanisms consisting primarily of a coil spring-mounted on the lower pivot to exert friction against the mounting support. They were of the push-out type and could be latched closed with a lever handle against the division channel. A pop-up vent door was still used for taking in air at the top of the cowl.

With the addition of vent windows, the door glass was reduced in area from the 16⅜x28⁵⁄₁₆-inch size previously used to 16⅞x18¼ inches. Only one screw was now used to hold the upper glass run channel in place. Another change, inside the cab, was the use of new seat adjusters designed with ball and roller assemblies between the upper and lower channels of the seat adjuster mechanism.

Front suspension stabilizer bars on half-ton models were redesigned in 1951, to place the transverse section of the stabilizer shaft in rubber bushings. These were retained in U-shaped brackets and attached to the bottom of the front cross-member with a reinforcement plate. Two arms extended rearward and were fastened to the axle with rubber insulated links (metal rods) that were fastened to the I-beam. There was also a minor change in front shock absorber attaching hardware.

Some braking systems received significant attention in 1951. Used on the front and rear of all half-ton models were new Duo-Servo single-anchor brakes. These were self-energizing in that they utilized the momentum of the vehicle to assist in brake application. Bonded linings and eleven-inch diameter rear drums

New, massive crossbar grille was used on 1954 trucks and carried over for the 1955 first series. They were usually painted, although parts books list an optional chrome grille for these models.

were used. Front brakes were two inches wide, rears 1 3/4 inches. Rear drums were changed in design, now being held to the hubs with three slotted screws easily removed with a screwdriver. A soft paper gasket was used to ensure a seal between hub and drum, and was supposed to be replaced during servicing. Three-quarter-ton trucks continued to use double-articulating Huck brakes with bonded linings.

Other brake system changes were adopted, such as the use of rubber sealing boots for both sides of the wheel cylinders on half-ton models. Brake tubing of 3/16-inch diameter, instead of 1/4-inch diameter, was now used on all half-tons. As a result of the new features, both hydraulic and mechanical adjustments and service procedures were changed for 1951 half-ton models.

Engine changes were not in the picture for 1951 Chevrolet half- and three-quarter-ton trucks, although some larger models had minor service procedure changes. Transmissions, fuel and exhaust systems, steering and electrical specifications were all the same as in 1950.

Revisions to the tire options for 1951 affected GVW ratings and required (mandatory) rear spring options. The 3100 series trucks now had 6.00x16 six-ply tires as base equipment and were rated for 4,200-lb. GVW when so equipped. This went up to 4,800 lb. with the series' only option, 6.50x16 six-ply tires at the rear. The 3600 series trucks were also down to a pair of tire options. With 15-inch six-ply rubber on the rear, the GVW rating was 5,400 lb. Available at extra cost were 7.00x17 tires, six-ply in front and eight-ply at the rear.

This option required the ordering of two-stage eight-leaf rear springs.

Tire specifications differed for the new JT series, which offered a three-quarter-ton forward control delivery chassis suitable for vocational-type bodies and having three higher GVW rating possibilities. These forward control delivery vans lie beyond the scope of this book, as do several other new truck lines introduced in 1951. There was now a total of twenty-five basic series, including about eighty-three factory-offered configurations of chassis or body designs.

Other minor changes for 1951 were a new 22 1/2-inch-long nonadjustable rearview mirror reinforcement assembly, new front-door rain deflectors, new door-window regulators and new door-window garnish moldings. Also redesigned were certain rear body parts on panels, Suburbans and canopy express trucks. Front wheel bearing assemblies on three-quarter-ton models also had new part numbers. Another change was made in the spare wheel carrier plate. From 1946–1950, this bolted parallel to the frame side-member. On the 1951 half-tons, it was designed to bolt to a diagonal cross-strap and swing out.

Calendar-year production dropped off a bit for 1951, peaking at 426,115 units, which was 30.17 percent of all US-built trucks. Dodge had a substantial 2.61 percent market-share increase, although Ford's business fell off another 3.26 percent. Chevrolet's drop was a big 6.62 percent.

To a large degree, Chevrolet's decline was not directly related to product appeal. Rather, the National Production Authority (NPA) had applied controls on

Sidemounted spares were reintroduced in 1953 and required special welled rear fender on half-tons like this 1954 3100, seen at the 1986 Hoosier Auto Show. Hoodside nameplates are the same as 1953 style.

Here's a restored 1954 3100 pickup with the grille chrome-plated. Note the accessory grille guard and external sun visor. Truck was displayed at Straits Area Old Car Show, in St. Ignace, Michigan.

production due to the Korean War buildup. The quota for Chevrolet was originally set at 34.93 percent, with a proposed revision to 34.95 percent later. Although Chevy's overall percentage in all weight classes was lower than these figures, the company's normal share of the light-duty category would have been higher. So light-duty truck makers Chevy (and Ford) wound up bearing the brunt of the NPA restrictions.

This clearly shows up in calendar-year statistics that break down production by weight class. Consider the comparison of the 1950 and 1951 figures in terms of heavy- and light-duty trucks and you'll see that the drop-off was mainly in small-truck production.

1952

Chevy truck experts can spot a 1952 model immediately by checking the hood-side trim on half-tons and the door handles of all models.

The half-tons no longer had 3100 call-outs below the Chevrolet nameplate at the rear corners of the hood. Korean War material restrictions may have prompted this change, but it was a money-saver, too. This part sold for eighty-five cents, which would amount to $435,000 in reduced costs by deleting two call-outs from each side of the hood on 250,000 trucks!

Three-quarter-ton trucks still used 3600 call-outs, meaning that they were identical in appearance to 1951 models except for the new outside door handles. These were now of a stationary design, with a push-button-type latch control in each handle. They were also used on half-tons. An outside key lock was built into the right-hand button only.

Cab door striker plates now had raised beads and serrations that mated, in assembly, to movable plates in the door pillar for in-and-out or up-and-down adjustments. Mounting holes were changed from round to oblong openings.

New differential carriers and torque tube assemblies (which were adopted as a mid-1951 running change for half-tons) were now standard. These had the depth of the bore in the differential carrier reduced 0.015 inch and used only one shim (instead of two) between the double row bearing and the bottom of the bore.

A feeler gauge slot, formerly incorporated in half-ton truck brake drums, was no longer provided. This changed the brake adjusting procedure as outlined in the *1952 Chevrolet Truck Shop Manual Supplement* (copies of this book are available from Crank 'N Hope Publications, 450 Maple Ave., Blaresville, PA 15717).

Chevrolet added a positive crankcase ventilation system to the engine of 1952 forward control models. If you find your pickup has this feature, however, don't assume that the engine has been switched from original. A factory-issued service kit was released for use on all other 1949-1952 truck engines. This unit—part number 3693661—sold for only $15.

New, revised GM model B carburetors were released for 1952 production and service use on all 1932-1951 Chevrolet trucks.

For 1952, two cooling system thermostats were serviced. A 151-degree model was standard and a 181-degree thermostat was available for use when permanent antifreeze was used. Early Advance-Design trucks had come with a 143-degree thermostat as regular equipment and three accessory types: 151-degree for alcohol antifreeze and 160- or 180-degree for permanent antifreeze. Another change was the switch to a pressure-type radiator cap rated for 3½ to 4½ psi,

Year	Up to 5,000 lb.	5,001–10,000 lb.	10,001–14,000 lb.	14,001 lb. & up
1951	215,175	76,659	26,701	104,580
1950	265,515	102,669	27,848	98,541

Part no.	Supersedes	Model useage & engine	Parts
7004600	7004039	'32–'36 216 ci	7004475 carburetor
		'41–'52 216 ci	3692797 insulator
		'41–'49 235 ci	839632 gasket
7004040	7002540	'37–'40 216 ci	7003966 carburetor
			3692797 insulator
7004476	7003864	'50–'52 235 ci	7004476 carburetor

Note: Since the old and new model B carburetors looked identical, brass tags bearing the part numbers were affixed. In addition, the last two digits of the part number were stamped on the carburetor air horn.

which was previously used only on cab-over-engine trucks.

A new toe and floorboard mat was released for commercial models with four-speed transmissions. It was made of black ribbed rubber. The new mat was designed specifically for the floor-mounted gearshift used in trucks with the four-speed option.

1953

As mentioned earlier, 1953 Chevrolet trucks had a new arrangement of trim on the rear corners of the hood. It featured the numerical series designations above a chrome molding that looped up and partly back on each end. This type of trim was also used in 1954. The 1953s still had the original Advance-Design grille and front hood ornament, however, which the '54s did not. A new option introduced for all trucks in 1953 was tinted glass for the windshield, side windows, back window and even the optional rear corner windows. A new sixty-pound oil pressure gauge appeared on the 1953 dash.

Mechanical changes of a minor nature were also seen. The three-quarter-ton models had new front wheel bearings, which were still of the roller type. A GM (Rochester) model B carburetor was employed again. This year's carburetor model number was 7004468, indicating no major change but some additional refinements.

Improved front suspension geometry was reflected in new wheel alignment specifications for 1953 models. Caster and camber changed for both half- and three-quarter-ton models, and the three-quarter-ton also had new toe-in settings.

Side-mounted spare tire carriers were introduced in 1953. The assembly consisted of three $7/16$x20x1-inch wheel mounting bolts, front and rear rail brackets meas-uring $1 3/16$x$2 1/2$x$17 1/2$ inches, and side and center wheel carrier cross braces. Also available was a wheel carrier locking mechanism consisting of a case, lock cylinder, plunger and spring. A special left-hand rear fender with a tire well, part number 3705885, was required when a side-mount spare was ordered for half-tons. Three-quarter-ton pickups could also be ordered with side-mounted spares, but did not use a welled fender because they had longer, 75¾-inch running boards, which set the rear fenders back far enough to allow space for the wheel carrier.

Thirteen different paint colors were available for 1953 Chevrolet trucks. Only three of them, Omaha Orange, Mariner Blue and Cream Medium, were carryover colors. A new shade called Juniper Green was used as the standard color. The other choices were called Transport Blue, Burgundy Maroon, Coppertone, Autumn Brown, Ocean Green, Commercial Red, Yukon Yellow, Jet Black and Pure White.

Calendar-year production totals for all 1953 Chevrolet trucks stood at 361,833 units. This represented 30.06 percent of the entire industry's output.

While records of model-year output or production by type of truck have never been released to the public, the above figure can be further broken down by referring to trade publications that kept statistics on production according to GVW classes.

For Chevrolet trucks with GVW ratings up to 5,000 pounds, the calendar-year output was 203,242 units. This figure equates mainly to production of the 3100 series half-ton models. For trucks in the 5,001 to 10,000 pound class, assemblies totaled 71,517 units. This probably includes all three-quarter-ton models, plus some one-tons and, possibly, small sixteen-passenger school buses. Together, these two GVW classes accounted for 274,759 sales and represented the major bulk of Chevy's truck business.

The ladder supports on this 1954 3100 pickup are after-market. This truck is a standard model with painted bumper and hubcaps, and black rubber windshield trim.

1954-1955

By 1954, Chevrolet's Advance-Design trucks were getting a bit dated. As a result, the new models introduced in December 1953 had the most changes seen yet in the series. Among them was an all-new grille, one-piece windshield, larger displacement base engine and optional automatic transmission.

Effective October 28, 1954, these same trucks were carried over as first series 1955 models. The only real change made at this time involved the switch to an open driveshaft, replacing the old torque-tube type. Prices were slightly increased, too. This carryover line lasted only three months. Then, on March 25, 1955, the Advance-Design era came to an end with release of the first totally redesigned and re-engineered Chevrolet trucks since 1947.

The 1954 truck grille consisted of an upper baffle with striker plate assembly, a down-curving upper molding stamped with the Chevrolet name, a short vertical center molding, left and right horizontal center moldings and a lower molding including two end panels housing the rectangular parking lamps.

Some sources indicate that these grille moldings came only with painted finish. The *1958 Master Parts Catalog*, however, indicates that the upper molding, vertical molding and both center members were available with chrome plating, too. The chrome moldings were much more expensive and the steep price difference—$60 dealer cost—seems to have kept the number of trucks with deluxe grilles to a bare minimum.

1954 grille moldings

Description	Part number	Dealer cost
Upper (notched on flange)	3700399	$ 5.40
Center left horizontal (notched on flange)	3700451	4.10
Center right horizontal (notched on flange)	3700452	4.10
Lower (notched on flange)	3700439	6.60
Vertical (notched on flange)	3700511	4.50
Upper (chrome)	3710262	26.05
Center left horizontal (chrome)	3701113	18.20
Center right horizontal (chrome)	3701114	18.20
Vertical (chrome)	3701112	16.10

When assembled, the new grille had a more open, crossbar appearance and ran across the full width of the front end. The bumper used with the new grille was the same used since 1947 on half- and three-quarter-ton models. It also shows up in the parts catalog as being available with either painted or chrome finish, although I have seen only one 1954 panel truck with a chrome bumper.

It should be noted that it is possible the Korean War material restrictions played a role in how 1954–1955 truck grilles were finished. Chrome plating may have not been offered at first but was then made available later.

Hood-side trim used for all of the 1954 series of trucks was of the same design as used on 1953 models,

Though not specifically covered in this book, the 1954 one-ton 3800 pickup could be had with this type of extra-long cargo box. This truck teams the Nu-Vue corner windows with Deluxe Cab moldings and has chrome wheel trim rings.

although the ornament decorating the front of the hood was redesigned. It now had a Chevrolet bow tie emblem at the bottom of a chrome horizontal molding.

Chevrolet promoted its new, one-piece curved windshield as a Comfort Master Cab feature. It was said to increase comfort, safety and convenience and to provide extra visibility. This windshield measured 15⁹⁄₁₆x51¼ inches in maximum dimension, as compared to 15¼x25⅝ inches for each pane in the old two-piece windshield. It came in clear or tinted versions.

A new Ride Control seat was an option. It was designed so that the seat cushion and back moved as a unit to eliminate back rubbing. The ad copywriters claimed that it floated the operator over rough roads with ease.

Standard powerplant for the 3100 series was a new Thriftmaster 235 ci six. It had 3.5625x3.937-inch bore and stroke measurements and a higher 7.50:1 compression ratio. Maximum brake horsepower was 112 at 3700 rpm. Maximum torque was 200 pounds-feet at 2000 rpm. The clutch used with three-speed manual transmissions was also redesigned and the transmission was said to be more rugged.

A three-speed was again the standard transmission, but there were two versions, one built under Muncie nomenclature and the other under Saginaw nomenclature. Another new option was a heavy-duty three-speed made by Borg-Warner. Offered once more, at

extra cost, was a four-speed manual gearbox with floor shifter. In addition, the 1954 series introduced automatic gearshifting to Chevy truck buyers. This was GM's bullet-proof four-speed Hydra-matic and could be had on all trucks up to one-ton. The half-tons used the model-180-type Hydra-matic and the larger trucks were fitted with the model 200-54 type.

A heavier frame cross-member was installed behind the engine. This made for more rugged construction and was promoted as a feature of all models. The amount of rear frame kickup was reduced to give pickups a lower loading height. This also permitted the use of deeper sides on the cargo boxes, giving an increased load space with twenty-eight square feet of floor room. Consequently, all cargo box components—side assemblies, endgate and security chains—were redesigned. Body (cab) mountings were also improved.

A 3.90:1 ratio rear axle was used in 3100 series trucks having synchromesh transmissions. A 5.14:1 axle was used on 3600 series models.

Both vacuum and electric windshield wiper motors were available and both were new. The 11¼-inch-long Trico wiper blades were more effective than the 10-inch blades used for 1947–1953 trucks. New, dark beige cab sun visors had the same 5¼x18-inch dimensions as the previous type. Also redesigned was the cab instrument panel, which had a different 1⅜x3⅜-inch radio control plate. A lamp switch was now available in the

From this view, it's hard to tell the 1954 half-tonner from a 1953. One hint is the new square front parking lamps show- *ing above bumper ends. This factory photo clearly illustrates a new hubcap design, too.*

glove compartment for the first time. The glove compartment door was redesigned, but had the same $5\frac{15}{16}$x$15\frac{1}{4}$-inch size.

A new Deluxe Cab feature was a door ventilator assembly with chrome trim and chrome-plated window sash assemblies. Body pillar lock parts were changed again. Cloth seat trims for the standard cab interior came in brown or gray and maroon. Deluxe cloth options included combinations of maroon and beige, brown and white, or solid green. Molded carpets came in blue, brown, green, or black.

Other changes were made in parts used for the pickup box gate assembly and a $1\frac{1}{16}$x13-inch chain cover was made available for the endgate chain assembly. Available again was a side-mounted spare tire carrier requiring a special welled left-hand rear fender for half-ton models.

Except for the deletion of Burgundy Maroon, the paint colors for 1954 and first series 1955 trucks were the same as those offered in 1953. Wheel colors were modified and were Jet Black or Onyx Black for regular production, body color for deluxe trim models painted solid colors and lower body color for deluxe trim models with two-tone body paint.

Unit production figures for the calendar year indicated a ten percent drop-off in Chevrolet's total truck sales. This was due to a general industrywide decline, however, and the company's share of a smaller overall market actually jumped nearly two points to 31.83 percent. Total production was 325,515 trucks of all types. Of these, 170,824 had GVWs below 5,000 pounds and 64,599 were between 5,001 and 10,000 pounds. In addition, projections for 1955 were very positive, and work on a 74,000-square-foot factory extension got underway at Indianapolis, Indiana.

The above figures are for calendar year 1954 and do not include the Advance-Design trucks made during the first three months of 1955. In fact, there is no way to break out how many of these final, first series 1955 trucks were produced after December 31, 1954.

This factory photo is usually identified as a 1955 first series model. These trucks were identical in specifications to the 1954 editions.

35

Chapter 4

Task Force era: 1955-1959

Chevrolet's second series 1955 trucks had many departures from the Advance-Design models. They arrived at dealer level on March 25, 1955, beginning a new family of commercial vehicles, which lasted until 1959. The advertising slogan Task Force Trucks was adopted. This fleet of modernized light-, medium- and heavy-duty models totaled seventy-five factory offerings on fifteen different wheelbases.

These trucks had squarer, sculptured feature lines with rounded corners for hood, fenders and cabs. A wraparound Panoramic windshield was used on all cab models. Technical improvements included 12-volt electrical systems, tubeless tires and V-8 engines. Wheelbases were shortened on both 3100 and 3600 series.

About the only similarity between the second series 1955 half-ton and previous models was the 3100 series designation. The running boards were made much shorter this year, too.

During the five years of the Task Force era, many significant new models appeared. They included a sporty Cameo pickup, the 3200 series long-box pickup, the Fleetside model with steel double-well cargo box construction and, in 1959, the passenger-car-based El Camino pickup. All models got fancy new interior trim options and more colorful exterior paint and trim packages.

Historically, the Task Force trucks helped Chevrolet stay ahead in the light-duty sales race. The company's real market strength remained with the standard six-cylinder pickup, but the fancy models added a whole new class of buyers. They also brought a basic change in commercial vehicle marketing strategies: the adoption of annual model-year restyling.

It was clear that Chevrolet product planners had helped change the image of the light truck. Instead of being strictly a utilitarian workhorse for farmers, contractors and businessmen, this type of vehicle came to be viewed as a product that could be made sporty, luxurious or hot-performing.

1955

By April 1955 Chevrolet had shaken up the truck industry with its most changed models of all time. They had all-new styling. Single headlamps were nestled below Frenched visors that blended into the new fadeaway fenders. The trapezoid-shaped radiator opening, with rounded corners, housed an egg-crate grille. Round parking lamps were placed below the headlamps. A straight, massive bumper with wraparound ends protected the front. On the hood was an ornament with the Chevrolet emblem below a chrome delta wing. Long

36

side emblems bearing the company name and series designation were seen behind the wheel opening, below the front fender feature line.

Rear fenders had a feature line crease, too. Again available, for use with the optional side-mounted spare wheel carrier, was a welled left-hand rear fender. Now there were actually two special fenders. Because of the shorter 123¼-inch wheelbase used for three-quarter-ton pickups, they also required this type of fender. In addition, a new long-box half-ton, being the same size as the three-quarter-ton, used the same component. The part numbers were 3722269 for the welled fender used on 114-inch wheelbase models and 372233 for the welled fender used on 123¼-inch wheelbase models.

Base engine in the half-ton and three-quarter-ton trucks was the Thriftmaster 235 six, but a Trademaster 265 V-8 was optional in both weight classes. The six gave 123 hp and the V-8 was good for 145 hp. Both were available with five transmission options: three-speed, heavy-duty three-speed, overdrive, four-speed manual or four-speed Hydra-matic. Rear axle choices included 3.90:1 or 4.11:1 with overdrive for half-tons and 4.57:1 for three-quarter-tons.

A new half-ton series with a single model was introduced. This was the 3200 series pickup with a 123¼-inch wheelbase and extended eight-foot-long cargo box. A 114-inch wheelbase and 6½-foot-long box were provided for 3100 series half-ton pickups. The

A 1955 Series 3600 pickup was used as a fire truck at Indianapolis Motor Speedway. Nameplate was below front fender crease on 1955s. This truck has standard cab with small rear window. Indianapolis Motor Speedway Corporation

The Suburbanite pickup of 1955 soon became popularly known as the Cameo to Chevrolet fans. It was a limited-edition model, available only in white with red trim on the rear of the cab. Fiberglass "skins" were used to give rear quarters a contemporary slab-sided look.

Somebody slipped a camper shell on the back of this 1955 Cameo pickup. Otherwise, it's a fairly original and well-maintained stock truck. The dark-colored lights in the grille look like a small modification.

3600 series three-quarter-ton trucks also had the 123¼-inch wheelbase. Base tires were 6.70x15 four-ply on 3100/3200 models and 7x17.5 six-ply on 3600s. White sidewalls were optional for all half-tons.

Belonging to the 3100 series was the high-style half-tonner that soon became popularly known as the Cameo or Cameo Carrier. In GM engineering department lingo, this was called a "suburbanite pickup," which described its dual-purpose car/truck nature. Up

front, it had the same styling as other half-tons, but the cargo box was hidden behind slab-sided rear fender skins made of fiberglass. Special interior and exterior trim features were included.

The bolt-on fiberglass panels brought the exterior width of the cargo box out flush with the sides of the cab. They were sculptured so that the bodyside feature-line continued straight to the rear of the truck on the outside of the box. A gap between the cab and box was chrome-trimmed. Unique chrome-plated finned taillamp housings held a vertical lens.

Stylish full wheel discs with eight Chevrolet emblems were standard. A hidden compartment, concealed below the endgate, held the spare tire under the bed. This was designed so that a portion of the rear bumper swung down on hinges, exposing a fiberglass well where the spare tire was stored. There was also a fiberglass panel, over the normal steel tailgate, which concealed the hinges. Inside latches, at each upper corner, released the tailgate. It lowered via cables on spring-loaded reels that kept it level with the bed floor. The endgate had a Chevy bow tie logo at the center.

The Cameo came with exclusive paint finish using Bombay Ivory in combination with Commercial Red on the rear cab posts. The interior was of red and white cloth that resembled the upholstery used for the 1954 Bel Air Sport Coupe. There was lots of chromed trim in the interior. Cameos with 16x5K wheels had Commercial Red wheel striping.

Models other than the Cameo came standard with painted grilles and bumpers. Trucks with deluxe trim (and all Cameos) had these parts chrome-plated. The

Series nameplate moved above the front fender crease on 1956 trucks. This Cameo, with some incorrect features (such as the black-finished grille and 1955 hood emblem) has an accessory-type hood ornament available for dealer installation. This truck was for sale at $7,000 in 1986 Hoosier Auto Show.

The 1956 Cameos were available with more color combinations than the 1955s, but they didn't come with the wheels, mirrors, tires or headlight shields seen here. The Cameos were the first Fleetside trucks and significantly affected pickup styling trends.

availability of individual rear corner windows as an option was discontinued. Instead, buyers could replace the standard $10^{11}/_{16}$x35⅛-inch rear window glass with a larger Panoramic rear window that wrapped around the corners of the cab. Cameos used this feature, too.

Other new options introduced on 1955 models included power steering and power brakes. The *Master Parts Catalog* also lists 1955 as the first year for a regular factory-installed radio and illuminated cigar lighter. Apparently earlier trucks had radios that were dealer-installed. A jet-airplane-type hood was also a dress-up accessory.

The rear axle used in 1955 half-ton trucks was again of the semi-floating variety and of open Hotchkiss design. Full-floating axles were still employed in the three-quarter-ton (and larger) models and were of the same type used since 1952. The 3100 models had a 60.5-inch front tread, sixty-one-inch rear tread and overall length of 185.687 inches. The 3200/3600 trucks were 205.56 inches long.

Thirteen colors were used on the exteriors of regular trucks. There were twelve two-tone combinations, too. Wheels were done in the lower body color on 3100 models and in black on all others. Deluxe equipment and two-tone options were not available for Suburbans.

Calendar-year production (this included some first series Advance-Design models made in January, February and March) came to 393,312 units total. This gave Chevrolet first place in the truck production race with its 31.55 percent share of industry. Trucks with GVWs under 5,000 pounds amounted to 219,805

Chevrolet name was again seen across the tailgate panel on the 1957 pickups. Rear bumper was optional equipment. This picture illustrates the standard small-window cab. Gas filler is on the left rear of the cab.

The Task Force styling was carried into its third season in 1957, but with a new grille design. Hood emblem was slightly redesigned, too. And the fender-side identification emblems were repositioned along the main feature-line. This standard version has painted finish on grille, bumpers and hubcaps.

39

This beautifully restored 1957 Cameo is finished with many factory accessories like foglamps, bombsight hood ornaments, dual spotlights, exterior sunshade and whitewall tires. Standard trim ring gives the look of full wheel covers. The V emblems on door and hood signify installation of an optional V-8 engine.

units, while 64,589 more were made in the 5,001 to 10,000-pound category.

1956

On February 1, 1956, the Task Force trucks began their second model year. Few changes were made, which was probably because of the late introduction of the all-new 1955 series. The hood emblem was changed so that the chrome wings extended from the bottom of the centerpiece bearing the Chevrolet bow tie. It was attached right on the lower edge of the hood, closer to the grille. A large V was added below the

Chevrolet logo to signify V-8 models. Also, the front fender-side nameplates were moved to a position above the feature line, instead of below it.

Horsepower in the standard Thriftmaster 235 six was increased to 140 at 4200 rpm. This engine had the same bore and stroke, but used a higher 8:1 compression ratio. Maximum torque jumped to 210 pounds-feet at 2000 rpm. The Trademaster 265 V-8 gained ten gross horsepower, also due to an 8:1 compression ratio. It put out 155 hp at 4200 rpm and developed 249 pounds-feet of torque at 2200 rpm. Late in the year, a Super Turbo-Fire version of this 265 ci V-8 was released. It had 9.25:1 compression, 205 hp at 4600 rpm and 268 pounds-feet of torque at 3000 rpm.

Transmission choices for 1956 models were the same as offered in 1955 second-series trucks. The model 180 Hydra-matic, which carried an orange identification plate, was again used in 3100/3200 trucks, while the model 200-55 Hydra-matic, identifiable by its black plate, was installed in three-quarter-tons. Rear axles were the same as 1955.

This year's Cameo Carrier came in eight two-tone color combinations: Cardinal Red over Bombay Ivory; Cardinal Red over Sand Beige; Jet Black over Golden Yellow and Arabian Ivory over any of five colors, Cardinal Red, Regal Blue, Granite Gray, Ocean Green or Crystal Blue. This truck was still generically known as the Suburban pickup but was popularly called the Cameo. In contrast to the 5,220 Cameos built in 1955, the 1956 version had a production run of only 1,452 units. (This would be followed by 2,244 assemblies in 1957 and 1,405 in early 1958.)

This Cameo illustrates some 1957 trim changes, including a new grille and hood emblem, and relocation of nameplates above fender crease again. Contrasting trim panel on rear bodysides was used only on Cameos. Whitewalls on this truck are a modification.

Major changes for the Cameo pickup model 3124 in 1957 were the redesigned grille and a wider selection of optional color choices. Standard color scheme was still Bombay Ivory and Cardinal Red, as seen on this restored example at the Appleton, Wisconsin, car show. The V behind the bow tie on the hood emblem indicates a V-8 engine.

Instrument panel styling in the 1956 models was the same as 1955 and typical of all 1955–1959 trucks. The panel itself was very clean, having only buttons, an ashtray, heater controls and a glove compartment breaking up the expanse of plain metal. All instruments were housed in a fan-shaped panel dominated by the speedometer face above a Chevrolet bow tie. The temperature gauge, ammeter, oil gauge and gas gauge (left to right) were inside small rectangles spaced across the top. A round-cornered upper panel covered the top. It bulged up slightly just above the instrument cluster, forming a hood.

The Deluxe Cab equipment package again included the Panoramic Full-View rear window, deluxe seat, chrome instrument knobs, cigarette lighter, dual sun visors, dual armrests and two-tone upholstery combinations.

For non-Cameo models, there were again thirteen exterior colors available. New ones included Forest Green, Cardinal Red, Golden Yellow, Regal Blue and Crystal Blue. Twelve two-tones were offered.

Cameo pickups came standard with chrome grille and bumpers up front. Bumper guards were optional and are not seen on this '57 model. Grille consisted of 21 separate moldings, panels, brackets and deflectors, not including nuts, bolts and hardware.

A total of 2,572 Cameo pickups were manufactured in 1957. The wraparound windshield, introduced in 1955, was first promoted as a safety and styling improvement, although it was later found to cause distorted viewing through windshield. Cameos were 77 inches wide. Turn signals were standard equipment on this model.

The scooped-out trim molding on the fender-sides of 1957 trucks carried series identification. On this Cameo pickup, the inscription was Chevrolet 3124 as on other half-ton models. The hubcaps are nonstandard. These whitewalls have just about the correct width of the era. Note that the twisty-type rearview mirror is painted.

Chevrolet's calendar-year output of 353,509 commercial vehicles included the company's four-millionth truck of the postwar era. This meant that production since 1947 had virtually equaled the entire prewar output. Chevy's traditional first-in-industry ranking was maintained, with second place Ford more than 56,000 units behind in 1956. Chevrolet registered a 32.01 percent market share.

Production included over 250,000 light-duties: 194,015 in the 5,000-pound-and-less GVW class, and 59,182 with GVW ratings between 5,001 and 10,000 pounds.

Up front, the 1957 Cameo resembled other Chevrolet 3100s. In back of the cab, the changes began. Moulded Fiberglass Company, of Ashtabula, Ohio, did the fiberglass outer skins for double-wall cargo box. Note brightmetal moldings around outside of window.

1957

On April 1, 1957, Chevrolet introduced a new way to further expand its light-duty truck market penetration. Four-wheel drive (Chevy wrote it "4-wheel drive" at this time) was made available as an option for a dozen 3100/3600/3800 models. Sales literature indicated that it could be had on pickups, panels, chassis-cabs, Suburban Carryalls and stake trucks.

Basic components for providing the extra traction were a rubber-mounted power divider and precision-engineered front axle equipped with Rzeppa constant-velocity universal joints. Drive to the wheels was controlled by a single lever with four positions: neutral, two-wheel direct drive, four-wheel direct drive and four-wheel underdrive. When the truck was operated in the

Cameo door panels had a ribbed appearance on the bottom and an upholstered panel at top. Colors were coordinated with exterior finish for an attractive appearance. Door sills were wide, like a running board. Vent windows were used at front of window opening. They were of push-out design, with a swivel-lever for locking them.

last two modes, the power divider distributed power equally to the front and rear axles. Shifting between the two- and four-wheel-drive modes required no clutching. It could be done at any time with the truck stopped or moving.

Four-wheel-drive models used the Thriftmaster six powerplant. Combined with the mandatory four-speed synchromesh transmission, the four-wheel-drive unit provided a total of eight forward and two reverse speeds. Four power takeoff openings were provided for operating special eqiupment. Standard tires required were 6.50x16 six-ply rated for half-tons and 7x17.5 six-ply rated on three-quarter-tons.

Both four-wheel-drive and conventional models had a number of modest, but noticeable, styling revisions for the new model year. The most obvious was a new grille design in which an oval loop in the center was

attached to a more massive grille surrounded by four short bars on the top and the bottom. Painted or chrome finish was available.

Two small wind-splits were sculpted into the top surface of the 1957 hood. Chrome bombsight ornaments could be ordered, at extra cost, to dress up the wind-splits. At the front edge of the hood was a large chrome handlebar-shaped molding with a Chevrolet logo in the center of its raised section. A chrome V was placed below the bow tie on V-8 models.

Fender-side trim became an oval piece of chrome scooped out in its center, where the Chevrolet name and series designation appeared. The ornaments were moved backward, but still sat above the feature-line crease. Also, just above the crease on the doors of V-8 models was a chrome V badge.

Cab styling was again unchanged and once more came with the choice of a small window or Full-View

All of the 1955–1959 Task Force-era trucks used basically the same instrument panel, with wedge-shaped gauge cluster. Cameos, like this '57, had the Custom Cab treatment as standard. It included brightmetal dashboard knobs. Steering wheel is standard.

Standard controls on the 1957 Cameo included hand throttle and choke, headlight and dome-light switch, headlight beam control, speedometer, ammeter, fuel, oil pressure and engine temperature gauges, and high-beam indicator light.

43

Custom Cab with Panoramic rear window was a regular feature of the Cameo pickup. These are often called Big Window trucks. Chrome moldings—part of the Custom Cab package—bordered the rear window, too.

Another new 1957 feature was contrasting trim band (with brightmetal decorations) along the side of the fiberglass rear fender panels. A vertical brightmetal molding was also used directly behind the cab to trim the edge of the fiberglass panels.

Cameo pickups were half-ton rated models with a 6½-foot-long bed. Taillights were very similar to those used on 1954 passenger cars, with flat lenses. Back-up lights, incorporated at bottom of lenses, were standard. The tailgate was fifty inches wide, and when lowered, it was supported by special cables attached to reels behind the fenders. This is the 1957 model.

option. All pickups except Cameos had pontoon-style rear fenders in conjunction with running boards. Special welled left-hand rear fenders were again used with trucks having side-mounted spares and had the same part numbers listed for 1955s.

Suburban pickups featured a new trim assembly to decorate the entire length of their seventy-eight-inch-long box. It consisted of a ribbed emblem with bow tie logo directly behind the cab, a Cameo script nameplate behind the emblem and two horizontal moldings. The upper molding ran from in back of the cab to the middle of the taillamp. The lower molding started behind the cab and ran to the bottom of the taillamp, wrapping fully around the rear corner of the cargo box. A secondary body color was used between the two moldings, creating a contrast band.

Cameos came in nine two-tone color combinations. Other trucks could be had in fourteen solid hues or thirteen different two-tones. At the rear, the Cameo's special endgate carried a large red Chevy bow tie badge in the center, about two-thirds up the gate. Endgates of other models had a rectangular embossment on the back with the word Chevrolet spelled out across the center in capital block letters.

Power teams remained the same as in 1956, according to a factory-issued *Special Information Catalog* that has also been reprinted by Crank 'N Hope Publications. This catalog indicates that a new Task-master 283 V-8 was used only in larger 1957 trucks. It should be noted here, however, that the sedan delivery could be had with this hotter engine, the same basic powerplant that arrived in passenger cars at midyear.

A nonglare inside rearview mirror was introduced in 1957. There were also minor changes to the wind-shield wiper valve assembly. New sun visor assemblies for regular and Cameo models appear in the *Master Parts Catalog*, and the instrument panel had new part numbers, too. A glovebox lamp was another new option. Door armrests and pads also had subtle alter-ations, such as coming in light blue, dark blue or green for Cameos.

A new cloth seat-cushion-trim choice for standard pickups was gray synthetic fabric, while blue and green cloth trims were released for Cameos. Seatback cushions released in 1957 included gray for standard models; charcoal or gray for trucks with deluxe equipment pack-ages; and blue, light blue, dark blue, green, light green, dark green, red, or beige for Cameos. A new black toe and floorboard mat was used for all models except trucks with four-speed manual transmission. Standard and deluxe cabs (except in Cameos) could be had with a charcoal-colored fiberboard top lining panel.

The number of Chevrolet trucks produced in facto-ries within the United States from January 1957 to January 1958 was 351,739 units. This gave the com-pany a 32.26 percent market share, compared to 30.92 percent for second place Ford and 11.17 percent for International Harvester, the third largest producer. Of this total, 198,538 trucks had GVW ratings of 6,000 pounds or less and 55,575 fell into the 6,001 to 10,000 pound GVW category.

Cameo tailgate had a fiberglass cover with chrome bow tie painted red in the center. Latches were on the inside. Rear bumper unit had seven separate components: a pair of chrome bumper ends, a pair of chrome bumperettes and three-piece main bumper. The center piece was hinged along bottom edge and secured by chrome bolts at top. It could be dropped down to reveal spare-tire carrier.

Dual headlamps and a very elaborate grille were among changes for 1958. All trucks, cheap or fancy, were called Apaches. This one has optional exterior sun visor and special double mirrors. George Crocker, of Rearview Mirror Museum, in Nags Head, North Carolina, was asking $9,500 for it.

1958

"Task Force Trucks" was again the slogan used in advertising and promotion of 1958 Chevrolet trucks. This was a year of relatively major changes to the vehicles and the product line-up, although there was not a total break from the past three years.

To go along with the heavily sculptured new body, the 1958 pickups had a new hood with large finlike bulges at each side. Fleetside model name appeared on rear of cargo box outer wall, above the missile-shaped bulge.

Basically, the same chassis and cab structure was used, as well as the same rear fenders on models with exposed running boards. These trucks also had the same cargo box components—side assemblies, endgate and security chains—employed since 1954.

All trucks had completely new front-end sheet metal. Fenders were more heavily sculptured and had a tubular look at the top, plus a deep, rounded feature-line extending forward from the wheel opening. At the front a wide, Frenched-style opening housed dual headlamps behind a door with two round openings. These doors were painted on standard models and plated on Deluxe-equipped trucks. The hood panel was completely re-sculptured with long, narrow blisters bulging up along the side contours of the raised portion. Between the blisters was a broad, flat expanse of sheet metal.

A new grille filled the reshaped radiator opening. It was a one-piece stamping with a massive horizontal center bar housing rectangular parking lamps at either end. Chevrolet was stamped across it in block letters, which were painted black. Above this was a louver-like arrangement of three horizontal blades. This portion of the grille and the border around the radiator opening (as

Just out!... new, wide and handsome!

NEW '58 CHEVROLET   FLEETSIDE PICKUPS

They're beauties to behold . . . they're built for more load . . . and they've just joined the Task-Force line!
Three new Fleetside pickup models, in two body sizes, are here to handle your light-duty hauls in style!

How about those high-styled lines! You'll be seeing the distinctive new Fleetside look all over town in no time at all. That, you know, is an advantage in itself—fine, fresh styling that attracts attention and puts your business name in a new light!

To make it even better, Chevrolet's new Fleetside design lets you put more cargo in the box. That handsome high-styled body's long and wide—a full six feet wide—and with more load space than you'll find in any other low-priced pickup in the Fleetside weight

class. Two high-capacity body lengths are offered: 78 and 98 inches, with G.V.W. ratings up to 6,900 pounds. Fleetside body side panels are double walled where it counts—built to handle rugged body-punishing loads . . . yet still stay new-looking a whole lot longer!

New Fleetside models bring Chevrolet's pickup total to ten. Ten fast-working ways to haul the widest possible variety of pickup loads. With your own kind of cargo in mind, consider just a few Chevrolet advantages: its low loading height, high-capacity box and

sturdy tailgate design. With your costs and schedule time in mind, consider the most famous truck 6-cylinder engine ever built: Chevy's gas-saving Thriftmaster, standard in any Task-Force pickup you choose. Short-stroke V8's are optional at extra cost.

Your Chevrolet dealer will supply complete specifications on everything from new Fleetside pickups to 30,000-lb. G.C.W. haulers. He's the right man to see for all your hauling needs. . . . Chevrolet Division of General Motors, Detroit 2, Michigan.

High-capacity box features a full-width graintight tailgate

With that extra-wide opening and steel skid strip in the hardwood floor, your loads slide in with ease. Sleek, sturdy side panels are double walled. Notice the twin taillight feature, too.

Replacing the Cameo Carrier in mid-1958 was the slightly styled Fleetside shown in this original advertisement. These trucks had all-steel double-wall box construction, rather than fiberglass outer walls. Note the Panoramic rear window in the smaller drawing showing rear styling.

well as the back portion of the parking light housings) were painted, even when chrome-plated finish was ordered for Deluxe trucks. The front bumper was also new, although not noticeably changed from the late-1955 to 1957 type. It was contoured only slightly differently.

Trim included an emblem mounted on the crease along the bottom lip of the hood. It was shaped somewhat like an inverted trapezoid with wings extending from each side. A large red Chevrolet bow tie was in the center, against a black background having short vertical ribs. A chrome V was added for V-8 models. A large jet-plane-shaped nameplate decorated the fender sides. The center section of this ornament was indented and carried a two-digit designation for the series code on the tail of the "jet." These designations were 31 for the 3100 series, 32 for the 3200, 36 for 3600, and so on. In front

of the numbers was a Chevrolet nameplate. Behind the tailfin of the jet was the word Apache.

All trucks in the 31, 32, 36 and 38 series were designated with this Indian name, which simply signified light-duty. According to Ward's *1958 Automotive Yearbook*, Apache models were all trucks with GVWs up to 9,000 pounds, available on six wheelbases. An Apache molding did not indicate deluxe chrome trim, special paint or Custom Cab upholstery. It simply differentiated the light-duty trucks from models in the 40–60 series (such trucks with GVWs up to 21,000 pounds were Vikings, while those with GVWs from 21,000 to 26,000 pounds were Spartans). This has fooled some modern-day writers and historians into thinking that only deluxe-trim trucks were Apaches.

The Cameo pickup reappeared during the early months of the 1958 model year and was now called a

Original advertising artwork shows the 1958 Apache half-ton Fleetside, with standard painted grille and bumper, in a typical workaday scene.

Cameo Carrier. It had the same rear fender trim as the 1957 version. Ten paint schemes were available, with the regular production colors remaining Bombay Ivory with Cardinal Red accents. This, the opposite combination and Bombay Ivory over Granite Gray were the only carryover color schemes, while the Jet Black and Golden Yellow combination was reissued in reverse of 1957 style with black as the main color. The six other choices were new. After 1,405 of these Cameos were built, the model was discontinued at midyear.

The reason for dropping the Cameo was that it was an expensive-to-make, pricey, limited-edition model. Although the price wasn't way out of line (just under $500 extra), it was high enough to keep sales to a minimum. Buyers had purchased more of the 1955 models because they were the only slab-sided pickups around and such styling was new at that time. In 1957, however, Ford responded with the Styleside pickup, a slab-sided (fenderless) model of all-steel construction. It sold for the *same* price as the old-fashioned pontoon-fendered Flareside, but immediately captured 64,050 orders compared to 13,122 for the Flareside.

It didn't take long for Chevrolet to realize that it needed a similar model to stay competitive. So in mid-1958 it replaced the Cameo with a similar-looking Fleetside model featuring steel double-wall cargo box construction. Unlike Ford, Chevrolet charged extra for the more modern looking trucks, but the difference was a modest six dollars.

The Fleetside box had a concave upper portion and flat lower side panels with tubular, missile-shaped bulges running the entire length of the box at midlevel. Simple round taillamps were housed at the ends of the tubes in a fender extension panel. A Fleetside chrome script was positioned just above the feature line, near the rear of the side panels. A wider endgate was used on this model, with the Chevrolet name spelled out across it in white-painted block letters. The chain assembly was attached to hinged latches that secured the flat upper endgate girder to the fender extension panels. The half-ton bed

Four-wheel-drive K series option was introduced in 1957. This view of the 1958 edition clearly shows the front drive axle and heavily sculptured hood.

48

length was the same 78½ inches as Stepside models offered. The cargo box was seventy-five inches wide, compared to fifty inches on Stepsides and forty-eight inches on Cameos. The inner wheelhousings protruded into the cargo area. The box floor was crafted from chip-resistant select wood with flush steel skid strips.

Fleetsides were also offered in half-ton long-box (32) and three-quarter-ton (36) series with the 123¼-inch wheelbase. These had a ninety-eight-inch long box offering 75.6 cubic feet of load space. Maximum GVW ratings of Fleetsides ranged from 5,000 pounds to 7,300 pounds. With standard 6.70x15 four-ply tires, the short-bed pickup's GVW was 4,000 pounds, but six-ply rubber was mandatory on long-box models. Base equipment for these was size 7x17.5 tires.

The regular suspension featured solid front axles. The six-leaf longitudinal springs used in front measured forty-two by two inches. Rear leaf springs were of two-stage design, and rear axles were again semi-floating on

The early Chevy four-wheel-drive models came only in Stepside configuration and only with manual transmission. The four-wheel-drive model line-up included 12 pickups, panels, chassis-cabs, Suburban Carryalls and stakes in the light-duty field (Series 31, 36 and 38).

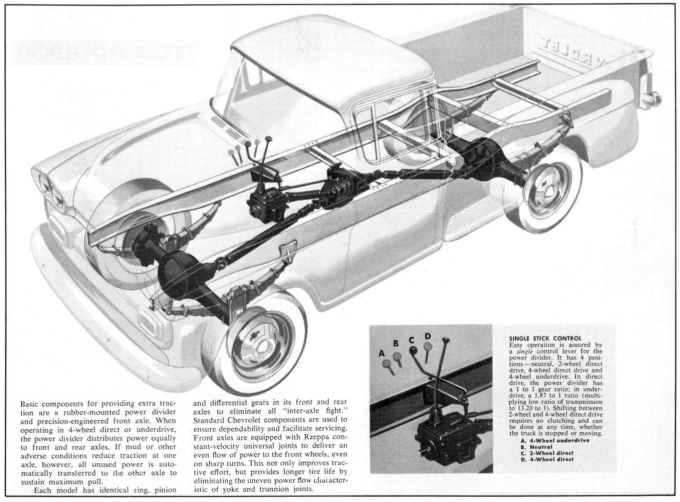

Basic components for providing extra traction are a rubber-mounted power divider and precision-engineered front axle. When operating in 4-wheel direct or underdrive, the power divider distributes power equally to front and rear axles. If mud or other adverse conditions reduce traction at one axle, however, all unused power is automatically transferred to the other axle to sustain maximum pull.

Each model has identical ring, pinion and differential gears in its front and rear axles to eliminate all "inter-axle fight." Standard Chevrolet components are used to ensure dependability and facilitate servicing. Front axles are equipped with Rzeppa constant-velocity universal joints to deliver an even flow of power to the front wheels, even on sharp turns. This not only improves tractive effort, but provides longer tire life by eliminating the uneven power flow characteristic of yoke and trunnion joints.

SINGLE STICK CONTROL
Easy operation is assured by a *single* control lever for the power divider. It has 4 positions — neutral, 2-wheel direct drive, 4-wheel direct drive and 4-wheel underdrive. In direct drive, the power divider has a 1 to 1 gear ratio; in underdrive, a 1.87 to 1 ratio (multiplying low ratio of transmission to 13.20 to 1). Shifting between 2-wheel and 4-wheel direct drive requires no clutching and can be done at any time, whether the truck is stopped or moving.

A. 4-Wheel underdrive
B. Neutral
C. 2-Wheel direct
D. 4-Wheel direct

Basic components in 1958 four-wheel-drive system were a rubber-mounted power divider and precision-engineered front

drive axle. Easy operation was assured by using a single control level for the power divider.

half-tons and full-floating on larger trucks. Chevrolet's four-wheel-drive option was carried over for 31, 36 and 38 Stepside models with six-cylinder engine and four-speed manual transmission. In mid-1958, two four-wheel-drive Fleetside pickups were added to the line-up, raising the total of 4x4 trucks to fourteen models including panels, Suburbans and chassis-cabs.

Power teams for all 1958 trucks had some changes. Compression on the Thriftmaster 235 six was up to

The 1958 Apache continued to be available in pontoon fender style with small running boards; the famous Stepside.

Cabs on all Task-Force-era trucks had basically the same general design. The gas filler was now located on the left-hand side of cab, behind the door handle.

8.25:1, boosting horsepower to 135 at 4200 rpm. The base V-8 was now the 3⅞x3-inch bore and stroke Trademaster 283 engine with two-barrel carburetor and 160 hp at 4200 rpm. Overdrive was no longer available, but all other transmissions previously offered were back again. Rear axles for half-tons were 3.70:1 or 3.90:1, with the latter used on all four-wheel drives. The three-quarter-ton trucks, including those with four-wheel drive, were equipped with a 4.57:1 ratio axle.

Chevrolet cabs for 1958 had double-cushioned Nu-Flex seats combining deep coil springs with Jack Stringer springs that dampened extra-large bumps. Air valves on the bottom of the seat helped reduce rebounds. Combining the Panoramic windshield with the optional Full-View rear window gave 1,902 square inches of viewing area front and rear. The High-Level ventilation system, with air intake at the base of the windshield, allowed clean, dry air to enter the cab. A new feature was a redesigned accelerator pedal said to be easier and more comfortable to operate.

Chevy's hard-wearing upholstery included new color combinations, with silver and charcoal gray two-toning in either vinyl (base-level Deluxe) or vinyl-and-pattern-cloth combination (extra-cost Custom Cab). Also featured was an eighteen-inch diameter deep-dish steering wheel and No-Glare instrument panel. Custom Cabs had two armrests and sun visors, a cigarette lighter, foam rubber seat cushions and backrests, bright-metal control knobs and chrome window moldings.

Solid colors for regular pickups totaled fourteen choices for 1958. Jet Black was the regular production color. Six others were carried over, and seven were brand new. There were thirteen two-tone combinations for non-Cameo models. Five were the same as in the past and eight made their debut. The patterning for two-tone paint application used the main color on the entire lower body and windshield posts and had the roof and rear corners of the cab done in the secondary color.

New options available this season included Cool-Pack air conditioning and factory-installed seatbelts.

The four-wheel-drive trucks again required optional tires. On the series 31 half-ton, the sizes used were

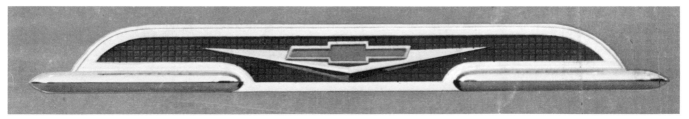

The 1959 hood ornament had a large red bow tie against a black waffle-pattern background inside chrome outlines. The V emblem behind the bow tie indicated use of a V-8 engine.

6.50x16 or 7x17.5 six-ply. The three-quarter-ton trucks in the 36 series came with either 7x17.5 or 8x19.5 six-ply tires.

GVW ratings again varied according to the tires used. The 31 models ranged from 4,000 to 5,000 pounds (5,600 pounds with four-wheel drive). The same ratings were specified for the 3,200s, except that these did not offer the four-wheel-drive option. GVW ratings for the 36 series trucks ranged from a low of 3,200 pounds to a high of 6,900 pounds (7,500 pounds with four-wheel drive).

During 1958, Chevrolet retained its role as industry leader in truck sales and production, although totals throughout the industry were down. The calendar year saw 278,615 commercial vehicles leave Chevrolet factories in the United States, giving the company a 31.98 percent share of market. The figure included 157,911 trucks in the 6,000-pound-and-under GVW class and 46,310 in the next-heavier category, ranging up to 10,000 pounds. As mentioned earlier, only 1,405 Cameos built to 1958 model specifications were produced before the model disappeared from the line.

1959

The 1959 line of Chevy trucks went on display at dealerships across the nation on October 16, 1958. New to the pickup truck offerings was the El Camino, which combined car styling features with the utility of a truck. Though built for personal transportation, it could carry loads up to 1,150 pounds.

The Massive-Functional styling of 1958 was generally retained in the new model year. Hood and front fender decorations were revised, while paint and trim got even brighter. New Color-Break two-toning was offered for the Fleetside pickups, and interiors were made even more colorful.

This was a recession period, a fact that inspired a wave of buyer interest in foreign cars. In the truck market, fuel economy gained even greater significance. Chevrolet's standard six got a new camshaft that promised better gas mileage; the improvement was estimated at ten percent. There was also a second six-cylinder option offering even greater fuel savings.

Another option added to the pickup line-up was a new Stepside with a nine-foot-long cargo bed. Ford had already introduced such a model, and Chevy was simply playing catch-up.

Conventional pickups had the same styling as in 1958, with changes in finish details. Most striking was the Color-Break paint treatments. The upper color was used on everything above the hood-level feature-line (except the rear of the cab), plus on the missile-shaped

side bulge and wheels. The lower body was finished in the color used on the rear of the cab.

Front fender emblems were moved above the wheel opening and changed to a missile-shape. The forward section was black-finished and now carried the Chevrolet and Apache nameplates. Next came a chrome piece, and then the two numbers designating the series, which were placed against a red background. As in 1958, all trucks—plain or fancy—with GVWs up to 9,600 pounds were identified as Apaches.

Chevrolet's sales literature dated October 1, 1958, announced that the Thirftmaster six had new features to improve fuel economy by as much as ten percent. The gain was attributed to a new camshaft design that helped boost torque to 217 pounds-feet at 2000 rpm (up from 210). This engine's 135 hp at 4000 rpm rating was also a change. The 31 and 32 models could also be bought with a Maximum Economy Option using a different carburetor and 3.38:1 rear axle. The early catalog didn't specify how much fuel this option saved.

The Apache 31 (3100) Stepside was now viewed primarily as a workingman's truck. This one has the standard cab with small rear window, and the grille, bumper and hubcaps are painted white. Optional bumper guards are also painted. Lack of V emblem below red Chevy bow tie on front indicates it's a six-cylinder model.

Apparently, it took about another month to figure out the fuel-savings. A four-page brochure released in December headlined twenty percent improved fuel economy. For the standard six, the gas savings were put at ten percent in normal operation and up to twenty-five percent when the engine was idling. This was due to the so-called Economy Contoured Camshaft design with smaller lobes and less valve lift. Next came the advice that the Maximum Economy Option for the small trucks "boosts fuel economy by still another ten percent." This version of the 1959 Thriftmaster six, with the smaller carburetor and economy rear axle, provided 110 hp at 210 pounds-feet of torque.

Although it was not mentioned in the December brochure, the original catalog also showed the Trademaster 283 V-8 option, calling it "a most modern and efficient short stroke design." This engine was said to have been improved, however, it still had 8.5:1 compression, a two-barrel carburetor, 160 hp at 4200 rpm and 275 pounds-feet of torque at 2400 rpm.

Transmission offerings were the same as in 1958. Despite the new emphasis on economy, overdrive was not available, even though it had been a Chevrolet option up to 1957. The wide-faced helical gears, designed to mesh smoothly and run quietly, were carburized and shot-peened for extra strength. Carried over were the same smooth-working clutch and ball-gear steering mechanism.

Leaf springs were retained at all corners, with the two-stage type at the rear. On these, the first stage functioned with the truck empty or lightly loaded, while the second stage met the requirements of heavy loads. There were no changes in the standard rear axles, but posi-traction was optional for 31 and 32 models.

The 1959 half-ton models had larger Torque-Action brakes. These were duo-servo units manufactured by Bendix. Trucks in both the 31 and 36 series could, again, be equipped with the four-wheel-drive option.

A total of twelve pickups were supplied in the one-ton and under light-duty lines, five of them with Fleetside styling. These came with bodies in lengths of seventy-eight or ninety-eight inches with GVWs between 5,000 and 7,300 pounds. Stepsides still had exposed rear fenders and running boards. Box lengths of 6½, 8 and 9 feet were offered, with a top GVW rating of 7,400 pounds.

For 1959, Chevrolet promoted its driver's compartment as a Flight-Ride cab. Features included a sweeping Panoramic windshield with 1,000 square inches of viewing, plus High-Level ventilation, door steps and Nu-Flex seats with deep comfort coil springs.

Foam rubber seat cushions and backrests, brightmetal dashboard control knobs, brightmetal windshield moldings, armrests, sun visors and a cigarette lighter were part of the Custom Cab package. New interiors were fashionably trimmed with durable vinyl and nylon-faced upholstery. Five new exterior colors were among the fourteen solid hues offered. Bombay Ivory was used as the second color in all thirteen two-tone color combi-

A new hood emblem was used in 1959, and the nameplates were repositioned above the front wheelwell on the fender crease. This is about as deluxe as the Apaches came. The 32 series was a half-ton on the longer wheelbase, shared with the three-quarter-ton 36s.

nations. Wheels were painted black with solid-colored trucks and main (upper) body color with two-tones. Chrome moldings were optionally available to highlight the missile-shaped bulges on the sides of the cargo box.

For Chevrolet, 1959 was a year of increased truck production despite the fact that an outside factor had a negative effect on business. A 116-day-long strike by the United Steel Workers of America took place between mid-July and early-November. At that point, an eighty-day injunction under the Taft-Hartley Act got the steel mills back in action. This caused a shortage of steel parts, resulting in a critical supply problem. During November, most Chevrolet assembly lines were shut down or operating at low capacity.

As a result, Ford was able to out-produce Chevrolet in light-duty trucks, while Dodge also made a slight gain in output. Even more importantly, Ford was able to increase its market share significantly. At the same time, International Harvester had an exceptionally good season.

For all classes of trucks, the calendar-year production and share of industry figures for the four companies looked like this:

Manufacturer	Units	% share
Ford	347,266	30.46
Chevrolet	326,093	28.61
IH	143,199	12.56
Dodge	71,680	6.29

Chevrolet continued to see the bulk of its production go to its popular light-duty models. Trucks with GVWs up to 6,000 pounds accounted for 196,307 units. Those in the 6,001 to 10,000-pound class totaled 49,566 units. In terms of sales, Chevy could still not be beat. Its calendar-year registrations stood at 305,837 commercial vehicles versus Ford's 292,338.

Promoted under the Flight Ride banner, the 1959 cab was little changed from 1955 except for colors and trim. Custom Cab equipment included foam seats, chrome dash knobs, chrome window moldings, dual sun visors, two door armrests and cigarette lighter.

Chapter 5

The V-8 era: 1960-1966

In 1960, more than eighty-six percent of the trucks built by Chevrolet were six-cylinder-powered, outselling V-8s six to one. In addition, Chevy's leadership in the truck industry was linked directly to the six-cylinder models' sales. For example, in 1961, Chevy built nearly 100,000 more sixes than its closest competitor, Ford.

By the end of 1966, the production ratio of sixes to V-8s was changed to the point where more than one of every three Chevy trucks had a V-8 engine. About forty percent of total output was so equipped. This included some thirty-nine percent of half-tonners and fifty percent of three-quarter-tonners. In unit terms, V-8 production leaped from just under 50,000 trucks in 1960 to nearly 250,000 trucks in 1966. Moreover, the popularity of optional V-8s climbed twenty-four percent in 1966 alone, with six-cylinder sales dropping eleven percent the same season.

A big reason for this change was the development of the recreational vehicle craze. Between 1961 and 1966, shipments of travel trailers, truck campers and camping trailers increased steadily every year. This segment of the market tripled in those six years.

Trucks with V-8 engines were recommended—in some cases required—to carry or pull trailers and campers up hills. This was a big factor in the changing character of the entire light-duty truck industry. In addition, gas was still cheap, V-8 engines were reasonably priced and the nation's vehicle buyers were generally in a horsepower race state-of-mind.

Perhaps the V-8 era was best summed-up by the release of a new 327 ci powerplant. According to *Automotive News*, this V-8 was designed "to meet the needs of the booming recreational vehicle market." Then in mid-1965 came a factory-issued Camper Special with the powertrains and chassis beefed-up to accommodate cab-over camper units in the pickup's cargo box.

The 1960 Chevy trucks were lower, roomier and stronger up front. The body had a pinch-waist look with pod-type fender bulges. This 3200 Fleetside has the Apache package, which was now optional.

	1961	1962	1963	1964	1965	1966
Travel trailers	28,800	40,600	54,500	64,200	76,600	87,300
Truck campers	15,800	16,700	26,800	34,800	44,300	54,500
Camping trailers	18,000	23,400	40,300	52,000	67,220	72,300

While the V-8 engine made great strides in popularity in the first half of the 1960s, this era was also a strong one in terms of total deliveries. At the end of 1959, Chevy's all-time sales of trucks since 1918 stood at seven million. By 1964, this figure had leaped upwards of nine million, and the ten-millionth unit was assembled during 1966. This meant that thirty percent of all trucks sold by the company since 1918 were manufactured in the seven-year-period 1960–1966.

1960

Chevrolet's Task Force era had brought a steady, modest expansion in the overall model line-up. For example, 136 different trucks had been marketed in 1958, and the count increased to 139 the next season. But now all stops were pulled out. The factory offerings exploded to 165 different basic products for 1960. Chevrolet described these as the most extensively changed trucks in its entire history.

The general styling was changed from the Massive-Functional look of 1955–1959 to an appearance that the division called "clean, functional lines." Sheet metal was said to be integrated with a new chassis design for a lower, roomier cab and stronger front-end assembly. A drop frame was used on the light-duties. This lowered the cab floor height, permitting floor pans to extend to the full body width, which eliminated the concealed steps formerly hidden inside the doors. Cabs were rubber-mounted and had larger windshields for better visibility.

New wheelbases were used for the 1960 models. Half-tons with the seventy-eight-inch-long short box had a 115-inch stance. Those with the ninety-eight-inch long box shared a foot longer wheelbase with three-quarter-tons. Styling was squarer than before. Below the mid-body feature-line, the Fleetside models resembled a big box with a full-width rectangular opening at the front. The low-mounted grille unit housed dual headlamps positioned side-by-side, at each end, with three louver blades running horizontally across the center opening.

The Indy 500 Safety Patrol used these Stepsides in 1960. Lead truck is a C-14 model on 115-inch wheelbase. Behind it is a C-15 pickup with longer 127-inch wheelbase. Both are half-tons. Indianapolis Motor Speedway Corporation

The Chevrolet name was stamped at the base of the grille. Below this was a wider, squarer and more massive bumper.

The body pinched in along the feature-line on the sides, then flared outward again before it curved back inward. This curve was interrupted at the rear by the inner wall of the cargo box. In the center of the truck it continued to the upper beltline. At the front, the curve blended into a flat, scoop-like "jet pod" on the outer portion of the hood and fendertop line.

Each side of the trucks had one of these jet pods. There was a flat, lower, center hood surface between them. The front of each pod was cut off to form an oval opening in which the parking lamps were mounted between vertically louvered wedges trimmed with thin chrome moldings. The lower center section of the hood was curved over at its front, where a bow tie badge was placed. A V-shaped emblem was seen behind the bow tie badge on V-8s.

Below the hood ornament was a hand slot through which the hood latching mechanism was accessible. The entire panel above the mid-body feature-line lifted on hinges at the cowl for access to the engine. Below the rear seam of this hood, under the pinch-waist sculpturing, was a Chevrolet nameplate.

Cab styling was also wider and squarer. A much bigger wraparound windshield was used. Behind the cab, the door pillar slanted forward at about the same angle as the windshield pillar. The rear corner of the cab, however, itself was only slightly forward-angled.

The roof had a flat-top look with a slight overhang all around. At the rear of the cab, there was an extension panel around the rear window. The overall design was a bit contrived, although not unpleasant for its era. It was much more modern-looking than a Ford or Dodge of the same year and seemed especially nice on panel trucks and sedan deliveries, on which the beltline and roofline continued to the rear.

Series coding for all trucks was changed to a letter and number system instead of the previous 3100, 3200 and 3600 codes. The half-ton to one-ton commercial models with conventional drive used the letter C followed by two digits, 14 for half-ton, 25 for three-quarter-ton, 36 for one-ton and 40 for one-and-one-half-ton. Trucks with the four-wheel-drive option substituted a K as the prefix letter.

Another variation from past practice is that Apaches were now merchandised as a trim package. This included chrome-plated grille bars and front bumper, bumper guards, special fender nameplates and a body-

Basic styling was carried over for 1961, but pod-mounted parking lights now had winged ornaments. This truck has deluxe chrome grille and bumper. The V insignia behind the bow tie emblem indicates V-8.

side molding that began under the nameplate, ran toward the taillights and curved back to the top of the rear wheel opening. On these trucks, the cab sides between the rear door pillar and extension around the back window were finished in contrasting color.

Another two-tone treatment seen this year had the color break at the mid-body feature-line completely around the truck. The roof and rear of the cab were done in the lower color, as were the wheels. Everything else was in the upper color.

Styling at the rear of the trucks varied between the Fleetside and Stepside models, the latter having separate fenders and running boards. Fleetsides had flat rear-end panels. They followed the fender contours on the outside and dropped straight down along the tailgate seam on the inside. The wide Fleetside tailgate had a flat, raised panel along the top and bottom, with the Chevrolet name in wide-spaced block letters along its indented center. The Stepside box had tubelike top edges and a narrower tailgate. This also had the company name across it, but in closer-spaced letters. Taillights were mounted in chrome housings at the bottom of each Stepside fender. Rear bumpers, when ordered, were different from both types of pickups, the Fleetside type being more modern-looking.

The design of the dashboard was the same for all models. There were large, wide arches at either side. The left one had a semicircular speedometer at its center, above the steering column. Two large round instrument dials were clustered in curved rectangles on each side. Furthest to the left was the temperature gauge, then the generator telltale indicator. On the right were the oil pressure indicator and gas gauge. Small circles below each cluster were signal indicator lamps. Heater and

This Chevy pickup owner shows how to use the small running boards on Stepside models effectively. His working half-tonner has the painted bumpers and grille treatment.

radio controls were at the center. The right-hand arch housed a glovebox.

A major engineering change was a switch to independent front suspension, said to be the first such system offered for trucks. The design used on all but two models had ball-joints and torsion bar springing. Other improvements for half- and three-quarter-ton models included a two-link coil spring rear suspension, while medium and heavy-duty models stuck with variable-rate leaf springs. Frames, steering and other components were redesigned to complement the new suspensions.

Design of the front suspension for C-10 to C-40 trucks was the same and included the frame front crossmember, control arms and shafts, ball-joints, torsion bars, steering knuckle and attaching parts. The ball-joints connected each steering knuckle to a set of upper and lower control arms. Each torsion bar was supported in a steel tube in the lower control arm, being held firmly in place in the hexagon section of the tube. The rear of

Pinch-waist beltline was kept in 1962, but lower Work Styled hood was used. This truck was Custom Cab with ribbed trim plate on rear quarter post and Custom molding package.

Canfield Two Bar Company was one of several Chevrolet-approved vendors of vocational equipment that supplied a four-ton wrecker package for the C-25 three-quarter-ton Fleetside pickups.

the torsion bar was supported in an adjustable anchor connected to a special cross-member. The upper end of each shock absorber was bolted to a frame bracket. The lower ends were bolted to the lower control arm, and vehicle height could be adjusted by turning the torsion bar anchor bolts.

Chevy's steering gear was of the recirculating ball type. A ball nut connected to the steering worm meshed with the sector gear. Precision-finished helical grooves inside the ball nut matched the helical grooves in the worm. Ball-bearings rolled around in the grooves as the steering wheel was turned. Two adjustments could be made in this type of gear.

The steering ratio for both C-10 and C-20 trucks was 24.0 to 1:17 inches. With optional power steering, hydraulic booster equipment was added. An improvement for 1960 was locating the control valve directly on the steering gear. This simplified the powerline arrangement and gave better response.

Engines available for C-10 and C-20 models included the Thriftmaster six of 135 hp and the 283 ci

Trademaster V-8 of 275 hp. An improvement in the latter engine was a neoprene rear main bearing seal, replacing the old wick type. Also, new carburetors were used on both engines. These were of the same basic type as before, but had different model numbers.

Four-wheel-drive models came standard with three-speed synchromesh transmission, and a four-speed was optional. Conventional truck buyers had the same choices, plus heavy duty three-speed manual and automatic. Hydraulically operated clutch controls were used on all stick-shift C-10s and C-20s (except for forward control models). A dual master cylinder—one side for clutch operation and the other for braking—was employed. Rear axles were the same as used in the past.

Chevrolet dropped the use of Hydra-matic transmission in half- and three-quarter-ton trucks in 1960. The company instead switched to the Powerglide automatic.

Another change for 1960 was seen on four-wheel-drive trucks, for which Chevy adopted a Spicer front axle. This replaced the system used since 1957, employ-

Standard equipment on this 1962 C-10 Fleetside included electric wipers, directional signals and tubeless tires. Torsion bar independent suspension smoothed out rough roads. A

new High Torque 261 six-cylinder engine offered extra power on light-duty jobs.

58

ing an axle with Rhezeppa constant velocity joints. Also different on these models was the suspension system, which employed leaf springs at all four corners.

For calendar 1960, Chevrolet's truck production hit 394,014 units, the highest since 1950. This stood as the third best year in the company's entire history of truck making. The market share credited to Chevrolet was a strong 32.88 percent, which was the second highest of all postwar years up to this point. The production figure included 339,229 six-cylinder models and 54,785 V-8-powered trucks.

1961

Chevrolet's complete truck line grew again in 1961 to now include a total of 186 models. The increased model count reflected the introduction of the innovative Corvair 95 models and a trio of new four-wheel-drive units. Other product alterations were so minor that the same artwork was used in sales catalogs, with detail changes air-brushed in.

The grille stamping was redesigned slightly. It now had a narrower hot-dog-bun-shaped opening. Inside this was a similarly shaped molding divided by four short vertical moldings, which had the Chevrolet name across them.

Full-width sheet metal forming the fendertop-hood panel again had jet-pod bulges at each side and a wide, flat center portion of the hood between them. The middle

of the hood still carried a bow tie ornament in the front with a V-shaped piece behind it on trucks with V-8 engines. The parking lamps were in the same location as 1960, but were changed in design details. They were now supported at the center of an ornament having wings or arms extending from each side. Side nameplates were moved from below the mid-body feature-line to above the feature-line along the top of the body.

Heavier tires were required for 1962 C-15 Fleetside long-box pickups when a camper unit like this one was added. It also helped to have a V-8 engine to pull the extra weight. This was the era when sales of RVs were starting to boom and increased steadily year to year.

Trucks like this 1962 Fleetside with Custom Cab and Custom chrome equipment were now identified as C-10, C-15 or C-20 models. Bumper guards were a factory accessory. New hood design was said to increase forward view by as much as 10½ feet.

Upholstery designs were changed from a style with three rectangles on each side of the seatbacks and cushions (as used in 1960) to an overall pattern. Otherwise, the cab interiors seemed mostly unchanged. The color choices were, of course, slightly revamped.

Technically, the 1961 models were about the same as the 1960s. The 135 hp Thriftmaster six was the base powerplant, and the 160 hp Trademaster 283 ci V-8 was a $120 piece of optional equipment for the half- and three-quarter-ton trucks. Standard transmission was a Chevrolet-built three-speed manual gearbox with gearshift controls on the steering column and all-synchromesh gearing. For an average of $80 extra, buyers could add the heavy-duty Warner model T898 three-speed or the Chevy-built four-speed with floor shift. Powerglide automatic transmission was a $190 extra that could be ordered for all trucks not having the four-wheel-drive option.

Starting with 1961 production, the Powerglide clutch drive (faced) plates were flat. A green stripe of dye was used to identify the new type plates, which, with the proper parts kit, could be adapted to the earlier transmissions.

The three new four-wheel-drive models were the long-box ninety-eight-inch bed half-tons, which had not previously been available with the go-anywhere-type driveline. They came as a chassis and cab, Stepside pickup or Fleetside pickup.

On a calendar-year basis, Chevrolet's leadership in the truck industry was seriously threatened this year. It out-manufactured Ford by a slim 3,670 units. Total output in all series came to 342,658 trucks, of which 294,183 were six-cylinder-powered and 48,391 had V-8 engines. The remaining eighty-four trucks were four- or six-cylinder diesels in the various delivery van or heavy-duty series.

I do not have any weight-class breakout of this production total, although trade journals did break down the calendar-year state registration figures (for licensing) this way. These figures show a total of 202,697 Chevrolet trucks with GVWs of 6,000 pounds or less being sold. In the 6,001 to 10,000-pound weight class, the registration total was 44,903 units.

1962

Introduced in September 1961, the new Chevrolet commercial vehicles were promoted as Jobmaster trucks. "A new world of worth" was promised in advertisements that stressed money-saving high-torque engines, independent front suspension, lower work-style hoods and improved mufflers. The total line-up was composed of

Several aftermarket companies supplied crew cab conversions that Chevrolet dealers could promote to customers through use of their Silver Book. This is a 1962 C-20 Fleet-side with a conversion that showed up at a VCCA show in Green Bay, Wisconsin.

203 models, including fifteen new medium- and heavy-duty diesel-powered trucks.

Light-duty Chevrolet models included two lines of C-10 half-tons: the 115-inch wheelbase C-1400s and the C-1500 subseries of long-box pickups riding on a 127-inch wheelbase. Three-quarter-ton C-20s also used the 127-inch wheelbase. Standard engine in all of these was a 235 ci High-Torque six, which had the same specifications as the former Thriftmaster six.

Pinch-waist body styling was used again, and the cabs were also unchanged. The main appearance alteration was a lowered hood without jet-pod scoops at each end. Instead, the outer surfaces were actually lower than the midsection, which had a slight sculptured bulge and a peaked center. The front edge of the hood simply carried the bodyside feature-line around to the front. Rectangular parking lamps were incorporated at each corner, and the mid-section had two hand slots, one on either side of center. There were no emblems or ornaments. This hood was said to permit drivers to see the road as much as 10½ feet closer when looking directly ahead.

Standard models came with electric windshield wipers, directional signals, left-hand sun visor, outside rearview mirror and black tubeless tires. Tire sizes were 6.70x15 four-ply for half-tons and 7x17.5 six-ply on

The rear end of C-10 Fleetside models had an extra-wide tailgate with Chevrolet lettering across it. The taillights were incorporated in the rear fender end panels. This 1963 truck has the standard small-window cab, but includes the optional rear bumper. Bed floor was still select wood reinforced with steel skid strips.

The primary styling changes for 1963 included a new grille that ran from end to end between headlights. This is the chrome version. Bodyside nameplates were also relocated to the front fenders, behind wheel openings. This is a C-10 Fleetside with Custom Cab and Custom side moldings.

Standard 1963 model came with painted grille. This bumper is a special-order heavy-duty type designed to carry a Chevrolet-approved Ramsey winch. This particular winch is Ramsey's Model 200 L-265, which came in an aftermarket kit including bumper.

three-quarter-tons. A spare was standard on half-tons only.

With optional V-8 power, an oil filter and oil bath air cleaner were included at no extra cost. Bumpers—both front and (optional) rear—were restyled to have a slightly more modern appearance. The fronts were rounder and the rears could be described as flatter and wider on the top.

On standard trucks, the grille and front bumper were still painted, and a painted rear bumper was available for pickups with a painted front bumper. A Custom Chrome Option added plating for all of these parts, with prices based on the number of bumpers ordered. For pickups with only a front bumper, the chrome package was $25.10 at dealer cost; with a rear bumper it came to $40.33.

A separate option, restricted to Fleetsides, was a Custom Side Molding package for $16.75 dealer cost. This included one molding along the entire mid-body feature-line, with a second one branching off at the center of the door and continuing from there to the back of the truck. White paint was applied to the front of the

This is why '63 Chevrolet Trucks are called the "New Reliables"

THEY HANDLED THIS KIND OF PUNISHMENT! These are the trucks that showed how tough they are on the toughest run under the sun—Mexico's Baja (bah'hah) Run—over terrain that punished new engines, frames, suspension systems, all components . . . harder than you ever will.

THEY CAN HANDLE YOUR KIND OF WORK! You can be sure 1963 Chevrolet trucks are the strongest we've ever built . . . built to do the work you buy them for reliably for years at low operating expense with just normal care and attention.

CHIEF ENGINE & CHASSIS ADVANCEMENTS FOR '63

 QUALITY TRUCKS ALWAYS COST LESS

Chevy's 1963 model trucks again used the wide-bottom-type wraparound windshield and flat-top-style roofline. The C-10

Stepside showed up in many ads, like this one, as Chevy seemed to be stressing their pickups' utility value.

upper molding and between the two branches along the door and bodyside.

Two-tone paint treatments used one color on the roof and window frames and the second on the body and wheels. On trucks with the Custom Side Molding package, fancy trim plates with Custom Cab identification were added to the rear quarter of the cab.

Chevrolet returned to the use of single headlamps in 1962. They were mounted behind oversize oval doors in each side of the redesigned grille. These had horizontally ribbed trim plates and chrome moldings circling the edges. The grille consisted of two long horizontal bars and two wide-spaced vertical bars forming three segments within three horizontal openings stacked on top of each other. The wide lower surround carried the Chevrolet name across it. This ensemble was set into an unchanged grille opening with wide moldings around the edges. Badges were used on the side of the cowl section, between the hood and door seam. They carried a red Chevrolet bow tie and two numbers—10 for half-ton and 20 for three-quarter-ton.

For 1964, the bodies looked the same, but the cabs were heavily restyled, with totally new windshields that also changed shape of vent windows and gave A-pillars a backward slant.

A 1965 C-10 Fleetside, virtually identical to the 1963 trucks. This truck was shown at the Elkhorn, Wisconsin, show in 1987.

Standard cab interiors featured a deep-cushioned three-passenger seat, driver's sunshade, left-hand door lock, heavy rubber floor mat, dome light and hooded nonglare instrument panel. Vinyl upholstery was used. The Custom Comfort Option, for $42.66 extra dealer cost in pickups, added full-length foam cushioned seats with nylon upholstery, plus twin sunshades and a horn ring. A Full-View rear window, with larger glass opening, was a separate option priced at $33.45 at dealer level.

For the first time since 1959, Chevrolet light-duties were available with an optional six-cylinder engine, and it was not an economy version. Called the High-Torque 261, this powerplant used a larger three-inch stroke to get its increased displacement, developing 150 hp. Some sources also refer to this as the Jobmaster Six, and state that it was not really a new engine. Larger trucks had used it since 1955, but this was the first year of availability in C-10 and C-20 models. The heavier-duty eleven-inch Chevrolet clutch was employed with this engine, which cost $65 extra on dealer sheets.

Also available for all light-duties was the Trademaster 283 V-8 which wholesaled for $92 extra. This was essentially unchanged, again using a Rochester model 2G two-barrel carburetor and having 8.5:1 compression. The horsepower rating was unchanged, but the torque ratio was lowered slightly to 270 pounds-feet at 2000 rpm.

The trucks continued to feature independent torsion bar front suspension and coil springs at the rear. Rear spring rates were heavier for three-quarter-ton models.

Transmission options were the same as previously offered. The Powerglide unit used in 1962 was essentially unchanged, except for elimination of the throttle valve and low servo apply test plugs.

Power steering was a $188 option. Rear axles were semi-floating on C-10s and full-floating for C-20s. Steering was again of the recirculating ball type. The new Delcotron alternators were available in two models: 42-amp and 52-amp. Dealer cost on this option was $22.62 or $29.30, respectively. C-20 models used larger brakes than the half-tons.

Four-wheel-drive trucks were again quite different from conventionals in some regards. They used a heavier frame, heavy-rated leaf springs front and rear, a

Rear styling was basically the same as the 1963 rear view shown earlier. Custom Cab, back-up lights and chrome rear bumper were among available options. This truck, with modern tires and wheels, is the long-box style.

64

Spicer tubular front driving axle and a two-speed transfer case, and boasted higher GVW ratings. Transmission choices were limited to three- or four-speed synchromesh. Also, the brakes used on half-tons with four-wheel drive had a slightly larger total lining area than the standard C-10 brakes

Chevrolet's production for calendar year 1962 was the third highest in the company's truck-making experience. Assemblies of all types of Chevrolet trucks in the United States peaked at 396,819 units. Of these, eighty-two percent were six-cylinder powered. Model-year production, at 396,940 units, was amazingly close to the same total. A milestone hit this season was building the eight-millionth Chevrolet truck since 1918.

1963

Numerous changes of an engineering nature were incorporated in the "New Reliables" that Chevrolet's truck division introduced in the fall of 1962. They included two different High-Torque six-cylinder engines that weighed less, but pulled more, than the previous sixes. Another update for conventional light-duty models was independent front suspension with variable-rate coil springs that stiffened as the load increased. All models now had ladder-type frames fabricated of extra-high-strength steel.

One might suppose that such a high degree of mechanical alteration would be accompanied by significant appearance changes. Not so! The major styling revisions amounted to no more than a different grille and relocation of the bodyside emblems.

The grille retained low-mounted single headlamps set into smaller, drum-shaped doors at either side, with the bottom portion of the surround again embossed with the Chevrolet name. The grillework in the center of the one-piece stamping consisted of three long horizontal

moldings and thirteen tighter-spaced short vertical moldings. Decorating the bodysides were large badges below the feature-line, near the rear edge of the front fenders. They consisted of a bow tie emblem and tall vertical numerical designations: 10 for half-tons and 20 for three-quarter-tons. Side trim moldings similar to 1962 were available as part of a Custom Cab option for Fleetsides. This again included rear cab corner trim plates.

Many ads seen this year highlighted the Stepside model, as one of these had been used in a promotional stunt in which a convoy of six-cylinder Chevrolet trucks were driven in the Baja Run in Mexico. "These are the trucks that showed how tough they are on the toughest run under the sun," said the copywriters. "Over terrain that punished new engines, frames, suspension systems, all components . . . harder than you ever will." Later in the year, these vehicles were displayed at auto shows around the country.

Chevy's new sixes were more efficient and powerful than their predecessors. The smaller engine had a 3⅞x3¼-inch bore and stroke giving 230 ci. It was an overhead valve design with wedge-shaped combustion chambers. With 8.5:1 compression and a Rochester model B carburetor, it put out 140 hp at 4400 rpm and had a 220 pounds-feet at 1600 rpm gross torque rating.

For additional pulling power, there was an optional 292 ci six with 3⅞x4⅛-inch bore and stroke, 8.0:1 compression, aluminized inlet valves, chrome top piston rings and a model B carburetor. It developed 165 hp at 3800 rpm and gross torque was 280 pounds-feet at 1600 rpm. Thin-wall-casting techniques were employed to make these engines lighter than their earlier counterparts. Although both engines were completely new, they were still promoted under the same High-Torque banner advertised in 1962.

This trade name was also used to describe the optional 283 ci V-8. Changes for this engine in 1963

Bed detail of the 1965 C-10 Fleetside.

Hubcap detail on the 1965 C-10.

included a higher 9:1 compression ratio, plus a different Rochester model 2G carburetor. Some features retained from the past included the overhead valve arrangement with aero-type mechanism, hydraulic valve lifters, five-main-bearing crankshaft and steel-backed Babbitt bearings. Both sixes and V-8s now came standard with Delcotron AC alternators, and DC generators were no longer used.

Chevy's driveline setup continued basically the same, with regular or heavy-duty three-speed or four-speed manual gearboxes offered in C-10 and C-20 light-duties. A new automatic transmission—the aluminum Powerglide—was also used. This had a welded-type three-element torque converter. The case and converter housing were a single cast-aluminum unit. The K-10 and K-20 four-wheel-drives came only with standard three- or four-speed manuals. The easy-acting diaphragm-spring clutch operated via mechanical linkage. A ten-inch clutch was standard on all light-duties, with an eleven-inch type optional.

Something new for 1963 was the design of both types of rear axles. The semi-floating rear axle housing and differential carrier were cast into an integral assembly, and the drive pinion assembly was mounted in two opposed, tapered roller bearings. Spacers, instead of nuts, were now used for preloading bearings. A lock pin rather than a lock screw held the pinion shaft in place. The full-floating rear axles were also redesigned. The straddle-mounted drive pinion was supported at the front by a one-piece double-row ball-bearing, and the pinion rear bearing was a roller-type assembly with precision-ground diameter on the pinion pilot which functioned as an inner race. Two- and four-pinion differentials were used in mixed production.

The new front suspension consisted of upper and lower control arms pivoting on steel threaded bushings on upper and lower arm shafts, which were bolted to the front suspension cross-member and bracket assembly. These arms were connected to the steering knuckle through pivoting ball-joints. A coil spring was located between the lower control arm and a formed seat in the suspension cross-member. The lower control arm functioned as the load-carrying member. Double-acting shocks attached to the lower control arms and connected with the frame, behind the suspension's upper end. Shims were now used for caster and camber adjustments. The 1963 steering gear was of the same type, although it required only three steps, instead of six, to remove it from the vehicle for repair.

Rear springs were two-stage coils on both C-10 and

For 1965, series identification was moved above the upper feature-line on front fenders. This small change helps to distinguish these trucks from 1964 models, which were virtually identical otherwise.

66

C-20 models, with standard ratings of 1,250 pounds and 2,000 pounds respectively.

The K-10 four-wheel-drives again used leaf springs, and the front units were increased one-half inch in width, with everything else the same as 1962. Heavier-duty axles, brakes, front springs, tires and wheels were employed on the three-quarter-ton four-wheel-drive trucks. Freewheeling front hubs were optional at extra cost on all K series models.

Among other new-for-1963 items was a larger nineteen-gallon gas tank as standard equipment on all half- and three-quarter-ton models. The new ladder-type frames compared to the 1962 units in section modulus as follows:

Frame section modulus

Series	1962	1963
C-10	3.39 in. cu.	2.98 in. cu.
C-20	3.91 in. cu.	3.71 in. cu.
K-14	5.09 in. cu.	3.62 in. cu.
K-15	5.09 in. cu.	6.19 in. cu.
K-20	5.09 in. cu.	6.19 in. cu.

An interesting historical point concerning 1963 models is the stability of vehicle prices at this time.

Nearly all Chevrolet trucks were listed within a few dollars of their 1962 retail prices, with some actually costing a few dollars less this season.

Calendar-year production for 1963 soared to 483,119 units, second only to the all-time high set in 1950. This included some 378,000 six-cylinder models and 102,400 V-8s. It was the first time that V-8 assemblies topped 100,000. The other 2,700-odd trucks had either four-cylinder engines or diesel powerplants. Chevrolet was on a roll and it was not about to stop, as 1964 would prove to be an even better season.

1964

Chevrolet's 1964 trucks bowed on September 29, 1963. The big news was the reintroduction of the El Camino on an intermediate-size chassis and the release of the Chevy Van series, early in the 1964 calendar year.

Pickups, panels and Carryall Suburbans underwent a number of important styling revisions that greatly modernized their appearance. Among them was a recontoured windshield, a redesigned dashboard, new eye-catching interior trims, a different grille and head-

In 1966, the series identification nameplate was slightly redesigned and moved below the front fender "pinch" again. The famous 327 ci V-8 was optional in pickups for the first time this year. This truck has modernized wheels and tires, but is otherwise mostly original.

lamp treatment, restyled hubcaps and new model identification badges. A tachometer was now included on the options list.

Cabs got the most attention. The old wide-bottom wraparound windshield was replaced with one having straight up-and-down sides and a piece of glass that curved only slightly around each cab corner. As a result, the angle of the cab A-pillars was completely changed. They now slanted backward instead of forward, making the vent windows triangular and wider at the bottom than the top. The cab rear corner panels also looked taller and thinner.

Chevy's new easy-to-see instrument panel was incorporated into a flat full-width dashboard that angled slightly away from the driver. The upper section was more shelflike, with a lip protruding along the top and sides to hood the entire dash and reduce glare. A rectangular panel at the left-hand side housed all the gauges in front of the driver. The center section had two vertical rectangular impressions with two squares stacked between them. These housed heater controls, ashtray, radio dials, and so on. At the right was a large, sculptured glovebox door of basically trapezoid shape. The ivory-colored steering wheel was a two-spoke deep-dished type.

Standard cab features included a deep-cushioned three-passenger seat with easy-to-clean vinyl upholstery having short lengthwise ribbing in the center of cushions and backs, with long horizontal pleats near the borders. There was improved insulation, a left-hand sun visor, left-hand door lock, heavy rubber floor mat and dome light.

The Custom Comfort Option included a full-depth foam seat upholstered in a handsome striped nylon fabric and trimmed with vinyl in red or beige, depending on exterior color. Also featured was a driver's door armrest, right-hand door lock, chrome-trimmed control knobs, cigarette lighter, passenger-side visor and steering wheel horn ring. White-accented trim moldings were again used on the outside of the doors and along the dispatch box between double moldings. A ribbed trim plate reading Custom was also applied to the rear sides of the roof to identify these Custom Cab trucks.

The 1964 grille had a narrower insert with thin horizontal and vertical moldings in a tight cross-hatch pattern. Stamped into the upper surround molding was the Chevrolet name. The lower surround molding was plain. Single headlamps were positioned on each side of the grille in square doors. The balance of sheet metal was unchanged from 1963. Series identification badges with red numbers below a chromed bow tie were in nearly the same location as last year. New hubcaps carried the bow tie emblem within a painted circle in the center of a somewhat gear-shaped raised section. Over-

all, the new model-year features made the trucks seem more up-to-date with a minimum of retooling.

Engineering features were basically a direct carryover from the previous year, the engine line-up being unchanged. A close comparison of specifications in the 1963 Chevrolet *Silver Book* and a 1964 sales brochure, however, shows slightly higher horsepower ratings and slightly lower torque figures for the 229 ci six and a lower compression ratio (with no change in horsepower or torque) for the 283 ci V-8. In addition, the part number for the Rochester model B carburetor used on the 1964 High-Torque 292 six was changed from 7023013 to 7024009.

Beginning in February 1964, an oil-pan drain plug was added to the aluminum Powerglide transmission, and by April 1 all transmissions were so equipped. Also, Chevrolet switched to self-adjusting brakes this season and extended recommended chassis lubrication intervals to 6,000 miles.

Exterior colors available in 1964 included Balboa

Here's a closer view of the half-ton series 10 model identification badge used on 1966 pickups. Push-button door handles were placed within a scooplike depression toward upper rear of doors. Custom moldings separated into branches on doors and boxsides, with contrasting finish between the branches.

Blue, Cameo White, Cardinal Red, Fawn, Gray Green poly, Light Blue, Light Gray, Light Green, Omaha Orange, Pure White, red, Tangier Gold poly, Turquoise poly, Woodland Green and Yuma Yellow. Four colors—Charcoal Gray poly, Fawn poly, ivory and red—were listed as interior colors. Sales literature indicates that most painted interior parts were Fawn-colored, with Charcoal Gray on the steering column, seat frame, pedal arms, gearshift lever and brake handle. The steering wheel was ivory, and red was used on the top of the armrest on red trucks with Custom trim.

The nine-millionth Chevrolet truck of all time was put together in 1964, which also became the best year ever for Chevrolet's truck business. Model-year production peaked at 523,791 units.

1965

Changes in all Chevrolet trucks were of a very minor nature for 1965. The pickups, panels and Carryalls were among the least changed of all models. Series identification badges were moved above the upper feature-line. This small change is helpful to collectors for recognition, as the 1964 and 1966 models, which are otherwise virtually identical, have this type of identification above the mid-body feature-line.

Among other new 1965 features was the long-overdue release of a factory-installed air conditioning system for light-duty models. Cars had offered this option since the late 1950s, and the big Chevy trucks also had it for both conventional and low-cab-forward models in 1964.

In mid-1965, Chevrolet introduced another long-awaited option, a Camper Special package for pickups. This included beefed-up chassis components and V-8 powerplants.

Standard equipment for 1965 trucks was the same assortment used since 1962. Available again were Custom Chrome (bumper and grille), Custom Appearance (Custom Cab) and Custom Side Molding (on doors and dispatch box) option packages. Cabs still came with a small rear window, unless the Full-View type was added at extra cost. Tu-tone paint (as Chevy spelled it) was also an extra, $12.55 dealer cost for pickups.

Horizontally ribbed brightmetal plate with center inscription decorated the Custom Cab models with larger back windows.

When California-style mirrors were ordered, the mounting for the standard mirror was filled with plugs.

Exterior color choices for the 1965 models included the same Cameo White, Dark Blue, Fawn, light blue, light gray, Light Green, Omaha Orange, Pure White, red, Turquoise poly, Woodland Green and Yuma Yellow finishes offered last season, plus two new shades: Maroon poly and Yellow. Colors of Charcoal, Charcoal Gray poly, Fawn poly, ivory and red were used for interior parts.

Engine and chassis specifications were unchanged from 1964. Higher output alternators were available, probably due to the growing list of options—especially air conditioning—that demanded more electrical power. Manual transmissions were again the standard Muncie three-speed, heavy-duty Saginaw three-speed and Muncie four-speed. The two Muncie units were available with four-wheel-drive trucks. An aluminum Powerglide ($146.30 dealer cost) was optional in all models, except four-wheel-drives.

Chevrolet promoted the 1965 models as "Work Power" trucks and advertised "The Long Strong Line For '65." This is the first model year for which I was able to locate complete model-by-model production breakouts, and the chart at the back of the book shows these figures in the far right-hand column. A small number of additional light-duty configurations, such as cowl-and-windshield or cowl-less-windshield, were also built for ambulance conversions and such. The figures cover production at US plants, including a small number of units exported overseas.

Model-year production by series

Chevy Van	42,999
C1400 (C-10)	131,395
C1500 (C-10)	186,461
K1400 (K-10)	2,788
K1500 (K-10)	2,024
C2500 (C-20)	64,282
K2500 (K-20)	2,561
Total	432,510

Model-year output of all Chevy trucks at US factories was 552,482. Of these, 458,235 were one-ton or under models, not including El Caminos and vans. This grand total included 532,495 domestic and 19,987 export units, but this does not include the 36,584 additional trucks made in Canadian factories.

1966

Chevrolet produced 621,354 trucks in model year 1966, including 504,779 light-duty models. They included the company's ten-millionth truck of all time. It was the final appearance of the pinch-waist body introduced in 1960.

Chief among annual product changes for chassis and cab, pickup, panel and Carryall models was the availability of Chevrolet's 327 ci V-8. This engine, first released in mid-1965 for cars, had a four-inch bore and 3¼-inch stroke. Advertised horsepower was 220 at 4400 rpm. Maximum torque was rated at 320 pounds-feet at 2800 rpm.

The 292 ci six and 283 ci V-8 were also continued. New transmission options included overdrive and Turbo Hydra-matic. The latter was used with higher output versions (over 275 hp) of the 327 ci V-8. Powerglide was still the automatic used with sixes and less powerful V-8s.

A new Saginaw three-speed manual transmission, used in trucks with overdrive, was fully synchronized in that all forward gear changes were accomplished with synchronizer sleeves. This was said to permit quicker shifts with greatly reduced gear clash and to allow downshifting from third to second between 40 and 20 mph and from second to first below 20 mph.

Styling changes for the season amounted to little more than the relocation of the series identification badge below the mid-body feature-line near the rear of the front fenders. It was similar to the small, rectangular badge of 1965, but in the same place as the totally different 1964 emblem.

Due to government safety regulations affecting the auto industry, Chevrolet expanded its standard equipment list for trucks. It now included seatbelts, an outside rearview mirror, two-speed windshield wipers (with washers) and back-up lamps. Prices increased accordingly.

Another politically motivated change seen on light-duty trucks (with all engines) sold in California was that state's required Air Injector Reactor system. This was designed to fight smog problems in cities like Los Angeles and impose stricter emissions requirements. Tune-up specs for engines with the AIR systems were different.

New distributors were fitted to all engines. They had wider dwell angles and different centrifugal and vacuum advance settings. Also changed were the alternators, which had slightly lower output ratings.

Chrome bumper equipment was added to 66,733 Chevrolet trucks in the half-ton to two-ton range this model year. In the same class, 70,085 trucks had a new Custom Comfort and Convenience package that entered production in February 1966. Out of 72,282 trucks qualifying for Camper Special equipment, 9,144 vehicles were so equipped. Transmission attachments in the half- to two-ton range included 4,168 overdrives; 5,759 heavy-duty three-speeds; 90,837 four-speeds; 39,064 Powerglides; and 6,577 Turbo Hydra-matics; plus several other big-truck options. Chevrolet's records kept track of the number of trucks having each option and also included "percent usage" figures based on the number of options sold versus the number of trucks that each option could be ordered for. Publishing all of these figures in a book of this size would be impractical.

As far as engine choices, some figures for models in the half- to two-ton category included 2,946 trucks with 230 ci sixes; 54,667 with 292 ci sixes; 130,944 with 283 ci V-8s and 53,020 with 327 ci V-8s. These figures give a general idea of the popularity of different options on all but Chevy's largest truck models, vans, forward control units and El Caminos. After 1968, the figures for light-duties became even more detailed, since a separate breakout for half- to one-ton models was recorded.

Model-year production by series

Chevy Van	37,403
C1400 (C-10)	140,783
C1500 (C-10)	206,363
K1400 (K-10)	2,959
K1500 (K-10)	2,463
C2500 (C-20)	73,825
K2500 (K-20)	3,151
Total	466,947

Model-year output of all Chevy trucks from US factories was 621,354. Of these, 472,894 were one-ton and under models (excluding vans and El Caminos). This grand total included 461,774 built for domestic sale and 11,120 trucks for the export market. In addition, 31,885 other one-ton and under units were manufactured in Canada.

The 1966 Panoramic rear window continued to be sealed with black rubber gaskets. Two-tone finish, usually with the upper cab in white, was common. Top of cargo box had square openings widely spaced for lashing down the cargo. Gas filler was on left-hand side, behind the door handle.

Chapter 6

Custom Sport Truck era: 1967-1972

The restyled 1967 pickups can easily be distinguished by the lack of side-marker lamps. This is a standard three-quarter-ton with two-toned cab and Custom chrome. It also has the Camper Special package and an all-weather Wolverine camper unit.

In 1967, when Chevy completely restyled its light-duty pickups, the new CST (Custom Sport Truck) version was introduced. This was, in fact, what Detroit calls a model-option—a prepackaged assortment of extra-cost equipment with its own sports-luxury image.

This marketing approach began with cars of the 1960s like the Chevrolet Super Sport or Pontiac GTO. The Custom Sport Truck also had a distinctive identity. It appealed to young, upwardly mobile buyers looking for the type of truck that stood out in a crowd.

As is the case with any extra-cost option, the CST package was installed on only a percentage of all Chevy pickups. Still, it represented the heartbeat of new product developments in the 1967–1972 period and has become a feature that collectors search for today. For these reasons, it seems appropriate to think of these years as the Custom Sport Truck era.

The CST era was marked by fluctuations in sales and production within the truck industry. For most of the six years the popularity of pickups continued to grow, although labor disputes in the 1969–1970 period had a negative effect on overall business.

Sales and production (all US trucks)

Model year	Sales	Production
1967	1,518,426	1,539,462
1968	1,775,601	1,896,078
1969	1,888,812	1,923,179
1970	1,790,177	1,692,440
1971	1,993,186	2,053,196
1972	2,513,952	2,446,807

During this period, Chevrolet's production picture followed that of the total industry, with the figures growing steadily, except in 1970, when a drastic decline was felt. The company entered this period building fewer than 550,000 trucks per year and by 1972 was up to nearly 750,000 units annually. Some of the improvement was related to product innovations, such as the introduction of the Blazer in 1969 and redesign of the Chevy Van in 1970. Pickups, however, remained a popular Chevrolet model line.

1967

Introduced September 11, 1966, was an all-new Chevrolet pickup described as having "the most significant cab and sheet metal styling change in Chevrolet history." A new, low-silhouette cab was designed to improve road handling stability due to a lower center of gravity and to reduce wind resistance. The lower hood gave a better view out of the larger windshield, and the size of the side windows was also increased.

Chevrolet said the new design "reflected the importance of an attractive appearance in the light-duty truck field as more and more trucks were purchased for personal transportation and camper use." Wheelbases on half- and three-quarter-ton models increased to 115 and 127 inches.

The front of the trucks featured a rectangular panel with square headlamp housings on either side of the radiator opening. A thin horizontal panel—with bow tie emblem in its center—ran across the opening, dividing it into two horizontal slots. Rectangular parking lights were tucked into the outer ends of the lower slot. Both slots were trimmed with thin brightmetal molding. The headlamp lenses were round and the new bumper was flatter and more sculptured, with a license plate recess at its center.

Above the grille, the hood lip was angled back and carried the Chevrolet name across it. All sheet metal

Rear view of the 1967 C-20 Fleetside with Wolverine's Pup-ette camper shell. The Camper Special package included heavy-duty suspension and electrical components, along with special fender badges identifying the option.

Here is the 1967 C-20 Fleetside with Wolverine's Pup slide-in camper and tailgate removed. Wolverine Camper Company was an authorized Silver Book vendor located in Gladwin, Michigan.

above the upper beltline, at the sides and rear, had an inward angled curve. Bodysides had a sort of rounded, slablike look. A prominent feature-line ran around the entire perimeter of the body (at bumper-top height), curving up over each front and rear wheel opening.

The cab had a more modern appearance with its much larger expanse of glass area (a panoramic window was available again). The roofline was shorter and more up-to-date. Double-wall construction was now featured for the cowl, windshield pillars, roof and door openings, as well as the Fleetside cargo box. All sheet metal had greatly improved rust protection; smooth-surfaced, undercoated front fender liners were used to protect against road splash.

Full-coil-spring ride was a new Chevrolet feature, said to be stronger and smoother-riding. Rugged two-stage coil springs were used at the rear. They were designed to adjust automatically to the weight of the load carried, thus providing a balanced ride whether the truck was empty or piled high with cargo.

The engine line-up included both sixes and V-8s. Base engine in the C-10 and C-20 series was the 250 ci, 140 hp six, with the 292 ci, 170 hp six available at extra cost. A 283 ci V-8 with 175 hp was the base V-8 for these models, while a 327 ci, 185 hp V-8 was optional.

Chevrolet advertised the 1967 models as Job Tamer trucks. In addition to the external identification on the front, they carried bow tie badges above the two-digit series call-outs on the front fender-sides, behind and above the wheel opening. Trucks with the CST option also had trim moldings along the lower perimeter feature-line, plus CST lettering high on the middle of the door, just under the side window.

In 1967, only three percent of the trucks manufactured had the Custom Sport Truck option. It consisted primarily of carlike features such as a cigarette lighter, door-operated dome lamp, bright trim on doors and the instrument panel and bright window framing all around. CSTs also had chrome front bumpers, full-width vinyl seats, pedal trim, roof moldings, carpeting and extra insulation.

Along with the CST package came an expanded list of extra-cost options and accessories for the 1967 pickups. These trucks could now be ordered with bucket seats, side trim moldings, transistor ignition, a tilt steering column, wheel trim covers, a speed warning indicator, tachometer, Custom and Custom Appearance equipment, dashboard assist handle and a Custom Comfort and Convenience package.

Half-ton C-10 pickups continued to come in Stepside and Fleetside models on two wheelbases. The 6½-foot short-box models had the 115-inch wheelbase, while long-box editions with an eight-foot-long box had a 127-inch span. The three-quarter-ton C-20 series also offered eight-foot-long Stepsides and Fleetsides on the 127-inch wheelbase. Four-wheel drive was a $651

An obvious change on 1968 models was the addition of federally required safety side-marker lamps on the front fenders and rear boxsides. Otherwise, they looked much the same as the 1967 Chevy pickups.

option for C-10s and $676 extra for C-20s. A K prefix was still used for four-wheel-drive trucks, which came with either a three-speed or optional four-speed manual transmission.

Automatic transmission was available on pickups with conventional drive. The more powerful V-8s employed the three-speed Turbo Hydra-matic gearbox. Others used the two-speed aluminum Powerglide. Rear axles were again of the semi-floating type on C-10s and full-floating with C-20s.

Colors available for 1967 included Cameo White, Charcoal Gray poly, Dark Aqua poly, dark blue, dark green, Hugger Orange, Horizon Orange, light blue, light yellow, Medium Blue poly, Omaha Orange, Pure White, red, Silver poly, Vermillion poly, Woodland Green, white, yellow and Yuma Yellow.

Model-year production by series

G-10	42,133
C-10	288,356
K-10	6,055
G-20	8,032
C-20	6,781
K-20	4,271
Total	355,628

Model-year production of all Chevrolet trucks including imports from Canada was 526,776 units. For the 1967 calendar year, Chevrolet produced 549,665 motor trucks and buses, which was down 71,689 units

from 1966. The Custom Sport Truck option was available for all cab models up to one-ton. This option was added to just 12,588 of all trucks Chevrolet built for the model year.

1968

After the major design change of the previous season, 1968 brought modest refinements to Chevrolet's light-duty truck styling. Introduced this season was a new three-quarter-ton Fleetside model with an 8½-foot-long cargo bed, available only with conventional two-wheel drive.

At the front, the 1968 models had more bright-work, with the grille panel around the grille and head-lamps available with a silver-annodized finish. A new option was a trim molding along the upper-body feature-line, extending fully to the rear of the box on Fleetside models.

Chevrolet's optional equipment list continued to grow. New this year was a shoulder-harness-type passenger restraint system, upper bodyside moldings, body paint stripes and door-edge guards.

The number of Custom Sport Trucks (up to one-ton) increased to four percent of production, a total of 16,755 vehicles.

Engine choices were increased to what Chevrolet advertisements described as "two tough sixes and four big V-8s ranging up to 310 hp." The base six had its output boosted to 155 hp at 4200 rpm. The 292 ci option (also six-cylinder) was rated for 170 hp at 4000

This 1968 C-10 Fleetside has the long-bed cargo box. It is a standard cab version with Custom side moldings. Also seen here are the optional "California trucker" mirrors that many pickup users preferred.

rpm. A new 307 ci engine replaced the venerable 283 as the base V-8. It was good for 200 hp at 4600 rpm due to its quarter-inch-longer stroke.

The 327 ci engine, with four-barrel carburetor, was available with 8:1 compression (185 hp at 4000 rpm) or 8.5:1 compression (240 hp at 4400 rpm) in light-duty models. Although it was advertised as a 310 hp option,

most reference books list the new 396 ci four-barrel V-8 as a more powerful option with 325 hp at 4800 rpm. It used a 10.25:1 compression ratio.

These trucks were again promoted as Job Tamer pickups, with some advertisements pointing out that Chevrolet trucks had been "America's first choice every year since 1937." Other ads stressed the four major

There are no side moldings on this base-equipped C-10 Fleetside, which has the standard-type outside rearview mir-ror. Side identification consists of Chevy bow tie badge and 10 series call-out. Chevrolet name appears on lip of hood.

Custom Sport Truck package included CST plaques on upper edges of doors at center of window opening. Here's the half-ton Fleetside version with two-tone paint, Custom moldings and Custom chrome option. Note the long-arm mirrors.

advantages of Chevrolet half- and three-quarter-ton pickups as having full coil spring ride, job-tailored power, double-strong construction and functional styling. "Get more . . . get all four," read a sales slogan.

Other technical changes in 1968 models were slight. Some carburetors and related parts had new model numbers, and a refined version of the Muncie four-speed manual gearbox required some minor changes in step-by-step service procedures. Also, some tune-up specifications differed between certain 1967 and 1968 models.

Colors used for 1968 Chevrolet trucks included Charcoal Gray poly, dark blue, dark green, Hugger Orange, light blue, Medium Blue poly, orange, red, Saddle poly, Silver poly, Vermillion poly and white.

Model-year production by series

G-10	46,427
C-10	335,424
K-10	8,618
G-20	6,927
C-20	81,110
K-20	6,617
Total	485,123

Chevrolet's calendar-year production for 1968 was recorded by the Automobile Manufacturers Association as 680,931 units.

1969

Chevrolet truck designers made it easy to spot 1969 models by changing the trucks' faces and the arrangement of trim, although body styling was largely unaltered. New engines were released for those preferring or needing V-8 power and a six-cylinder engine was again used as base equipment.

Simply described, the grille for '69 looked like a barbell inside a large, round-cornered rectangular opening. The triple-steppe-style outer surround molding looked thicker than the 1968 style. Spanning the center was a wider horizontal band made of aluminum (be careful, it dents easily) with rectangular white parking lights at either end and the Chevrolet name stamped across it. The grille itself was made up of tightly spaced horizontal and vertical members in a cross-hatch pattern.

Chrome moldings trimmed the top and bottom of the aluminum centerpiece and extended up and around the square headlamp housings at either side. The centers of these housings were finished in matte black and held single, round headlight lenses.

A large blue bow tie emblem decorated the center of the hood, above the grille. Front side markers on standard 1969 trucks had amber-colored rectangular lenses. On deluxe models, these were placed in body-colored housings that allowed the lenses to show through two slotlike openings stacked atop each other.

Series identification appeared on the cowl sides, below the upper-body feature-line. Chrome letters spelled out the options available to light-duty buyers, such as C-10, C-20, Custom-10, Custom-20, Custom Camper 20, and so on. Below these nameplates, engine call-out badges were sometimes seen when optional powerplants were ordered. These narrow rectangular ornaments were horizontally mounted and carried cubic-inch-displacement numbers.

Here's another 1968 C-10 with the CST treatment. This one has styled wheel covers and California-style OSRV mirrors. Thin stripe whitewalls were an OEM equipment option.

Standard equipment on all 1969 pickups included the base six-cylinder engine; self-adjusting four-wheel brakes; dual brake master cylinder; back-up lights; directional signals; side-marker reflectors; left- and right-hand outside rearview mirrors; heater and defroster; padded dashboard; nonglare instrument panel; padded dual sunshades; ashtray; push-button seatbelt buckles; low-profile control knobs; two-speed electric windshield washer-wipers; safety glass; flexible fuel filler neck and deep-dish steering wheel with telescoping shaft.

Standard cabs came with a curved front windshield; panoramic rear window; three-passenger adjustable bench seat; embossed vinyl upholstery; dome light; rubber floor mat and a choice of six upholstery colors: Saddle, blue, green, red, black or turquoise. Fleetside and Stepside models came with short box six-foot bed or long box 8½-foot bed options. A big nine-foot box was also available in the C-20 line, but only with Fleetside styling. The C-10 pickups could be had on two wheelbases, of 115 or 127 inches. The C-20s also had a choice of two wheelbases, of 127 or 133 inches. Four-wheel drive was available for chassis and cabs, pickups, and Suburbans in both series. The price of this option was $650 for the half-tons and $680 for the three-quarter-tons.

An optional Custom Comfort and Appearance package was available. It included brightmetal windshield moldings, rear window trim, brightmetal venti-pane frames, Custom front fender nameplates, color-keyed vinyl-coated floor mats, full-depth foam seat with color-keyed fabric and vinyl trim, vinyl door panels with bright upper retainers, a cigar lighter, brightmetal control knobs, cowl insulation and full-depth armrests.

The top trim level was again the Custom Sport Truck option. It included most features of the Custom package plus a chrome front bumper, full-width vinyl seats, bright pedal frames, bright roof drip moldings, extra insulation, matching carpets and CST front fender nameplates. Bucket seats and a center console were separate options that could be teamed with the CST package.

Other new features for 1969 included a low-profile steering wheel, revised seatback construction and a change to a foot-operated parking brake. Optional body-side moldings were again available to trim the lower perimeter feature-line, but were of a new design. They were wider and fancier, with a contrast strip between two thin, bright moldings. Also, the moldings no longer curved up along the upper lip of the wheel openings; they ran only horizontally. A separate option was a molding for the upper-body feature-line.

At the rear, Fleetside trucks had thin, vertical taillight lenses with a wedge-shaped white back-up lens above them. The tailgate had an upper horizontal indentation, below which the panel was flat and stamped with the Chevrolet name in white letters. Custom moldings

The term Job Tamer Trucks was used to promote all 1968 Chevrolet commercial vehicles. The new grille, introduced a year earlier and carried over, had two full-width slots stacked on front, with bow tie badge in center.

ONLY CHEVROLET GIVES YOU ALL THIS INNER STRENGTH:

The lasting strength of double-strong sheet metal construction. Chevrolet puts double walls of steel in all the right places. In the cab roof, cowl, windshield pillars and door openings. And Fleetside body side panels. Also, new outer body sheet metal resists rust better because there are no external welded joints. And here's another Chevy rust fighter: new front fender liners that protect against road splash.

The riding strength of Chevrolet's exclusive suspension system. This is the truck ride you'll like best, whether you haul a cargo or a camper body. It gives you the exclusive smoothness of coil springs — strong truck-built coils — at all four wheels. Only Chevrolet ½- and ¾-ton models have them. And it gives you an independent front suspension that's proved its bump-leveling ability on more truck jobs than any other.

The working strength of more power for more purposes. Fact is, a Chevy gives you the widest engine choice of any popular pickup. You can get just what your work — or recreation — requires. Go with the 250 Six, biggest standard six in any leading make. Or specify a bigger 292 Six — or any one of *four* modern V8's. At your Chevrolet dealer's. . . . Chevrolet Division of General Motors, Detroit, Michigan.

CHEVROLET *Job Tamer* pickups

America's first choice every year since 1937

This 1968 Chevrolet ad shows the exterior and interior views of the C-10 Fleetside pickup. The ladder-type frame was exceptionally rigid and gave excellent riding strength. Sixes available were the 250 or 292 ci versions.

when ordered, emphasized the rectangular shape of the tailgate. A flush-style latch was integrated into the middle of the tailgate's upper feature-line.

Stepside trucks of all these years weren't much different, at the rear, than early-sixties models. The extended rear fenders were restyled, however, so that their sculptured feature-line now ran across the lower portion and up over the wheel opening. Also, large side markers were added on the fender-sides behind the wheel opening.

The standard pickup engine was the 250 ci six, with the 292 ci six optional. Base V-8 was the 307 ci with 200 hp introduced in 1968. Replacing the 327 ci V-8 was a new 350 ci powerplant with the same four-inch bore, but a longer 3.48-inch stroke. It came in four different forms: first, with 8:1 compression and two-barrel carburetor producing 215 hp; second, with 9:1 compression and two-barrel carburetor producing 250 hp; third, with 9:1 compression and four-barrel carburetor producing 255 hp; and fourth, with 10.25:1 compression and four-barrel carburetor producing 300 hp.

Another option was the 396 ci V-8 with 9:1 compression and a four-barrel carburetor producing 310 hp.

Truck-option production totals recorded by Chevrolet show that 27,827 trucks in the half- to one-ton class used the 292 six; 28,542 used a medium-duty version of the 350 V-8; and 121,217 used a light-duty version of the 350. The 396 V-8 was installed in 13,269 trucks (not including vans or El Caminos) during the model year. In this same category, 51,623 trucks had a heavy-duty clutch; 2,889 featured an overdrive transmission; 91,784 had the regular wide-ratio four-speed (3,368 had a special close-ratio version); 25,023 trucks had Powerglide automatic transmission installed; 53,021 had Deluxe 300 Turbo Hydra-matic; and 94,781 had a different three-speed Turbo Hydra-matic gearbox.

A slightly changed three-speed Muncie transmission was standard equipment on 1969 trucks with conventional drive, and was used through 1977. The main differences with this gearbox were in minor service operations. There were similar small variations, as usual, in

Chevy said that its exclusive full-coil-spring suspension system made Chevrolet pickups "the most comfortable campers." This was an important factor, since the RV industry was booming. This slide-in camper unit is mounted on a 1968 three-quarter-ton Fleetside with Custom Camper package.

small details like tune-up specifications, carburetor model numbers and adjustments, wheel alignment specs and so on. These can be found in Chilton or Motor truck repair manuals, and amounted to nothing more than year-to-year refinements to a well-engineered line of Chevrolet commercial vehicles.

By the way, this was the first year for Chevrolet's Jeep-like Blazer utility vehicle, which had a production run of 4,935 units. Nearly all of these came with an extra-cost removable top (4,636 white tops and 290 black ones were ordered), although the base model was really a pickup.

Fifteen colors were offered for exterior finish of Chevrolet trucks this season. They were black, Light Clematis Blue, dark blue, dark green, light blue, light green, Maroon poly, orange, red, Saddle poly, Silver poly, Turquoise poly, white, yellow and Yellow-Green poly. Paint colors used on truck interior parts included black, flat black, dark blue, dark green, dark red (gloss and flat), Dark Saddle, light green, red, Silver poly and Turquoise poly.

Model-year production by series

G-10	49,133
C-10	412,891
K-5/K-10	15,460
G-20	7,343
C-20	104,736
K-20	8,296
Total	597,859

If this was a good year for sales and production in general, it was also a season in which fancy trucks—especially pickups—continued to grow in popularity with buyers. More Chevrolet customers were spending the money to option-out their trucks with many appearance, convenience and high-performance extras. Total model-year production of pickups with the Custom Sport Truck option came to 29,942 units, while the Custom Comfort and Convenience equipment option was installed on 147,311 vehicles. Air conditioning of either standard or roof type was ordered for 61,568 trucks. As far as outside appearances, 204,568 trucks were sold with two-tone paint finish (not counting vans or El Caminos).

On a calendar-year basis, overall production of Chevy commercial vehicles (trucks and buses) climbed slightly to 684,748 units. This made ten years in a row that the company had held first spot on the January-to-January production charts.

It should be noted that, in 1969, Chevy became a full-line truck marketer, selling badge-engineered ver-

Pam-Top, made by Plastimet Corporation, of Portland, Oregon, on a 1969 Fleetside. Rear styling was unaltered from 1967. Custom moldings brightened up the rear end appearance considerably.

sions of GMC's heavy over-the-road models through Chevrolet dealers.

1970

Chevrolet advertisements for 1970 used the slogan "On the Move" and promoted the year's light-duty trucks as "The Movers for '70." Unfortunately, moving the trucks out of dealerships became quite a problem for the company. Early in the sales season, a sluggish US economy made buyers reluctant to purchase new trucks. In the fall, the United Auto Workers union called a strike against all General Motors divisions. It shut down the factories for sixty-seven days. When it was over, production was off twenty-eight percent and represented the lowest total since 1963.

Sales for the calendar year stood at 562,231 trucks. To make matters worse, Ford was not affected by the labor dispute, and moved easily into the number-one rank for both six-cylinder and V-8 models.

"You'll still be washing it when other '70s are washed up," claimed an ad showing a bikini-clad blonde toweling down her CST-10 short-bed. The copy noted that scrappage records proved the tough Chevys out-lasted other pickups. Nevertheless, with assemblies at a halt after September, Chevy couldn't outsell other brands. "The year 1970 was one of the worst in Chevrolet history," pointed out *Ward's Automotive Yearbook* for 1971.

Another 1970 ad read, "The first thing a Chevy has to move is you. And we never forget it. It shows in the way our '70s look. In their coil spring smoothness. Car-like options list. Power choices. And all the different ways they come: Fleetside, Stepside and camper-designed Longhorn, the second car that doubles as a second home."

Discussing these features one-by-one, looks come first. In general, the '70 Chevy line had modestly altered styling. Up front, the use of the barbell-shaped aluminum center piece continued in the grille design, although the texture of the background insert was changed.

Instead of cross-hatched screening, as used in 1969, the new insert had twelve groups of four short horizontal fins arranged with six stacks of fins spaced out above the center bar and six below it. There was certainly a more car-like look to the grille, although it did not greatly affect the appearance of the trucks otherwise. All in all, they seemed like customized 1969 models.

New exterior colors included Dark Bronze poly; Dark Gold poly; Dark Blue-Green poly; Dark Green poly; Dark Sandalwood; Copper poly; Dark Blue Suede poly; Flame Red; Hugger Orange; Light Sandalwood; Medium Blue; Medium Blue-Green poly; Medium Green poly; Red-Orange and Sandal poly (clear coat). Certain '69 exterior colors were dropped and interior finishes were revised to complement the new body colors.

A new grille was introduced with 1969 models. It was made of aluminum and had the Chevrolet name embossed across the center piece. Bow tie was now on center of hood in place of Chevrolet lettering. This truck has Custom chrome and moldings, and rally wheels.

Fender-side nameplates for trucks with Camper Special option differed from standard trim again in 1969. This three-quarter-ton has painted bumper and hubcaps, but features Custom molding packages. The unusual camper is by Travel Queen Coaches, of Louisville, Kentucky.

Coil-spring front suspension was carried over and was highly promoted. "We build our independent front suspension to expect the worst from a road. Without getting rattled," one ad noted. There were some refinements. Ball-joints were now used on the front axle of K-10 and K-20 four-wheel-drive models, instead of king pins. And new wheel bearings were also adopted for light-duties.

Among car-like options was the Z62 Custom Comfort and Appearance group. It included vent window and windshield moldings, chrome control-knob trim, Custom emblems, color-keyed floor mat, white hardboard headlining, full-depth foam seat with fabric upholstery (except vinyl bucket seats), cigar lighter, special insulation on C-10 and K-10 models, bright glovebox nameplate and dome lamp bezel.

Also available was the Z84 Custom Sport Truck option. Its features were bucket seats, console, right-hand sunshade and armrest, cigar lighter, CST emblems, special insulation, undercoating, chromed bumpers, bright control-knob and pedal trim, bright windshield, bodyside, tailgate, taillight and back-up light moldings, bright fuel filler cap, side-marker reflectors and dual horns.

Full wheel covers and G78-15B or H78-15 Highway Bias belted-ply white-stripe tires were among individual extras, which also included air conditioning, power brakes, gauge packages, tinted glass, push-button AM radio, automatic transmission and power steering. An unusual, no-cost option was a K plate for the state of Pennsylvania, apparently to identify four-wheel-drive units sold there.

Power choices were expanded with the release of an optional 400 ci V-8. It had bore and stroke measurements of 4.126x3.76 inches and actually displaced 402 ci; however, it was marketed as the "400 V-8."

Ad promoting the sale of Saginaw power steering for 1969 Chevrolet pickups with campers said, "Just 2½ pounds of finger pressure moves that pickup around like a car." Two-toning had white on upper cab and lower body perimeter.

Other features of this powerplant were an 8.5:1 compression ratio, four-barrel carburetor and 300 hp rating.

As usual, some new model-number carburetors were released this year for trucks with both two- or four-barrel carburetors. The basic type components—Rochester 2G, 2GC and 2GV and Quadrajet 4MX—were unchanged, but float levels, pump rod and other adjustments were slightly different.

Among the various models, the long-box 127-inch wheelbase Fleetside was the original popularity leader, far outselling other offerings in both half-ton and three-quarter-ton series. The Longhorn version with 133-inch wheelbase came only with the three-quarter-ton payload rating. This was the truck that Chevrolet ads described as being camper-designed, since its large 8½-foot-long cargo box was just right for accommodating a camper module. Nearly 21,000 Camper Special options were ordered from Chevy this season, despite the fact that overall sales in the RV industry were down 8.1 percent due to the economic recession. And still, production of Longhorn pickups peaked at just over 5,000 units.

The short-box 115-inch wheelbase Fleetside model—available in the C-10 line—accounted for almost 50,000 sales, including 2,554 four-wheel-drives. This truck is the top choice of collectors today, although it was about one-fifth as popular as the larger C-10 and C-20 pickups when new. The reason for this is that original buyers wanted utility value in their trucks, while today's collector goes for rarity and good looks rather than load-hauling ability.

Model-year production by series

G-10	8,261
C-5/C-10	338,147
K-5/K-10	25,489
G-20	1,435
C-20	92,550
K-20	10,431
Total	476,313

Despite the overall decrease in sales and production caused by the 1970 United Auto Workers strike, the popularity of trucks with fancy trim options and

The new-for-1969 grille had a delicate cross-hatch pattern latticework of vertical and horizontal bars. Parking lamps were incorporated into each end of the center piece. This truck has modern aftermarket wheels, tires and tonneau cover.

car-like accessory packages and extras was again very high. In fact, some of these options actually had increased installation rates. The Custom Sport Truck package was added to 49,717 of the 1970 pickups and Blazers in the half- to one-ton category. In the same category, 126,848 trucks had the Custom Comfort and Convenience package; 162,228 had regular two-toning and 62,251 had special two-toning. Lower bodyside moldings were added to 181,094 units, 20,900 had Camper Special equipment and 264,498 featured push-button radios.

As far as powertrain options, the 350 ci V-8 was used in 232,427 units, 17,427 came with the 396 ci V-8, automatic transmissions (Turboglide or Power-glide) were installed in 226,276 trucks and 85,502 had four-speed manual gearboxes.

1971

Chevrolet kept the same basic body for its Totally Tougher trucks in 1971, but there were numerous changes in appearance and engineering, plus a new top-of-the-line trim package with the richest interior appointments ever.

External updates included a new lattice-pattern grille with a Chevrolet bow tie badge at its center. This grille consisted of seven horizontal and fifteen vertical members. Familiar-looking round headlamps were now

The 1970 Chevy trucks introduced a new grille with six stacks of horizontal moldings above and below the center piece. A 400 ci V-8 was now optionally available. This ad makes it pretty obvious that farmers weren't the only buyers waxing enthusiastic about Chevy trucks in the seventies.

The sporty appearance of the 1970 Chevy Fleetside with high-level trim options was appealing to California surfers, too. CST identification was now found on the front fendersides, rather than the upper edge of doors.

A snazzy two-tone 1970 CST/10 Fleetside with a short box. This truck was shown at the 1987 Elkhorn, Wisconsin, show.

mounted in bright square housings, while the parking lamps were now mounted in rectangular slots in the front bumper. Fleetsides with optional two-tone finish could be had with the entire side panel, between upper and lower feature-lines, painted white. The 1970-style two-toning with lower perimeter in the second color was available again, too.

Technically, all 1971 truck engines were modified to operate on the low-lead fuels and to meet revised federal exhaust emission standards. A fuel evaporative system, formerly offered as optional equipment to satisfy California's Air Resources Board requirements, became standard in half-ton models.

Another regular feature of Chevrolet's new light-duty trucks was the use of disc brakes at the front. Power-assisted brakes were offered as standard equipment in three-quarter-ton and one-ton models, including all Suburbans, Blazers and four-wheel-drives. Power brakes remained an option on half-ton pickups.

Engines for 1971 were about the same, although a wider choice of horsepower options was offered for specific models like vans, Blazers, Step-Vans, and so on.

Wheel detail on the 1970 CST/10.

Call-out identification plate tells the essentials about this truck.

Here's a 1970 CST 10 Fleetside short-box pickup at an auto show in Jefferson, Wisconsin. Front fender call-outs indicate there's a 350 ci V-8 below the hood. The wheels and tires are of nonfactory design. Standard chrome bumper had no guards.

The highest of five ratings for the 350 ci V-8 was 270 hp. Most engines now had either 8:1 or 8.5:1 compression ratios. Top option was the 400 ci V-8 with 8.5:1 compression and a four-barrel carburetor, which developed 300 hp at 4800 rpm.

Chevy's new trim package was the Cheyenne Super level, with carpeting, vinyl trim, chrome bumpers and other stylish items. These were a step up from the popular Custom Deluxe and Custom Sport Truck trim levels. The panel delivery truck was no longer offered, since panel van models were the preferred choice of buyers.

Other new options appearing in factory installation records for the first time this season included an AM/FM radio and tilt steering column.

Dark Saddle, Parchment and Argent Silver interior paint colors were new for 1971. On the outside of the body, buyers could now select Medium Olive poly and Ochre finish. No longer available were Dark Blue poly, Bronze poly, Dark Sandalwood, Flame Red, Light Sandalwood, Medium Blue-Green poly, Red-Orange, or Yellow-Green poly exterior body colors.

Model-year production by series

G-10	35,509
C-5/C-10	278,774
K-5/K-10	33,132
G-20	28,412
C-20	76,271
K-20	10,060
Total	462,158

The year 1971 was a banner season in both sales and production of Chevrolet trucks. Record output, fanned by a strike recovery program, put Chevy back in the slot of number-one truck maker, although several plants had to operate the whole year, six days per week. For all Chevrolet trucks, the calendar-year output was 739,480 units, or 35.69 percent of industry.

A major contributor to the healthy figures was the Chevy Van and Sportvan line, which was totally revamped in the spring of 1970, but marketed as a 1971 series with an extended model year.

In Chevy's light-truck (pickups, Blazers and Suburbans) category, the merchandising of car-like acces-

A step down the trim level ladder from the CST 10 was the Custom 10 half-ton. This one has some aftermarket accessories like headlight shields. It is also slightly customized, with the bow tie badge removed from the hood and a plastic bug screen added.

sories, performance equipment and optional trim packages continued to play a major role in the truck division's developmental history. For trucks in the half-ton to one-ton bracket, the sales figures for options added to 1971 models looked like this:

Option	Sales
Deluxe air conditioning	97,203
Rooftop air conditioning	3,928
292 ci six-cylinder	13,392
350 ci V-8	250,382
400 ci V-8	21,010
Four-speed transmission	67,757
H-D four-speed transmission	1,122
Powerglide transmission	5,338
M-38 Turbo Hydra-matic	211,831
M-49 Turbo Hydra-matic	21,668
Tilt steering	12,279
Power steering	215,479
Custom Comfort & Convenience	98,895
Custom Sport Truck (CST)	72,609
Cheyenne Super	9,867
Camper Special	20,501
Wheel covers	101,893
AM/FM radio	5,282
Whitewall tires	77,266

The badge behind the wheelwell identifies this truck as a Cheyenne 10 Super. Front engine call-out indicates the 350 ci V-8 was ordered. Rally-styled wheels were a popular option. Inner liners continued to be used on front fenders to fight rust and corrosion.

The new-for-1971 Cheyenne interior trim package made for an extra touch of convenience and luxury. Also new for the year was a cross-hatch-pattern grille, redesigned outside mirrors and front wheel disc brakes as standard equipment.

89

Side-marker lamps again featured twin-slot styling in 1971. The liners inside the front fender wells were self-washing, and "Rust-causing elements can't find a foothold," Chevy advertised. Cowl had groups of horizontal louvers to direct air into cab. Radio antennas were mounted on right-hand side of cowl.

1972

The final season of Chevrolet's light-duty truck development covered by this book developed into another banner year. Spurred by the boom in light-duty trucks for personal transportation, customer demand climbed so high that Chevy was actually unable to produce enough 1972 models to meet it. A new record of 828,961 trucks of all types and sizes was produced by the company in the model year. Yet, calendar-year output of 770,773 units was 25,000 less than Ford built, based on its larger production capacity. Also lower, of course, was Chevrolet's share of the total industry, which was 31.1 percent versus Ford's 32.2 percent.

Few styling or mechanical alterations were made in the 1972 models. There were, however, slightly richer cab options than ever offered before. In addition, Chevy switched to the use of tougher, more stain-resistant acrylic enamel paint finishes. Otherwise, it was hard to distinquish full-size 1972 models from 1971 models without checking serial numbers. One truck that was easy to identify, however, was Chevy's brand-new LUV mini-pickup.

New grille for 1971 models had 15 thin vertical and seven horizontal moldings crisscrossing each other. A Chevrolet bow tie badge was mounted at the center. Parking lamps were relocated to a new position in the front bumper.

Same basic cargo box and tailgate styling was used through 1972. This is the 1971 pickup. Numerous trim levels were available for interior and exterior. The 350 ci V-8 was a new engine choice this season. The 1967–1972 sheet metal was engineered with a reduced number of external joints to reduce rust.

Extra-strong double-wall construction featured in the Fleetside cargo body stood up well to tough jobs. Cargo-area lamp, mounted above rear window glass, was an extra-cost option. All trucks had the big back window now, although sliding glass was available at extra cost.

This 1971 Cheyenne 10 short-box Fleetside has accessory type bed rails, bumper guards, rally-styled wheels and white sidewall tires. It was for sale at the Car Corral held in conjunction with the flea market in Carlisle, Pennsylvania.

Due to labor problems experienced in producing the Vega, Chevrolet realized that it was virtually impossible to build vehicles in the United States at a cost that would make them competitive price-wise with Japanese subcompacts. Thus, the decision was made not to manufacture a mini-pickup in this country. Instead, Chevy purchased 34.2 percent of Isuzu Motors Limited of Japan during 1971, and immediately launched a program to modify a small Isuzu pickup to meet American emissions, safety and marketing standards.

This Light Utility Vehicle (LUV) initially went on sale during March 1972 in West Coast and Gulf Coast marketing areas at selected dealerships. It had a 102.4-inch wheelbase, a six-foot cargo bed and a half-ton load rating. Power came from a single overhead camshaft, inline four-cylinder engine with 3.31x3.23-inch bore and stroke, two-barrel carburetor and 8.2:1 compression. This engine produced 88 hp at 3000 rpm.

Styling was slab-sided (like a full-size Fleetside) and included a miniature version of Chevy's lattice-pattern grille with a bow tie in the center. There were dual headlights, bow tie hubcaps and a Chevrolet name across the tailgate. The rear quarters of the roof had three short horizontal louvers, multiple round taillights, and back-up lamps were mounted in and below the tailgate.

Other technical features included a four-speed all-synchromesh transmission with floor shift, eight-inch diameter single dry disc clutch, 4.56:1 rear axle, ladder-type frame with six cross-members and boxed side rails, independent ball-joint front suspension with adjustable torsion bars, semi-elliptic rear leaf springs, power-assisted self-adjusting hydraulic drum brakes, manual recirculating ball steering and 6.00x14 six-ply tube-type tires.

Chevy again stressed the durability of its full-size trucks. "The trucks that last longer cost less in the long run," pointed out a sales brochure that stressed five ways in which Chevrolet trucks were built: durable disc brakes, tough double-wall construction, massive girder beam front suspension, fully aluminized exhaust system and steel-armored brake lines. The rear brake lines were wrapped with steel wire at critical points, to guard against impact damage and the effects of vibration.

As proof of the long-lasting characteristics of Chevrolet trucks, the company printed a chart (using

Last of Chevy's fifth-generation postwar pickups was the 1972 model. This is a Custom 10 half-ton version with the 350 ci V-8, according to the various fender badges. Camper shell is aftermarket.

The 1972 frond-end styling was identical to 1971. This truck has the optional sliding rear window, which can be seen through the windshield in this photo.

92

figures compiled by R. L. Polk & Company) showing the percentages of 1956–1967 Chevrolet trucks that were still on the road. The figures, which may be interesting to collectors, were as follows:

Model year	Percent in service (1972)
1956	55.7
1957	63.9
1958	65.1
1959	71.1
1960	78.9
1961	79.4
1962	87.4
1963	90.3
1964	93.1
1965	96.6
1966	97.9
1967	97.7

"No competitive make has as many as half its '56 models still on the job," claimed the sales brochure. "And nobody else matches Chevy's consistently high percentages in the years since then."

In its full-size 1972 truck line, Chevrolet offered sixteen different Fleetside models on three different wheelbases, plus the traditional Stepside, and most models came with either two- or four-wheel drive. This was the last year for the body introduced in 1967, which is now considered a classic by Chevy truck collectors.

Engine choices were again listed as two sixes or three V-8s, with some changes in certain compression ratios and all-new net horsepower ratings. The six-cylinder engines were the 250 ci, 110 net hp and the 292 ci, 125 net hp jobs. Optional V-8s were the 307 ci, 135 net hp, 350 ci, 170 net hp and 400 ci, 240 net hp engines.

A new Highlander luxury interior package was offered to Chevrolet truck buyers in 1972. It was available on pickups and Suburbans with the Custom Deluxe package and Blazers with the CST option. The High-

Profile view shows the 1972 Cheyenne Super long-box in two-tone paint treatment. Styled wheels were an extra-cost item. Note how upper molding on cargo box slants slightly downward at rear, to follow body contours.

Interior of the 1972 Custom 10 features a full complement of gauges directly in front of the operator. Two-spoke steering wheel has squarish horn button in center.

The 1972 Chevy C-30 one-ton with optional dual rear wheels made a good base for mounting this El Dorado frame-mounted camper unit.

lander interior consisted of contemporary plaid upholstery in a choice of four color combinations: orange, avocado, blue and gray, with thick-pile carpeting in rich-looking black nylon blend.

Many new exterior colors were seen this year, with a number used exclusively on the LUV mini-pickup.

During 1972, Chevrolet entered the mini-pickup market with a model built by Isuzu of Japan. It was marketed by Chevy dealers as the LUV, which stood for Light Utility Vehicle.

These included Dark Acanthus Blue, Adonis Yellow, Blue-Gray poly, Light Clemathis Blue, Crimson Red, Dark Argent, Desert Tan, Horizon Blue, Jasmine Yellow, Madder Red, Matte Black, Midnight Blue, Palm Green, Red-Brown poly, Shannon Green, Silver, Sky Blue, Strato White, Walnut Beige, Weldenia White and Westway Tan. The small truck also came in Ochre, a color it shared with full-size models, although the codes were different for both.

Full-size pickups also offered a few new colors, including blue, Dark Green poly and Medium Gold poly, plus most of the same shades available in 1971.

Model-year production by series

G-10	30,618
C-5/C-10	365,778
K-5/K-10	74,047
G-20	30,543
C-20	113,010
K-20	22,461
Total	636,457

A 1972 Custom 10 Stepside Shortie. This truck has been customized further with a three-inch top chop and heavy-duty tires. Shown at the 1987 Elkhorn, Wisconsin, show.

Wide lower bodyside molding	333,417	M-49 Turbo Hydra-matic transmission	41,555
Deluxe air conditioning	195,061	Tilt steering column	62,137
Bucket seats	31,416	Cheyenne Super option	40,636
Body paint stripe	35,086	Custom Comfort & Convenience	
292 ci six-cylinder engine	7,796	package	156,391
350 ci V-8 engine	467,968	Custom Sport Truck	142,645
Four-speed manual transmission	90,826	Camper Special equipment	32,226
M-38 Turbo Hydra-matic transmission	372,279		

The 1972 Custom 10 four-wheel-drive Fleetside Shortie owned by Glenn Benzel.

Chapter 7

Chevrolet commercial cars

Now that we've traced the development of Chevrolet's full-size pickups and taken a little look at the little LUV, let's briefly turn our attention to the other models on the periphery of the Chevy light truck's history.

First, there are three models that differ from conventional Stepsides and Fleetsides, but are still best described by the term "pickup truck." They are the El Camino, the Loadside and Rampside Corvair, and the Blazer. There are also a number of models that aren't pickups at all, but still interest those interested in light-duty Chevy trucks. This group includes chassis and cabs, platform and stakes, sedan deliveries, panels, Car-

A predecessor of the half-car, half-truck El Camino concept was the Chevrolet coupe pickup of the late-1930s and early- *1940s. This is the 1941 edition. Such a model did not reappear after the war.*

Totally new for 1959 was the El Camino from Chevrolet. It represented a cross between a passenger car and a pickup.

The El Camino came in just one trim level, but offered many options and accessories.

The full-size El Camino's second and last season was 1960. The model name was again carried on the front fender-sides.

Styling was considerably revised, but still used the flat-top cab roof.

ryall Suburbans, compact vans and Vega panel express trucks.

These models vary in their significance to collectors and their impact upon Chevrolet truck history. For example, the El Camino and Corvair pickups are paramount to collectors, although both have been fully researched in separate books. Sedan deliveries, panels and Suburbans are also very collectible; they are not, however, part of the pickup truck family, the main topic of this book. Chassis and cab and platform and stake models are little more than configurations of pickup trucks and, therefore, warrant only light consideration.

The El Camino sedan pickup returned in 1964 on the midsize Chevelle platform. Otherwise it was much the same as the original concept. It was even available as a Super Sport model-option with bucket seats.

Finally, vans, Blazers and Vega trucks are primarily of interest to a different kind of truck fanatic who can best be described as an enthusiast rather than a collector due to the models' time frame. While other books have been—and will be—written about these models, their history is not directly linked to the pickup truck.

For these reasons, this chapter covers the other Chevrolet trucks as a group, giving a concise picture of major product developments and the relation they may have to the pickup story.

El Camino

The first El Camino bowed in model year 1959 as the answer to the Ford Ranchero, introduced two years earlier. Based on Chevy's two-door wagon, it combined the appearance and trim of a passenger car with a double-walled pickup box measuring 76¼x64½x12¾ inches. Chevy's 119-inch wheelbase, X-built Safety-Girder frame was used under the sedan pickup, which also featured full-coil-spring suspension, a 135 hp High-Thrift six and column-mounted three-speed stick shift.

A flat overhanging roofline, like that of the Impala Sports Sedan, was combined with a wraparound windshield and large 1500-square-inch rear window. The all-vinyl bench seat interior featured a two-spoke Bel Air steering wheel. Bodyside trim was like that of the Bel Air, with El Camino fender scripts. The full-box-width, grain-tight tailgate required special split cat-eye taillights, and lowered on a hinged bracket that held it parallel to the ground for floor-level loading.

One of the hottest pickups to ever leave an assembly line was this 1968 Chevelle-based El Camino SS-396 sports pickup.

All three versions of the 396 ci high-performance V-8 were available in it. Note the flying buttress cab roofline.

98

Additional powerplants included the 283 ci, 185 hp Turbo Fire standard V-8 or the 283 ci, 230 hp Super Turbo Fire option. Transmissions were three-speed with overdrive and Powerglide or Turboglide automatics. El Caminos came in thirteen solid or ten two-tone color combinations, and offered most passenger car extras, plus special options like bed railings. They boasted a rated load capacity of 1,000 pounds.

Some observers believe Chevy's controversial passenger car styling held down sales. Actually, the recession of the late-fifties probably had more to do with keeping deliveries at some 32,000 units. It's also believed that production cost was high since many bodypanels were unique to this model, requiring special tooling.

For 1960, the El Camino received the modestly revamped exterior styling of the year's passenger cars and continued to borrow Bel Air trim, which was somewhat plainer-looking than before. Design characteristics included an oval grille, jet-plane rear quarter panel treatment and more angular gullwing fins. The sedan pickup was again based on the two-door Brookwood wagon, with a shortened version of the four-door hardtop roof.

While the base six was unchanged, the standard V-8 became a 170 hp version of the 283 ci engine, with the 230 hp edition as an extra. As in 1959, the El Camino was 56.3 inches high and stretched 210.9 inches overall. Tires were again 8.00x14 four-ply, with whitewalls optional.

Only some 16,000 El Caminos were sold in 1960, and the low sales of the two-door wagon were a problem. Since Chevy made nearly 200,000 four-door wagons versus 14,000 two-doors, it simply became impractical to continue offering both. When the two-door wagon was dropped, El Caminos and sedan deliveries disappeared.

This 1970 El Camino SS was for sale at the 1986 Hoosier Auto Show, in the Indianapolis Motor Speedway. The asking price was $3,300. Front-end styling was all new and the SS front-end treatment was also distinct from the base model's front end.

At Ford, the full-size Ranchero was also discontinued. It, too, found only modest acceptance, but Ford stuck with sedan pickups, transferring the model to its new Falcon compact car line. Between 20,000 and 23,000 of these were sold in each of the years 1960–1963, proving that there was a substantial—if not overpowering—market for smaller passenger-car-based pickups.

In 1964, production of the Falcon Ranchero tumbled to just over 10,000 units. A reason for this was, undoubtedly, Chevrolet's re-entry into the market with a similar, but slightly larger, sedan pickup built off the new mid-size Chevelle platform. A total of 34,724 of these second-generation El Caminos were sold in their first production year of 1964.

Production of El Caminos hit 48,400 units in model year 1969. The sedan pickup used the same 116-inch wheelbase as Chevelle wagons. This one has an optional camper shell.

The 1972 El Camino styling was a facelift of the all-new look introduced in 1971. Its features included single headlights and parking lamps in the front fender ends. The SS option was still available this season, but the 454 ci V-8 was dropped.

Merchandised as a personal pickup, the new El Camino rode a 115-inch wheelbase and stretched 198¼ inches long. It had the slightly square, lightly sculptured, stylish Coke-bottle shape of the Chevelle two-door wagon and came in two trim levels, available in both the six-cylinder or V-8 series.

The regular El Camino had the same trim level as the base Chevelle 300, which was fairly well equipped,

Traville Corporation, of Detroit, Michigan, offered this Vista Camper conversion for the Corvair Greenbrier wagon. It was promoted in the Chevrolet Silver Book and marketed by Chevrolet dealers. It included a rooftop Vista Dome, butane gas range, refrigerator, sink and water tank.

with features like color-keyed rubber floor mats, armrests, foam seats, self-adjusting brakes, electric wipers, dual sun visors and a heater-defroster. Also available was the Deluxe model, similar to the Chevelle 300 Deluxe, with a glovebox light and back-up lamps. While the passenger vehicle line offered the Super Sport (SS) package as a model-option, this equipment was a separate add-on for El Caminos. It included vinyl bucket seats, deluxe wheel covers and special namebadges.

Base engines were shared with Chevelles: a 194 ci six or a 283 ci, 195 hp V-8. A 230 ci, 155 hp six was $33 extra, and a 220 hp version of the V-8 could be added to base V-8 trucks for $42 extra. Three-speed manual transmission was standard. Overdrive was available with all engines, and a four-speed with floor shift was $147 extra on base V-8s. All sixes and V-8s could also be had with Powerglide attachments.

There wasn't much change in 1965, when Chevelles got a new grille with finer patterning and a heavier horizontal centerpiece. There was also a slotted front bumper and new extras like an AM/FM radio and simulated wire wheels.

A more exciting engine option, the 327 ci V-8, was made available in two versions: 250 or 300 hp. Two basic trim levels were again available: regular, comparable to the Chevelle 300, and Deluxe, which added the features of the Chevelle 300 Deluxe.

The Corvair 95 Rampside pickup was introduced in 1961 and changed very little, in appearance, from year to year. This is the 1962 version, which found only 4,102 buyers.

For 1966, the all-new Chevelle body was also used for El Caminos. It had more rounded sides, a slanted front end, wraparound front fenders, a horizontal bar grille and more pronounced Coke-bottle shape. Dimensions were about the same, except for optional powerplants, which included two new big blocks, both displacing 396 ci and offering 325 or 360 hp ratings.

The more powerful version was standard in the SS-396 introduced for high-performance fans this season; it included vinyl upholstery, special wheels and blackout-style graphics treatment. Most of these hot trucks came with bucket seats, a center console and floor shift. There was also a special hood, with power blisters on each side.

In 1967, El Caminos were restyled with a new radiator grille, a full-width slotted bumper, wraparound taillights and slightly recontoured front fenders and hood. Two basic models, regular and Custom, were offered in base form with a 230 ci, 140 hp six. The SS-396 was merchandised in a separate series, with the big-block V-8 as standard fare. This was the 325 hp version, priced at $142 extra.

Optional engines for the regular and Custom models included the 250 ci, 155 hp six at $21, the 327 ci, 275 hp V-8 at $74 and a 325 hp version of the 327. In addition, a 350 hp version of the 396 engine was also available for the SS-396 only. This option cost $226 in El Caminos.

The regular model again had the same standard features as the Chevelle 300, which meant everything formerly offered plus the addition of federally mandated safety equipment required on American cars this year. The new El Camino Custom was comparable to the

Another product of Traville Corporation was the Campside slip-in camper unit for this 1962 Corvair 95 Rampside pickup. The Rampside's drop-center design provided full stand-up room inside.

A ribbed rubber protective mat covered the top edge of the Rampside's drop-down side flap. This kept the paint finish from being damaged when the ramp was lowered for cargo loading.

Malibu passenger car, with bright bodyside and wheel-lip moldings, foam seats, deluxe steering wheel, glove-box light, electric clock and door-operated courtesy lights. The SS-396 was the Custom, and included vinyl upholstery, F-70x14 red stripe tires (whitewalls could be substituted at no cost) and the big-cube engine. Strato bucket seats ($88) and a console ($38) were strictly extras and not inclusive in the SS-396 package.

Dozens of other options were offered, too. They included power brakes ($33), metallic brake linings ($29), dual exhausts with the 327 ($17), air condition-ing ($283), AM/FM push-button radio ($106), Cruise control with automatic transmission ($40), power steer-ing ($67), tilt steering wheel ($33), stereo tape system ($99) and tachometer ($38). Trucks sold in California required an optional Air Injector Reactor, which cost $36.

Manual transmission options ranged from a special three-speed gearbox at $63 to a four-speed at $146 and overdrive at $92. Turbo Hydra-matic ($114) was available with SS-396 engines, while Powerglide ($150 average) was available with sixes or the smaller V-8s. Super-Lift shock absorbers were standard on all El Caminos. (All option prices given show the dealer prices, and retails would be somewhat steeper.)

For 1968, the El Camino was totally restyled on a 116-inch wheelbase, with overall length of 201 inches. The front end had the wrapover-fenders-look of the year's Chevelles and a new bumper slotted only behind the license plate. The dual headlamps were set into two square housings on each side of the fine-mesh grille. On SS-396s the grille was blacked-out and had an SS center badge. These models also had a power bulge hood, blacked-out lower body perimeter and special styled wheels. All El Caminos had a new flying buttress roof treatment.

There was a new 307 ci, 200 hp base V-8, plus 250, 275 and 325 hp versions of the 327 ci V-8 and 350 or 375 hp SS-396 options. The base SS-396 was still rated at 325 hp.

Also in 1968, the regular El Camino gained side-marker lights, and the Custom version added carpeting and woodgrain dashboard trim. Vinyl roof coverings in black or white were available for $54 extra at retail level. Accent striping was a new $30 option for the SS-396 only. Heavy-duty close-ratio four-speed manual transmissions were another added extra, selling for $242 and available on all models. Also listed as an extra, for the first time this year, were power disc front brakes at $102.

This beautifully restored 1963 Corvair 95 Rampside pickup was displayed at the 1987 St. Ignace, Michigan, auto show.

The owner has equipped it with a see-through Plexiglas floor panel over the rear-mounted engine for exhibition purposes.

The 1969 El Camino received a facelift that enlarged the center bumper slot and placed the front parking lamps inside it. Bright horizontal bars ran across a finned grille on the top, center and bottom levels. On the SS-396, the grille was again blacked-out.

Seven engines were available, a few less than in 1968, although most were based on the same blocks. However, there was a new 350 ci V-8 in place of the venerable 327 ci engine. Not much else was totally new or different, since Chevy was involved with launching its Bronco and did not have time or money to revise the El Camino. And it really wasn't necessary, as sales were strong. Production during the model year came to some 48,400 units.

A new more rounded front end characterized the first El Caminos of the 1970s. The SS option was readily identifiable through its identification badges and distinctive front end. The grille was divided into two sections by a prominent center bar carrying SS letters. All models had new instrument panel treatments. On base and Custom trim versions, the gauges were housed in wide rectangular units. Dashboards with round instrument

housings were a unique feature of SS-396s or the all-new SS-454.

Base engine for the series was again the 250 ci six with 155 hp. The 307, 350, 400, 396 and 454 V-8s were also available. Their horsepower ratings were 180, 255, 254, 350 and 360, respectively. About five inches of overall length were added to the sedan pickups this season. They also had a wider (60.2 inches, 59.2 inches) front and rear tread and a higher 54.4-inch overall height. Standard tire size was upgraded from 7.35-14 to F-78-14B.

El Camino models for 1971 had a new look, with single-unit Power Beam headlamps and stacked parking lamps that angled around the corners of the body. The grille also had a stacked horizontal theme, with sections that angled in-and-out around the V-shaped center. Engines began to drop off a little in gross horsepower (a loss of 5 to 10 hp was average) as the high-performance era drew to a close due to pressure from the government and the insurance industry. Nevertheless, the 454 ci powerplant jumped to 365 hp and also gained a 425 high-output option. Very few of the latter models were

Two working versions of the 1964 Corvair 95 included the side-door-loading Corvan panel (top) and the Rampside

pickup. One of the Rampside model's distinct advantages can be seen here.

manufactured, and they are among the most desirable El Caminos to serious collectors.

All of these engines were modified to operate on the new low-lead fuels and had fuel evaporative systems as standard equipment. Other new features included full-flow ventilation, maintenance-free sealed Delco batteries and a lighter, safer windshield that reduced the possibility of breakage in accidents.

Larger, one-piece corner lights were seen on the 1972 El Caminos. Four prominent brightmetal moldings split the bar grille into three horizontal segments. Chevrolet lettering on the left-hand side of the bottom segment replaced a bow tie badge in the center.

Regular and Custom series were offered again, plus the SS-454 model-option. Like other engines, the 454 ci big block (Code LS5) had a lower compression ratio. It produced 270 hp under the new net horsepower rating system that Chevrolet used this year. The SS package also included a blacked-out grille, cowl badges, a special domed-hood with locking pins, power front disc brakes, styled wheels with white-letter tires, vertically pleated door panels, round instrument panel gauges and several other extras.

Other engines offered in 1972 were the 250 ci, 110 net hp six, 292 ci, 125 net hp six, 307 ci, 137 net hp V-8, 350 ci, 170 net hp V-8 and 400 ci, 240 net hp V-8. Model-year output amounted to 21,098 El Caminos.

As mentioned, the El Camino is a popular enthusiast's model. It has particular appeal to collectors of both vintage vehicles and high-performance cars.

Corvair trucks

Corvair trucks and vans were produced from 1961 to 1965. There were four models the first two years, three models in 1963–1964 and just one the final sea-

son. The longest-lasting model was the Greenbrier, a passenger van that was actually merchandised as a station wagon although it was very similar to the trucks except for trim and seating arrangements.

During the 1950s, the Volkswagen forward control van or Kombi, had gained some degree of acceptance in the United States. Chevrolet's all-new Corvair, a compact car introduced as a Volkswagen-fighter for model year 1960, provided a vehicle platform that was well-suited for construction of a compact forward control van with a very Volkswagen-like rear-mounted air-cooled engine-transaxle arrangement.

Like Volkswagen, Chevy produced this model in the passenger van Greenbrier, Corvan panel and pickup versions. The latter simply had the upper rear part of the van body removed and the bottom rear portion converted into a cargo box. A panel with back light was added behind the driving compartment to create a cab.

This pickup came in two styles. The Loadside version featured fixed double-wall boxside panel doors just behind the cab. Also available was a Rampside model, with a door hinged at the bottom that dropped to the ground to become a loading ramp. This novel feature was reflective of the Corvair series' overall level of innovative design.

Greenbriers were identified by a script with the model name, while the other trucks were designated Corvair 95s. This code indicated the use of a ninety-five-

The new-for-1969 Chevrolet Blazer Utility Vehicle was actually an open-cap pickup. It used full-size truck sheet metal and was really a shortened version of the C-10/K-10 pickup.

The Go-Home motorhome, by Ultra Van Manufacturing Company, used the rear-mounted Corvair engine for power. The futuristic-looking machine was 24 feet long and eight feet wide. It weighed under 3,000 pounds and was said to be capable of doing 65 mph.

inch wheelbase. Other dimensions included a roof height of 68.5 inches, front and rear tread measuring fifty-eight inches and an overall length of 179.7 inches. The cargo box was 105 inches long and nearly forty-four inches wide. Size 6.70x15 tires were used in 1961, then upgraded to 7.00x14 in subsequent years.

Standard equipment on all models included the air-cooled "pancake" six, three-speed synchromesh transmission, electric wipers, directional signals and five tubeless tires. Chrome hubcaps and bumpers and a Custom trim package were available at extra cost.

Greenbriers had seating for six adults and windows built into the upper sides of the body. There were countless individual options such as posi-traction, whitewall tires and four-speed manual or Powerglide automatic transmissions.

The opposed overhead valve Turbo Air engine had a 3.437x2.60-inch bore and stroke, 8:1 compression and two single-barrel Rochester carburetors. It produced 80 hp at 4400 rpm and 128 pounds-feet of torque at 2300 rpm. This powerplant was renamed High Torque in 1962, although its specifications did not change in that year or the next.

In 1964, the Greenbrier offered a larger engine, with its stroke increased to $2^{15}\!/_{16}$ inches. This upped displacement to 164 ci and horsepower to 95 at 3600 rpm. For 1964–1965, the Greenbrier could also be bought with a High Performance 164 engine that featured a 9.25:1 compression ratio and 110 hp at 4400 rpm.

Independent front suspension, with a 2,500-pound rating, was used at both the front and rear of Corvair 95 models. Steering was of the ball-gear type with a 20:1 ratio. Coil springs with a 1,150-pound capacity were used at all four corners. Brakes were hydraulics with 11x2-inch drums front and rear, and 167 cubic inches of lining area. A 9⅛-inch-diameter clutch was used with manual transmission, and electrics were 12-volts. A 3.89:1 ratio rear axle was standard.

Corvair 95 styling was handsome and didn't change substantially over the years. The main characteristics included a large slanted windshield, dual headlamps in a chrome trim housing and a concave sculpturing treatment that ran around the entire midsection of the body. When the vehicle was two-toned, the concave area was done in a contrasting color. There were hori-

The 1971–1972 Blazers looked virtually identical with their cross-hatch grilles. Base engine was the 250 ci, 145 hp six for conventional drives and 307 ci V-8 for four-wheel-drives.

The 1970 Blazer shared the year's new light-duty truck grille. Base model was still topless, but most Blazers came with optional fiberglass hardtop that added $360 to price. Both 4x2 and 4x4 versions were offered.

Chevrolet's 1948 sedan delivery was part of the Stylemaster Six car line. Unlike other trucks, it had passenger-car front sheet metal and lots of appeal to small businessmen in need of light hauling capabilities combined with an upscale image.

Chevy built a record 23,045 sedan deliveries in 1949. This one was used by the California Highway Patrol's Technical Research Unit. The year's new passenger car styling was adopted to this truck and gave it a lower, wider and more modern appearance. California Highway Patrol

zontal louvers on the rear bodysides to admit air for engine cooling.

These trucks (including Greenbriers) initially pulled down some strong sales, as they had all the popular features of the Volkswagen Kombi, plus more power. At the same time, something that truck users did not like was the high load floor, created by the rear-mounted engine. Ford's Econoline van, also bowing in 1961, became the main competitor and outsold the Corvan because of the wider acceptance of its more conventional front-mounted inline six and more functional load-floor configuration. The Econoline, however, was not nearly as distinctive or handsome as the Corvair 95.

Production during the introductory 1961 model year totaled 47,557 units for the four Chevy models. This dropped to 35,969 in 1962; 26,968 in 1963; 15,199 in 1964; and 1,528 (Greenbriers only) in 1965. In mid-year 1964, the front-engined Chevy Van was released as part of the Chevy II model line, and Corvair trucks were phased out of production.

Several interesting "vocational" versions of the Corvair 95s were available from approved aftermarket companies that merchandised their offerings through the Chevrolet *Silver Book*. For instance, an ambulance conversion of the Greenbrier was offered by Franklin Body & Equipment Company, of Brooklyn, New York.

Highway Cruisers, Incorporated, did a neat Rampside camper conversion called a Sports Cab. It added a camper-back module on top of the cargo box, which had a flip-up hinged section above the bottom-hinged ramp.

Traville Corporation, Royden Industries and Travel Equipment Corporation marketed pop-top campers made out of Greenbriers or Corvans.

No doubt the ultimate in Corvair-based campers was the Ultra Van "Go-Home," a twenty-four-foot-long, eight-foot-wide motorhome. It used the Corvair powertrain to propel a monocoque aluminum body built using aircraft construction techniques. It was not, however, a direct conversion of Corvair 95 models, as the smaller van camper units were.

Blazer

The Blazer was Chevy's answer to the Bronco, which was Ford's answer to the original International Scout concept. In the early sixties, the Scout had taken the off-road versatility of the Jeep and added to it a dose of sportiness and some creature comforts. The Bronco was, in a sense, a luxury version of the same type of vehicle. And the Blazer was Chevy's equivalent model.

Chevrolet modified the equation by making the Blazer bigger than the competition when it was introduced in 1969. It was a short truck but not a small one—actually a full-size C-10 pickup with a shortened wheelbase. The basic body style, however, was a convertible having two doors and a single three-passenger front bench seat with a raised platform behind it.

Buyers could optionally add passenger and driver bucket seats ($158 or $179), a one-passenger rear auxiliary seat ($70) or a three-passenger rear bench

Between 1949 and 1952, the sedan deliveries featured the same basic body with annual revisions to the grille design. They had stainless steel belt and rocker panel trim, but black rubber gravel guards were used. Front grille guard was a factory accessory. This is a 1951 model.

seat ($105). The lower price for bucket seats applied when this option was teamed with a removable hardtop (priced at $269), which came in black or white. Nearly all Blazers in 1969 were sold with this particular option, the black top being the less popular choice. In later years, the black top would gain popularity.

This made the Blazer part pickup and part station wagon. In addition, the 1969 model—available only in four-wheel drive—was part Jeep as well. And it came with a wide selection of interior and exterior trim options rivaling those of the fanciest Chevrolet passenger cars.

Standard equipment on 1970 models included all federal regulation safety features, 104-inch wheelbase, 250 ci, 155 hp six, and E-78-15B tires. The 307 ci, 200 hp truck engine was available as a base V-8, and a four-barrel version of the 350 ci V-8 was just $37 more than the small V-8.

A Custom molding package with brightmetal highlights for the lower fenders, doors, bodysides and taillights plus a chrome fuel filler cap was $21 extra, or standard with the Custom Sport Truck option. The latter also added bucket seats, a center console, right-hand sun visor and armrest, CST emblems, pedal trim, special insulation, undercoating, dual horns and extra brightmetal trim for $283.

Blazers were rated for a half-ton payload and a gross vehicle weight of 5,000 pounds. They had a 60.4-inch front and rear tread, 68.7-inch overall height and 177.5-inch overall length. Chassis options included 1,350-pound capacity or 1,750-pound capacity front springs, 2,000-pound rear springs, front stabilizer bar, Super-Lift shock absorbers, free-wheeling hubs and a choice of 3.07, 3.73, 4.11 or posi-traction rear axles.

Extra-cost transmissions included a four-speed manual gearbox or Turbo Hydra-matic with heavy-duty radiator. A heavy-duty eleven-inch clutch was $5.85 extra with the base drivetrain but included with the optional drivetrains.

Blazers were merchandised in two series, KS and KE, with the second letter S indicating six and E indicating eight. The K, of course, meant four-wheel drive in Chevrolet lingo. Factory-issued production records also showed a CS and CE Blazer section, but production was not indicated, since no conventional two-wheel-drive versions were made in 1969 form.

Like most Chevy trucks, the 1952 sedan delivery could be custom painted to customer specifications for slight additional cost. This one has been two-toned and is equipped with wide whitewall tires. Although these trucks shared some sheet metal with station wagons, they were not strictly wagon-based, since there were no two-door wagons in the line.

For model year 1970, the Blazer used the same new grille insert as pickups, and a two-wheel-drive model was definitely added in both the six and V-8 series. Nevertheless, fewer than 1,000 of these were built.

The 1971 Blazer adopted the year's new egg-crate grille. Sales began to climb as the Chevrolet-built utility truck gained greater acceptance in the marketplace. Again, most of the Blazers were of the 4x4 type, and ninety-nine percent of them had the removable top, seventy-eight percent being the black-colored style.

In 1972, the Blazer had the same new features as Chevrolet pickups, which were headlined by the Highlander plaid interior package. This was available only in conjunction with the Custom Sport Truck option. It was an exceptionally good season for production, which jumped to a fantastic 47,623 units. Of these, only 3,367 trucks did not get four-wheel drive.

Sedan deliveries

Chevrolet introduced its first sedan delivery late in 1928 and continued to offer this model through 1960. The first postwar editions were a carryover of the prewar model, based on the 1942 passenger car. Major styling changes occurred in 1949, 1953, 1955, 1958 and 1959, so there were six basic generations of postwar sedan deliveries.

The early, 1946–1948, versions of this body style did not, of course, share the Wurlitzer styling of other

With the introduction of two-door station wagons in 1955, Chevrolet made the sedan delivery a wagon-based model. This brought the change to a rear liftgate arrangement in place of the panel doors used earlier. This is the 1956 version. Note that the liftgate is a one-piece type, not the wagon's liftgate-tailgate type.

Chevy's new-for-1953 body styling was used through 1954 on both passenger cars and sedan deliveries. This is the 1954 version with the year's full-width grille; however, the '54- *style taillights were left off the truck. Powerglide was optional for the first time on trucks.*

light-duty trucks. They had the front-end sheet metal of automobiles and were of three-door configuration, with one door on each side and a curbside opening rear door. On the right-hand side, the gas filler exited behind the side door. Upper bodysides were of steel panel design, and the rear of the body slanted straight down.

Sedan deliveries had a half-ton payload capacity and 4,100-pound GVW rating. They used the same drivetrain as passenger cars, with a 216.5 ci overhead

For 1958, the sedan delivery was considered part of the base-level Del Ray passenger car line-up. It had a new X-frame chassis and full-coil-spring suspension. The sedan delivery survived through 1960.

valve inline six. Tires were 6.00x16s, the same size as on pickups, but were of four-ply, rather than six-ply, construction. Wheelbase for the sedan delivery was 116 inches, an inch more than other half-ton trucks. Overall length was 207.5 inches.

These trucks were merchandised as part of the Stylemaster series. The 1946 models had a hood emblem with upright wings and a grille with four horizontal bars. A wider grille and different ornament were seen in 1947, and a vertical piece was added to the center of the grille for 1948. Two-tone paint, usually with the upper body in a darker color, was common.

Standard equipment included a single bucket seat for the driver, with an auxiliary bucket seat available for a passenger. These were upholstered in a durable imitation leather. Most accessories available for cars could be ordered for these trucks.

Sedan deliveries did not follow the other trucks' system of major styling changes in 1947. The all-new postwar models introduced for 1949 were lower, wider and somewhat slab-sided, although rear fenders were still pontoon-type units bolted on. The trucks—actually commercial cars—were now part of Chevy's Styleline Special series.

Wheelbase was reduced to 115 inches and overall length to 197.9 inches. The tires were smaller 6.70x15

This beautifully restored 1967 Chevrolet sedan delivery was at the 1986 Hershey Car Show. This truck was part of the One-Fifty passenger car series, and only 7,273 were pro- *duced for the year. Spotlights, whitewalls and full wheel covers were factory options.*

four-plys. A seventy-three-inch-long load space was provided. Inside panels were brown masonite painted gray. The headliner was tan imitation leather. Rubber mats were used on the driving compartment floor, and the rear cargo area was covered with linoleum.

Engineering features were the same as on 1949 passenger cars, with a valve-in-head six producing 90 hp and driving through a three-speed manual transmission operated via column gearshift controls. The sedan delivery continued to come with a mixture of trim features from other models. For example, the headlamp doors were brightmetal from the Styleline Deluxe, but the rear gravel shields were made of standard black rubber.

Year-to-year changes in styling and appointments followed those of the Chevy cars. The 1949 grille had seven short vertical members below the horizontal center bar, while the 1950 style had only two below the parking lights. The 1951 grille had a chrome loop at the

bottom, and the 1952 design was similar but had five teeth on the horizontal centerpiece. An all-time sales record for this body style was established in 1950, the same year that Powerglide automatic transmission became available. When this option was added, a different version of the 235 ci truck engine with hydraulic valve lifters was used, which developed 105 hp.

Chevy's all-new 1953 passenger car body was used for the year's sedan delivery. Changes from 1952 included a one-piece windshield, a different hood ornament, a new grille with three vertical fins on the center bar and a redesigned hood nameplate. The truck was part of the base 150 series with no bodyside moldings and rubber gravel guards.

Wheelbase remained at 115 inches and overall width was 74¾ inches. From bumper-to-bumper, the measurement was 195.5 inches. The 6.70x15 tires were used again. The stick-shift engine had a new 7.1:1 compression ratio that boosted horsepower to 108,

Chevy's 1946–1947 panel deliveries featured the Wurlitzer Juke Box front-end treatment. This is a 1946 version spotted at Hershey in 1986. It came with dual panel doors at the rear, which had double windows at their tops. Dual wipers indicate this is the Deluxe version.

The 1946–1947 Chevrolet panel deliveries continued with prewar styling and engineering. With the rear door open, the unusual shape of the rear windows is obvious. This is a standard model with single wipers, but has the chrome grille and bumper option and an accessory front grille guard.

Beginning in May 1947, the panel delivery adopted the Advance-Design look. This is a 1950 half-ton, judging by the lack of vent windows and 3100 call-outs below Chevrolet hood nameplate. This truck has the standard painted grille.

while the Powerglide six used a 7.5:1 compression ratio giving 115 hp. Power steering was a new option in 1953.

Inside, the adjustable driver's seat and separate hinged passenger seat were upholstered in durable leatherette. The rear cargo compartment had a black linoleum floor, and painted masonite panel board was again used to trim the walls, while the wheelhousings, rear corner panels and inside of the rear door were painted to match the interior. On the outside, since a rear bumper guard could not be used (due to interference with the rear door) the bumper was plain and the license plate lamp was relocated.

The 1954 sedan deliveries were essentially of the same basic style, with a full-width grille with five vertical dividers added, plus a new hood ornament, redesigned bumper and guards, new emblems and revised rear fenders. The little truck was still part of the base 150 series. Both engines were now at 7.5:1 compression with output ratings of 115 hp on stick-shift models and 125 hp for those with Powerglide.

The fourth generation of postwar sedan deliveries is probably the most collectible. Chevy's 1955–1957 passenger cars are widely considered as classics, and the trucks share the overall desirability of these years. These sedan deliveries were more like station wagons with blanked-out upper rear panels, and the styling of the rear end changed from a curbside door to a large liftgate arrangement.

For 1955, the wraparound windshield, slab-sided body, rectangular egg-crate grille and hooded head-lights set the styling theme. About the only throwover to the past was the 115-inch wheelbase. Overall length climbed to 197.1 inches, and tires were upgraded to size 7.15x14 tubeless models. Front and rear tread widths, formerly at sixty-two inches, were narrowed to fifty-eight and 58.9 inches, respectively. Six-cylinder models were more than 100 pounds lighter.

The base six was now the 235.5 ci engine with 7.5:1 compression. It produced 123 hp on stick-shift models and 136 hp in Powerglides. There was also a totally new V-8 series using a 265 ci, 162 hp engine. The stick-shift version used solid valve lifters, and the Powerglide trucks had hydraulic lifters. Buyers could also order a Power-Pack for the V-8 which added a four-barrel carburetor and dual exhausts. It's likely that more sedan deliveries have this option today than the factory built with it in 1955.

Something new for 1956 sedan deliveries was a three-quarter-length chrome molding on the bodysides. This served as a new bit of dress-up trim for the base 150 series and allowed Chevy to advertise that it was the only maker in its field to offer chrome trim as standard equipment. The 1956 models also boasted full-width grille and a general refinement of the 1955 appearance. As the horsepower race was in full swing, Chevy made its new Hot One even hotter, with options up to 205 hp in a Super Turbo Fire V-8. Base powerplant—and the most common in the commercial cars—was a 140 hp six-cylinder with raised 8.1:1 compression.

Chevrolet added fins to its 1957 models, and the sedan delivery was no exception. It also had the updated

This 1951 panel delivery (note the vent windows and non-push-button door handles) has the Deluxe chrome grille and accessory brightmetal fender trim bars. Chrome hubcaps were also optional. Double rear panel doors had windows to allow viewing traffic at rear.

integral bumper-grille with bomb-type guards, wind-split-style hood and slightly revised molding treatment. New V-8 engines included four based on a larger displacement 283 ci block with 185, 220, 245 or 283 hp. The last two were strictly high-performance options,

This 1952 half-ton panel delivery is one of a fleet built expressly for the United States Navy. Extra windows were added when the trucks were new, making them resemble a Suburban. Apparently, they were used by Navy survey teams in the San Francisco Bay Area. At least two such trucks survive today.

using either two four-barrel carbs or a fuel-injection system producing one horsepower per cubic inch (and probably *not* available in sedan deliveries, at least as a regular production option).

A new triple-turbine Turboglide automatic transmission was added to Chevy's extra-cost list in 1957 for use with larger, more powerful V-8s. Three-speed manual, overdrive and Powerglide gearboxes were also available. As in 1956, the sedan delivery continued to feature the 150 series side trim without the vertical sash molding used with other bodies.

Longer, lower and wider bodies were used for the 1958 model. It now had an X-type Safety Girder frame and full-coil-spring suspension. The sedan delivery was built on the new 117.5-inch wheelbase and stretched 209 inches long. It measured 77.7 inches wide and stood merely 58.5 inches high.

Chevrolet described its new styling as the Sculpturamic Gull-Wing look and this seemed fitting to describe its contrived, but not unpleasant, contours. Sedan deliveries were trimmed like base-series Del Ray models, with that model name at the leading edge of the rear cove and a plain single side molding. There was a chrome molding surrounding the wraparound windshield, but none on the side windows. Dual headlamps and parking lamps were used up front, along with an elaborate custom car grille.

For sedan deliveries, powerplants ranged from the 145 hp six to a pair of 283 ci V-8s with 185 or 230 hp. Air conditioning and a posi-traction rear axle joined the

Birmingham Cleaners was probably a fictitious company name applied to this 1952 half-ton panel delivery for taking publicity photos with appeal to small businessmen. New this *year were push-button door handles. The 3100 call-out no longer decorated the hood, although the 3600 three-quarter-tons still had their call-outs for identification.*

114

The hoodside nameplate seen on this half-ton panel delivery was used from 1953 to the 1955 first series. The 1953s used the original Advance-Design grille with horizontal bars, while the 1954 and 1955 first series trucks had this crossbar grille. This is identified in factory photos as a 1954 model.

Here's a 1954 3800 one-ton panel delivery with Deluxe-type fender bars. Grille, hubcaps and bumpers are the painted type, however. The one-ton hubcaps were of a similar design to those of other light-duty trucks, but larger in diameter.

ever-growing factory options list. The sedan delivery continued to come with a swing-up endgate that looked like the Chevy station wagon's liftgate-tailgate arrangement combined into a single unit. A single bucket seat for the driver was still standard equipment.

Second series 1955 panel delivery had completely modernized styling and engineering. V-8 engines were now optionally available. This '55 was used by the Carnation Milk Company. It has the standard painted trim and blackwall tires.

Since we have already described most details of the 1959 and 1960 El Caminos, there's no need to dwell on details of the sedan delivery for the two years, which were very similar except in roof and upper rear body design.

The hotter versions of the 348 ci ranged up to 335 hp with 11.25:1 compression, but these mills were not available in the sedan delivery, except possibly on special order. The 135 hp Hi-Thrift six was most commonly seen under the hood of the little truck, although the 185 hp Turbo Fire and 230 hp Super Turbo Fire versions of the 283 ci V-8 could be ordered as Regular Production Options.

Regular sales catalogs for trucks simply describe the 1959 sedan delivery as roomier and give few additional details. This model was now being constructed on a 119-inch wheelbase and had a 211-inch overall length, eighty-inch width and 56.3-inch height. These specifications also apply to the 1960 model, which was the last of the true sedan deliveries.

For all years, the sedan delivery body style is relatively rare, with highs in annual production never reaching much over 21,000 units and the typical figures being

This well-restored 1956 3100 panel delivery was at the 1986 Hershey Car Show to represent Chevrolet's Task Force era. The hood mascot shown was a factory accessory item.

Note the V (V-8) emblem on the hood ornament. Spotlights, outside sun visor, bumper guards and whitewalls were factory extras.

116

far lower than this. That's one big reason that light-duty truck collectors find the sedan delivery a desirable item. To this can be added the extra attractiveness of passenger car-like styling, a convenient size that's relatively comfortable to drive and easy to store, and the fact that these trucks could be had with lots of performance and dress-up options or accessories.

Chassis models

Because of the many vocational uses that trucks of all sizes are built for, there are hundreds of vendors involved in the business of supplying purpose-built truck bodies. Most of these companies construct their custom-designed bodies on chassis models supplied by manufacturers as a standard part of the line.

Chassis-only models are what the name implies: a bare chassis with frame, running gear, powertrain, suspension and tires. A front seat is also often included.

The chassis and flat-face cowl models (sometimes called chassis and cowl) adds other parts, such as front-end sheet metal up to the forward part of the cowl.

A third variation is the chassis, cowl and windshield, which includes windshield frame, windshield header and windshield glass. Station wagons constructed on commercial chassis usually start in this form.

The most expensive vocational truck is the chassis and cab, which adds the complete cab, with seats, upholstery, doors, door glass, and so on.

Prices, weights and, in some cases, production totals for Chevrolet chassis models are shown in the charts at the back of this book. These trucks were

This illustration from the 1958 Chevrolet four-wheel-drive model brochure illustrates the four-wheel-drive Apache panel delivery. Panel bodies provided double-walled steel doors with weathertight insulation, two-position (90- and 180-degree) door stops, durable one-piece plywood floors (grooved with protective steel skid strips) and protective asphalt-impregnated roof insulation.

offered in both the half-ton and three-quarter-ton conventional series. In addition, chassis versions of sedan deliveries were used as the basis for many ambulances and funeral cars made by aftermarket bodymakers.

Most postwar chassis-model trucks were delivered to their original purchasers with some type of body mounted, so that restorers and collectors today wind up with a complete truck, rather than a chassis version.

The panel delivery had the year's new truck grille styling for 1957. Also redesigned were hood emblem and fender-side model nameplates. This one has the painted bumper and grille. Its tires are of a more modern style with thin whitewalls. Mike Carbonella

Continued for 1959, with only minor trim variations, was the Apache panel truck. This one has the deluxe grille and bumper and two-tone paint with the panel sides in contrasting color. It's a very pretty truck.

117

This new pinch-waist body styling and dual jet-pod hood design was used on 1960–1961 Chevrolet light-duty trucks. Shown here is the 1960 panel delivery with Custom Chrome package.

Such owners may become interested in the historical aspects of how their trucks were built. In addition, knowing how many chassis and cowl or chassis and cab trucks were produced in a model year may help them narrow down the relative scarcity of their vehicles.

In addition, some restorers may find themselves returning an old truck to chassis and cab form in the cases where these components are in good condition but the rest of the body (cargo box, platform or stake racks) are rusted or damaged. They may start with a complete truck and wind up with a chassis and cab.

By and large, however, we do not see many chassis models offered for sale in publications, flea markets or auctions that constitute the collectors' marketplace, and it is not necessary to go into great detail on these trucks. In general, they followed the same styling and engineering development patterns as pickup trucks of the same

model year. Therefore, a chassis model of 1953 should look like a pickup of the same vintage and utilize the same engine, transmission, running gear and other features.

Panel trucks

Panel trucks (also called panel deliveries) go back in history and first evolved from one of the earliest types of commercial vehicle, the delivery car. These were first built on modified automobile chassis and came with open or closed cabs. Panel trucks were a bit lower and wider than delivery cars since they were built on the heavier truck chassis and shared the front-end sheet metal of regular trucks. Postwar panels generally have enclosed cabs and solid panels on the rear bodysides.

A variation of the panel truck, which Chevrolet offered as a regular model through the first series 1955 line, is the canopy express. This type of body also dates back to the early days of light-duty trucking, when express models (actually large pickups) were offered with four- or eight-post-canopy-style tops and roll-down sidecurtains. In the 1920s the same basic concept was used to create a version of the panel truck that had open sides to allow the display of items such as produce and fish.

In the postwar era, Chevrolet offered half-ton and three-quarter-ton panel trucks in 1946, plus a half-ton canopy express. In 1947 the three-quarter-ton panel was discontinued. The other two models were retained (along with one-ton versions of both) until the second series of 1955 trucks came out. At that point the canopy express was dropped.

Starting in 1957, K series four-wheel-drive versions of the half-ton panel were introduced, and they

The stock 1962 panel delivery was the basis of this ambulance conversion offered through the Silver Book. It is the standard model of Franklin Body Company of Brooklyn, New York. Notice the return to single headlamps and lower, less obtrusive hood.

A regular production model for many years, the canopy delivery sang its swan song in the early postwar era. This is the 1949 model with curtains. Hope Emerich

were produced from then on in relatively small numbers each year. The half-ton panel with conventional drive also remained available.

Half-ton panels using the same basic styling and engineering features of pickups were continued into the sixties. However, the release of the Corvan, which was actually another type of panel truck, gave the conventional panel some competition. While the Corvan did not generate sufficient sales to threaten the panel truck's existance, the forward control Chevy Van, introduced in mid-1964, was another story. This model appealed to the same basic type of buyer, but did its work better, with greater utility and economy. In addition, the Chevy Van was available with short or long wheelbases and in a three-quarter-ton configuration.

In 1967, Chevrolet introduced a new C-20 three-quarter-ton panel truck. This was a relatively rare model, especially in four-wheel-drive form. Still, it did little to increase sales of conventional panels vis-à-vis those of the forward control panel vans. As the following figures of production between 1967 and 1970 illustrate, the popularity of the G series panel van was up to seven times greater than the appeal of the regular panel trucks in this period, despite the reintroduction of the three-quarter-ton version.

Panel truck and panel van production: 1967–1970

1967 Panel vans

G-10 (90″ wheelbase)	18,293
G-10 (108″ wheelbase)	13,624
G-20 (108″ wheelbase)	6,013
Total	37,930

1967 Panel trucks

C-10 (2-wheel drive)	3,827
C-10 (4-wheel drive)	30
C-20 (2-wheel drive)	940
C-20 (4-wheel drive)	8
Total	4,805

1968 Panel vans

G-10 (90″ wheelbase)	18,617
G-10 (108″ wheelbase)	17,569
G-20 (108″ wheelbase)	5,504
Total	41,690

1968 Panel trucks

C-10 (2-wheel drive)	4,801
C-10 (4-wheel drive)	59
C-20 (2-wheel drive)	1,572
C-20 (4-wheel drive)	68
Total	6,500

1969 Panel vans

G-10 (90″ wheelbase)	18,456
G-10 (108″ wheelbase)	20,730
G-20 (108″ wheelbase)	6,030
Total	45,216

Last appearance of the Chevrolet canopy delivery was during the 1954–1955 first series period. This factory photo shows the 1954 3100 half-ton edition with curtains rolled up for access to cargo area. Security was a problem among tradesmen using this model.

Although the canopy delivery was on its way out in 1954, Chevy still offered the model in different weight classes. This is the 3800 one-ton. The canopy delivery used a curtain at top rear with a tailgate at the bottom.

A 1935 innovation of Chevrolet Motor Division was an all-steel station wagon, built on the light-duty truck chassis and marketed as the Carryall Suburban. This is the 1949 3100 half-ton version.

1969 Panel trucks

C-10 (2-wheel drive)	5,492
C-20 (2-wheel drive)	1,779
Total	7,271

1970 Panel vans*

G-10 (90″ wheelbase)	3,933
G-10 (108″ wheelbase)	3,069
G-20 (108″ wheelbase)	1,195
Total	8,197

1970 Panel trucks

C-10 (2-wheel drive)	3,965
C-20 (2-wheel drive)	1,032
Total	4,997

Van production in 1970 was affected by a strike that caused GM to halt production until changeover to a completely new line of vans.

With the close of production for model year 1970, the conventional panel truck was completely dropped from the light-duty line, and the panel van took its place as the truck for commercial users that needed an enclosed truck with solid panel bodysides.

Chevrolet's postwar panel trucks were in the same series as the pickup trucks and followed the same pattern of styling changes. The early postwar versions, of 1946–1947, had the Wurlitzer look. This was followed by the Advance-Design models, which are particularly handsome and appealing to collectors. They had double rear doors and running boards and could be ordered with Deluxe features such as chrome bumpers and grille, fender-side moldings, two-tone paint and fancy cab appointments.

In 1955, the panel trucks took on the Task-Force frontal styling, wraparound windshield and a flatter, squarer overall appearance. The pinch-waist models of the early sixties were also quite handsome, especially when painted in two-tone combinations, which were applied with the lower bodysides and the rear of the roof done in contrasting colors. The Job Tamer styling, adopted in 1967, was extremely attractive in panel truck form. This would also be the end of the road for the model that had been part of Chevrolet's truck line for half a century.

Panel trucks are relatively popular vehicles with light-duty truck collectors. They are also appealing to conversion van enthusiasts looking for something older and distinctive to turn heads at van rallies or shows. These enthusiasts usually keep the exterior in near original condition (they might add parkway camper-style windows to the sides) and turn most of their attention to updating the interiors.

This is another 1949 Suburban, and the lack of a 3100 nameplate identifies it as a three-quarter-ton 3600 series model. Suburbans came with a choice of double rear panel doors or liftgate-tailgate arrangement. The two versions were similarly priced and about equally popular. Note the sliding windows in center and rear of sides.

121

Suburban Carryall

The Suburban was introduced in 1935 and remained an exclusive Chevrolet model until the 1950s, when Dodge's Town Panel and International Travelall entered the same market segment. Checker had actually produced a similar commercial vehicle in the early 1930s, but it had wood framing in its body. Thus, Chevy's long-standing claim that the first Suburban pioneered the all-steel station wagon is probably true.

Postwar Suburbans used the same basic body as the panel truck, but used windows instead of solid sheet metal panels on the upper rear bodysides. This truck has the unusual distinction of having been produced with side door configurations of two-, three- and four-door styles. As far as I know, only some early touring cars could claim the same thing, and they had a fourth dummy door stamped on the driver's side. This meant they had four-door styling even if only three doors actually opened.

The Suburban did not reappear immediately after the war, as it was not included in the early 1946 CK truck line. The DP series of late 1946 reintroduced two versions, however. Both had one door on either side of the driving compartment, but a choice of cargo-access methods was provided at the rear. One option was double panel doors that opened from the center. The other was the endgate style with a tailgate hinged at the bottom and a liftgate hinged at the top.

From 1947 to 1949, the Suburban was offered only in endgate form. Beginning in 1950, the version with double panel doors was brought back for a permanent stay. Other features of early postwar models included the use of sliding glass in the rear side windows, which was available through 1966. The double panel doors or liftgate had fixed windows, while the driving compartment doors had lowerable glass (with vent windows after 1950).

Front-end sheet metal for Suburbans was shared with the other light-duty trucks and underwent styling changes at the same points in product development history, Advance-Design, Task Force, and so on. Accommodations for eight passengers were available on three bench seats, with the center and rear seats designed for quick removal to allow extra cargo space. Front bucket seats were optional from 1967 on.

Characteristics of all Suburbans were nicely summed up by copy in the 1958 sales catalog, which said, "Suburban Carryalls can be fitted for shuttle bus service, sportsman's activities and numerous jobs that combine passenger transportation with cargo hauling."

A 3100 hood nameplate was added to identify half-ton Suburbans of 1950. This one has the optional chrome grille and bumper. Long-arm rearview mirrors are also fitted. Lettering on door is in Hebrew.

The 1954 Advance-Design Suburban Carryall with panel door option. This is the half-ton. Most, if not all, 1954 Chevy trucks came with painted grilles and bumpers. Chrome-plated replacement parts were offered by the company in later versions of the Chevrolet master parts catalog.

This 1954, early-1955 style Suburban Carryall has the tailgate and liftgate option. Suburbans came with three seats, the rearmost pair being easily removable for increased cargo space.

Aftermarket companies used this model as the basis for mini school buses, ambulances, funeral coaches and small campers.

Suburbans also used the same engineering features as other Chevrolet light-duties, which included the availability of a four-wheel-drive system as an option after 1957. Engines and transmissions were the same as offered in pickup trucks.

Beginning in 1960, Suburbans adopted the new pinch-waist styling and attractive color-break two-tone paint combinations. These were applied with lower body-

Four-wheel drive was made available in 1957 and could be ordered for the 1958 Carryall Suburban seen here. Note that larger all-terrain tires were used with the option.

sides, wheels and the rear portion of the roof in one color, while the upper bodysides, hood, fendertops and cab portion of the body were painted a second color. Removable second and third seats and the choice of panel door or endgate styling was continued. There was still a single door on either side up front.

Three-door styling was introduced to the Suburban in 1967. There was one door on the driver's side and two on the curb side, which forced the rear-seat passengers to enter from the right side of the vehicle. Optional second and third seats were still of the removable type, and the two styles of cargo-access were carried over. A new model available this season was the C-20 three-quarter-ton Suburban. Custom CS trim and the four-wheel-drive K option were available at extra cost. Three-door styling was used through 1972, being replaced with a new four-door Suburban in 1973.

Few Suburbans are being seriously collected or restored, although they are popular with people in the vintage vehicle hobbies as cargo haulers or tow vehicles.

Vans

Chevrolet introduced its first compact forward control front-engine vans in mid-1964. These trucks are really a separate class of light-duty models that currently seem to have greater appeal to the modified vehicle enthusiast than the collector or restorer. There's no doubt in my mind, however, that good original or restored-to-original vans will start showing up in large

The building of Vega Dam near Collbran, Colorado, created a lake that became a popular vacation spot. Here we see a

1960 Chevrolet Carryall Suburban parked there. Department of Interior; Bureau of Reclamation

numbers at collector vehicle shows as they grow a bit older.

Since they have not yet caught on as collectibles and since they are not directly related to the development of conventional light-duties, we're back to skim over their product history as quickly as possible.

One basic thing to understand is that Chevrolet has merchandised its commercial vans and passenger vans differently. For example, there are separate catalogs issued for the panel-type Chevy Vans and the passenger-type Sportvans and Beauvilles.

Initially, only the panel van was available, and it was considered a part of the Chevy II car line, as it used that series' four-cylinder engine as base powerplant. This workingman's truck had one door for each side of the driving compartment, double panel doors on the curbside and another set of panel doors at the rear. A small 120 hp six was optional.

By 1965, the Sportvan models were added to the line. These were window vans available with various seating configurations and different trim levels. The following season, a pop-up camper option was a new product offering, and sales continued to climb.

Chevy added a longer wheelbase of 108 inches to the original ninety-inch wheelbase series in 1967. The G-10 half-tons came on both wheelbases, while a new G-20 three-quarter-ton series used the 108-inch stance only. The smaller trucks had 209 cubic feet of cargo space, and this jumped to 256 cubic feet in the big ones. Also new was an optional 283 ci V-8. Four models—Chevy Van, Sportvan, Custom Sportvan and Deluxe Sportvan—were available in the three lines.

The vans were continually refined, but not drastically changed until 1971, when a total revamp was accomplished. Actually, the UAW strike of 1969 had delayed development of the updated van and shortened production of the true 1970 series, so that the new style

The somewhat unusual three-door Suburban was introduced in 1967, as seen here. There were two entry doors on the curb-side of the vehicle, but only one (for the driver) on the road side. Styling was modernized, but a choice of panel doors or gate arrangement was still offered for the rear.

vans were introduced in May 1970 as 1971 models. They had a higher, wider and longer body with an extended front hood for easier engine service access. Everything from one end to the other was restyled.

Both the G-10s and G-20s now came on two wheelbases. The shorter one stretched 110 inches and the longer versions had a 125-inch stance. There were three models in each of the four series. These were Chevy Vans, Sportvans and Beauvilles. The latter represented a top-of-the-line luxury van available only with V-8 powerplants, which now included 307 ci and 350 ci engines.

Other innovations for 1971 included independent front suspension, an extra-cost Custom Appearance

The 1946–1965 Suburban Carryalls came with one entry door on either side. This is the 1962 half-ton edition with a 12-passenger school bus conversion by Coach and Equipment Corporation, of Penn Yan, New York. Bow tie emblems and 10 badges decorated sides of cowl.

The 1972 Suburban Carryall came in 32 different basic choices, not considering colors, engines or transmissions. It was still designed with a single entry door on the left, but two on the right-hand side. Cheyenne and Cheyenne Super interior options were available. This is the C-10, but K-10, C-20 and K-20 models were offered as well.

package and an optional sliding side door. Front disc brakes were standardized for half-tonners. For 1972, the van story was primarily one of refinements.

Vega panel express

The last of the other Chevrolet light-duties was actually a small sedan delivery, although Chevy called it a panel express. It was based on the subcompact Vega station wagon, also known as the Kammback model.

Conventional forward control vans replaced the Corvan in mid-1964. This 1972 version shows the slightly extended engine hood designed for improved serviceability which was adopted by this model year.

Chevy described it as the "kinky way to haul around your surfboard."

It came only with the Vega's standard all-vinyl interior, less passenger bucket seat, and with either black or green upholstery. An aluminum-block overhead cam four-cylinder engine was the powerplant. Also standard was a three-speed floor-shifted manual transmission, front disc brakes and below-the-floor storage compartments. It had a ninety-seven-inch wheelbase, 176.5-inch overall length and 51.8-inch height. It was listed as a half-ton with 68.7 cubic feet of cargo space. A total of 7,800 units were built in 1971, with 4,114 made the next year.

These trucks generated a lot of interest when they first appeared and are almost certain to become a late-model collector vehicle.

Additional notes

In addition to the models that I have touched on in this chapter, Chevrolet also offered light-duty versions of a platform-stake bed truck, small Step-Vans and commercial station wagons in certain postwar years. Leafing through a *Silver Book* of any vintage will provide an even better idea of the hundreds of different vocational light-duty trucks that utilized various Chev-

The basis for most Chevrolet conventional light-duty trucks was the chassis and flat-face cowl. This configuration is shown here. The illustration is of a 3100 half-ton model of 1954–1955 first series design.

Available in the light-duty line for much of the early postwar era was the platform truck. A 1949 three-quarter-ton model of the 3600 series is shown here.

Stanford Nursery used their three-quarter-ton Chevrolet platform stake truck for many chores in 1954. This configuration was extremely popular with farmers, too. The long-arm rear-view mirror helped the operator see around the wide stake body.

National Body Company offered this low-cost ambulance on the Chevrolet chassis in 1951. These professional vehicles were actually custom creations using some car and some truck parts to create a totally new type of vehicle. Some people consider them passengers cars; others say they are actually a type of light-duty truck. Crestline Publishing Company

rolet chassis. Going deeper into the history of these other models would probably be extremely interesting, but the main topic of this study is the postwar light-duty pickup truck.

Collectors seeking additional information about these trucks will then have to turn to original factory literature, such as sales catalogs and service manuals. Even such literature for trucks is relatively scarce, although the recent growth of this branch of the hobby has inspired flea market and mail-order vendors to start gathering more material on trucks.

The 1971 Chevy Vega panel express was the first domestic small truck with a fully enclosed body. It saw its debut on August 6, 1970. A total of 68.7 cubic feet of cargo area was offered with a payload capacity of 650 pounds. A 90 hp four-cylinder engine was standard. Overall length of this mini-panel was 14 feet.

Chapter 8

Factory factors

Although we'll be discussing modified trucks in the next chapter, the primary focus of this book is on stock postwar Chevy pickups. In other words, trucks in well-preserved *original* condition or those that have been or will be restored to *original* condition.

Since plain-looking, bare-to-the-bones vehicles aren't the first choice of collectors, most of the trucks that you'll see out in the hobby today will carry a number of original options and accessories, and be finished in original factory-issued colors.

Those who buy, sell and restore light-duty trucks rarely base their decisions about values or how much to invest in a particular truck on the thousands of option and model variables they'd need a computer to sort out. There is no way for one person to memorize the hundreds of different options available in each model year. So, in most cases a truck will be eye-balled and checked for its features and general condition. This will give the hobbyist, collector, investor or dealer an immediate idea of what the vehicle is worth and whether it will pay to restore it.

Such an expert will probably think, "This truck has the short box, the CST option, bucket seats, two-tone paint, air conditioning and a big V-8 and seems to be in good, rust-free condition; it's probably worth $7,500 in top shape." In most cases, the first thing that this expert will look for, beyond generally good condition, is the option packages or groups that the truck carries. While individual options such as high-performance engines, chrome wheel covers and a radio will figure into the overall equation, the existence of the more desirable packages will quickly reveal whether the vehicle is basically a plain or fancy model.

Around 1959, Chevrolet embarked on an aggressive program to merchandise some of its optional equipment in package form. This reflected the thinking of General Motors Chairman Alfred P. Sloan, Jr., who once noted that options enabled his company to make a small number of models appealing to a large group of buyers, since the add-ons permitted the personalization of the product to individual tastes. Sloan also said that different options could be combined in so many ways that it was possible for Chevrolet to build an entire year's worth of vehicles without making any two exactly the same.

As Chevrolet expanded its option list, the merchandising of basic packages of extras was adopted as a means of simplifying the selective process while promoting additional sales of extra-cost equipment. The various packages were grouped so that each selection gave the vehicle its own character and made it seem like a separate model.

For example, trucks with the Custom Side Molding package had certain features that made them fancier than base models, but less luxurious than top-of-the-line models. From there, buyers could step up to something like the Custom Sport Truck option, which *included* the Custom Side Molding package, plus even more features. This was called the building block approach to vehicle merchandising.

Modern-day collectors who are familiar with the different building blocks available from Chevrolet find them an easy way to help formulate their decisions about the value of a certain truck. In other words, if a truck has certain option packages, they know right away that it is worth closer examination as a collectible vehicle.

This doesn't mean that a plain-Jane truck won't be given any consideration. If such a vehicle is in mint condition, has extremely low mileage or uses a rare high-performance engine, it could be collectible, too.

But, in most cases, it is the fancier models that have the most desirable features and represent a good buy for the serious collector.

The following pages include a list of some of the more desirable option packages and groups for different model Chevrolet pickups, including El Caminos and Blazers. Each listing gives a general idea of the inclusive features, although there were minor variations in specific equipment for different model years.

Popular Chevrolet truck option packages

Custom Deluxe trim package

Full-width bench seat with comfortably padded seat cushions and backrest. Vinyl seat upholstery and door panels. Steel roof panel painted in main exterior body color. Black rubber floor mat extending to firewall. Padded armrests. Padded sunshades. Courtesy lamp. Prismatic rearview mirror. Foam-padded instrument panel. Exterior includes bright upper and lower grille outline moldings, bright headlamp bezels, bright outside rearview mirrors, bright door handles, white-painted front bumper, hubcaps and wheels, and bright Custom Deluxe nameplates.

Cheyenne trim package

Bench seat with full-depth foam cushions and backrests. Custom-grained vinyl upholstery or nylon cloth and vinyl upholstery. (Bucket seats also available with vinyl upholstery.) Special door trim panels. Cab headliner. Deep-twist nylon carpeting extending to firewall. Color-keyed garnish moldings. Ashtray-mounted cigarette lighter. Custom steering wheel. Cheyenne dashboard nameplates. Door- or manually-operated courtesy lights. Extra acoustical insulation. Exterior includes all Custom Deluxe items plus the following additions or substitutions: brightmetal cab trim and moldings, bright upper bodyside and tailgate moldings. Central taillight applique for Fleetside and Cheyenne nameplates.

Custom Cab option

Foam rubber seat cushions and backrests. Brightmetal dashboard control knobs. Brightmetal window moldings. Right-hand door armrest and sunshade. Cigarette lighter.

Custom Appearance option

Brightmetal grille. Brightmetal hood, fender, vent window and windshield moldings. Chromed control-knob trim. Custom emblems. Color-keyed floor mat.

Custom Comfort option

Special insulation. White hardboard headlining. Vinyl sidewall trim panels on Suburban. Spare wheel cover. Full-depth foam seat. Special upholstery. Cigar lighter.

Custom Side Molding package

Fender moldings. Door moldings. Bodyside moldings. In late 1960s and 1970s, also includes taillight moldings, back-up light moldings and bright fuel filler cap (included when Custom Sport Truck option is ordered).

Custom Sport Truck option

Right-hand sunshade and armrest. Bucket seats and console in Blazers. CST emblems. Special insulation. Undercoating. Chromed bumpers. Bright control knob and pedal trim. Bright windshield, bodyside, tailgate, taillight and back-up light moldings. Bright fuel filler cap. Side-marker reflectors. Dual horns. Bright transfer-case shift lever in Blazers.

El Camino Appearance Guard group

Front bumper guards. Door-edge guards. Two front color-keyed floor mats.

El Camino Operating Convenience group

(All models without special instrumentation.) Electric clock. Left-hand remote-control outside rearview mirror. When teamed with the special instrumentation option, left-hand remote-control outside rearview mirror only.

El Camino Center Console option

Available only when bucket seats were ordered. Includes storage compartment. Transmission gearshift is located on console. With standard three-speed available only in SS-396. Not available when overdrive transmission was ordered.

El Camino Special Instrumentation group

Electric clock. Tachometer. Ammeter. Temperature and oil pressure gauges.

El Camino Auxiliary Lighting package

Includes ashtray lamp. Courtesy light. Underhood trouble light.

Blazer Custom Molding package

Brightmetal lower fender, door and bodyside moldings. Taillight and back-up light moldings. Bright fuel filler cap. Included with CST option.

Blazer Custom Sport Truck option

Bucket seats. Console. Right-hand sunshade and armrest. Cigar lighter. CST emblems. Special instrumentation. Undercoating. Chrome bumpers. Bright control knobs and pedal trim. Bright windshield, bodyside, taillight and back-up light moldings. Bright fuel filler cap. Side-marker reflectors. Dual horns. Bright transfer case shift lever. With auxiliary top and rear seat, also includes bright vent window molding, embossed vinyl door and body trim panels with bright upper retainers, spare tire cover and front and rear color-keyed carpeting. With auxiliary top without rear seat, includes bright vent window molding, embossed vinyl door and body trim panels with bright upper retainers, spare tire cover, front color-keyed carpeting and rear color-keyed vinyl-coated rubber floor mat. Without auxiliary top, includes front color-keyed vinyl-coated rubber floor mat.

El Camino SS-396 option

Front and rear wheel-opening moldings. Body molding. Deluxe steering wheel. Glovebox light. Electric clock. Door courtesy light switches. Foam seat cushions. Vinyl interior. Blackout grille. SS identification. Redline or white stripe or raised-white-letter tires. Engine: 396 ci, 325 hp V-8.

El Camino Custom Model option

All standard El Camino equipment, plus carpeting, electric clock, glovebox light, deep-dish steering wheel and woodgrain trim on dashboard.

El Camino SS package

Special pattern and Custom vinyl seat trim. Matching right- and left-hand outside Sport-style rearview mirrors. Special body striping and/or identification. 15x7-inch Rally wheels. Extra-wide, low-profile raised-white-letter tires. SS emblems. Blackout grille finish. 454 ci V-8 engine with SS-454 model.

Paint colors

The use of factory paint colors on older Chevrolet pickups will be important to the collector of original light-duty trucks. Needless to say, a truck represented as a well-preserved original should be painted in a color scheme that was available from the factory. In this case, the color should also agree with the paint code indicated by the vehicle data plate on the firewall.

A truck that has been expertly refinished in proper factory colors will be quite acceptable to even the most discriminating collector. In fact, most experts would hardly blink their eyes if the color scheme isn't the same one called for on the data plate, as long as it's an original selection and the paint is correctly applied.

On the other hand, a nonauthentic color (or even an incorrect two-tone combination of original colors) will be a turn-off to a collector. Not that he or she can't have the truck properly refinished, but he will probably feel that doing the job wrong in the first place hints that shortcuts were taken and may have also been used in other phases of the restoration.

Trucks with totally improper paint jobs are bound to have lower collector value, even if they're in great mechanical and physical condition. So if you are thinking of selling that basically solid truck you've found in the collector's marketplace, don't decide that you should give it a quick coat of fresh paint in the cheapest color you find. The collector is going to refinish the vehicle anyway, but may think that the incorrect new paint is hiding imperfections. This means you have wasted your time and money to do nothing but raise suspicions that the repaint is hiding shoddy bodywork or buckets of bondo. It's much better to simply clean up the original as best you can—or else repaint it the right way.

On the following pages you'll find charts showing the paint codes for colors used on Chevrolet trucks from 1939-1951, 1953-1959 and 1964-1972. Although each of these charts has a different format, the essential paint code information is there.

As experienced restorers know, these codes were applicable years ago, when paints were formulated somewhat differently than they are today. Therefore, some colors cannot be exactly duplicated. Most restorers consider it acceptable to refinish collector vehicles with the closest matching colors that are currently available. To help these craftsmen, the major suppliers of automotive finishes—such as PPG, Ditzler and Martin-Senour—maintain color libraries.

The clerk at your local paint jobber or auto supply shop can help you contact the manufacturers to get the color-matching information you'll need through their color library services. These libraries will have a collection of original paint chips for your truck and be able to tell you the available colors that best approximate its original finish today.

Individual options

Another of the factory factors that truck collectors pay attention to is the installation of factory-approved extra-cost equipment, individual options and accessories on the pickups that they own.

These extras were merchandised to buyers for several reasons: to personalize or improve appearance; to increase operating convenience, comfort or safety; to raise the performance level of the vehicle; and to increase its utility to the commercial user.

There were also different methods of merchandising extras. Certain types of equipment were added to the truck on the assembly line. Other extras were installed as dealer accessories at local Chevrolet agencies. There are probably some items that could be added either way—for instance, if the buyer later decided he wanted an option that wasn't included in his original purchase order.

General Motors also followed the practice of sometimes adding equipment that a buyer demanded even though it was not included on a list of approved accessories for a specific model. These are known as Special Production Options (or SPOs). Extras included on the approved list were called Regular Production Options (or RPOs). Naturally, it's much easier to prove that an RPO was available as original equipment.

Proving the authenticity of an option may be necessary if the collector decides to have his pickup judged in a commercial-vehicle class at a car show. The existence of any nonoriginal features on a vehicle being judged will lead to point deductions in the authenticity

PER-MAX CHEVROLET COMMERCIAL COLORS (1939-1951)

PARTS		BASE COLORS	COUNTER SETTING	PARTS		BASE COLORS	COUNTER SETTING
colspan="4"	**2U711—CREAM MEDIUM**	colspan="4"	**2U314—SEACREST GREEN**
100	TE-02	H. H. Mix	100	100	TE-02	H. H. Mix	100
616	TE-91	White	716	298	TE-91	White	398
182	TE-74	Ferrite Yellow	898	232	TE-74	Ferrite Yellow	630
92	TE-76	Yellow Toner	990	232	TE-31	Organic Green	862
10	TE-41	Lamp Black	1000	138	TE-41	Lamp Black	1000
colspan="4"	**2U710—OMAHA ORANGE**	colspan="4"	**2U801—SUN BEIGE**
100	TE-02	H. H. Mix	100	100	TE-02	H. H. Mix	100
518	TE-54	Orange Red	618	568	TE-91	White	668
278	TE-72	Medium Yellow	896	178	TE-74	Ferrite Yellow	846
100	TE-74	Ferrite Yellow	996	108	TE-81	Burnt Sienna	954
4	TE-41	Lamp Black	1000	46	TE-41	Lamp Black	1000
colspan="4"	**2U708—ARMOUR YELLOW**	colspan="4"	**2U312—CHANNEL GREEN**
100	TE-02	H. H. Mix	100	100	TE-02	H. H. Mix	100
680	TE-72	Medium Yellow	780	318	TE-91	White	418
100	TE-74	Ferrite Yellow	880	274	TE-74	Ferrite Yellow	692
94	TE-51	Medium Red	974	250	TE-41	Lamp Black	942
26	TE-91	White	1000	58	TE-31	Organic Green	1000
colspan="4"	**2U502—SWIFT RED**	colspan="4"	**2U313—FATHOM GREEN**
100	TE-02	H. H. Mix	100	100	TE-02	H. H. Mix	100
780	TE-53	Toluidine Red	880	398	TE-74	Ferrite Yellow	498
82	TE-72	Medium Yellow	962	342	TE-41	Lamp Black	840
34	TE-91	White	996	124	TE-31	Organic Green	964
4	TE-41	Lamp Black	1000	36	TE-91	White	1000
colspan="4"	**2U601—CAPE MAROON**	colspan="4"	**2U328—BREWSTER GREEN**
100	TE-02	H. H. Mix	100	100	TE-02	H. H. Mix	100
570	TE-63	Light Maroon Toner	670	390	TE-41	Lamp Black	490
314	TE-66	Permanent Maroon	984	338	TE-31	Organic Green	828
8	TE-91	White	992	120	TE-81	Burnt Sienna	948
8	TE-72	Medium Yellow	1000	52	TE-72	Medium Yellow	1000
colspan="4"	**2U211—MARINER BLUE**	colspan="4"	**2U315—APPLE GREEN**
100	TE-02	H. H. Mix	100	100	TE-02	H. H. Mix	100
704	TE-24	Milori Blue	804	280	TE-91	White	380
116	TE-91	White	920	264	TE-71	Lemon Yellow	644
80	TE-31	Organic Green	1000	200	TE-41	Lamp Black	844
				156	TE-31	Organic Green	1000
colspan="4"	**2U206—WINDSOR BLUE**	colspan="4"	**2U203—EXPORT BLUE**
100	TE-02	H. H. Mix	100	100	TE-02	H. H. Mix	100
404	TE-91	White	504	350	TE-21	Chinese Blue	450
362	TE-22	Astral Blue	866	280	TE-91	White	730
134	TE-41	Lamp Black	1000	220	TE-22	Astral Blue	950
				50	TE-41	Lamp Black	1000
colspan="4"	**2U330—FORESTER GREEN**	colspan="4"	**240D22—BOATSWAIN BLUE**
100	TE-02	H. H. Mix	100	100	TE-02	H. H. Mix	100
504	TE-21	Chinese Blue	604	774	TE-21	Chinese Blue	874
300	TE-76	Yellow Toner	904	60	TE-66	Permanent Maroon	934
66	TE-72	Medium Yellow	970	36	TE-41	Lamp Black	970
30	TE-91	White	1000	30	TE-91	White	1000

The codes and color names for Chevrolet commercial colors between 1946–1951 appear on this chart. The information inside the boxes told the paint jobber which percentages (parts), colors and counter settings should be used in mixing the color above the box. Consult your local paint jobber about the best way to obtain the best approximation of these colors today. Rinchard-Mason Company

1953-59 PAINT CHARTS   1953-55 (1st Ser.)

BASIC COLOR	STRIPING COLOR⊕
*Juniper Green	Cream Medium
Mariner Blue	Cream Medium
Commercial Red	Argent Silver
Jet Black	Argent Silver
Ocean Green	•Jet Black
Transport Blue	Cream Medium
Omaha Orange	•Jet Black
Copper Tone	†Shell White
Autumn Brown	Shell White
Pure White	Juniper Green
Cream Medium	•Jet Black
Yukon Yellow	•Jet Black
▲Bergundy Maroon	Gold Bronze

*Juniper Green is standard on all models.

•1954 striping color may also be named Onyx Black.

†Original striping was Onyx Black.

▲1953 only.

⊕Striping color for 1953 models. Wheel stripe for 3100 series models in 1954-55 (1st. Ser.).

OTHER WHEEL COLORS 1954-55 (1st. Ser.)

Regular Production..........................Black

Deluxe Solid Body Color......................Body Color

Deluxe Two Tone Body Color..................Lower, Body Color

1955 (2nd Ser.)

SOLID COLORS All Models (ex. 3124)	TWO TONE COLORS⊕ BODY		Wheel Stripes	Wheels
	Upper	Lower		
*Juniper Green	Bombay Ivory	Juniper Green	Bombay Ivory•	
Commercial Red	Bombay Ivory	Commercial Red	Argent Silver•	
Sand Beige	Bombay Ivory	Jet Black	Bombay Ivory•	
Jet Black	Bombay Ivory	Empire Blue	Bombay Ivory•	
Omaha Orange	Bombay Ivory	Cream Medium	Bombay Ivory•	
Granite Gray	Bombay Ivory	Yukon Yellow	Bombay Ivory•	Lower body
Empire Blue	Bombay Ivory	Ocean Green	Bombay Ivory•	Color on 3000 Series;
Cream Medium	Bombay Ivory	Crystal Blue	Bombay Ivory•	All others, Black
Yukon Yellow	Bombay Ivory	Granite Gray	Bombay Ivory•	
Ocean Green	Bombay Ivory	Omaha Orange	Bombay Ivory•	
Crystal Blue	Bombay Ivory	Sand Beige	Bombay Ivory•	
Russet Brown	Sand Beige	Russet Brown	Bombay Ivory•	
Pure White				
Standard—3124	Commercial Red	Bombay Ivory	Commercial Red▲	

• Deluxe equipment and two-tone options are not available for models 3106-16.   * Regular production on all models except 3124.

• On 15-5K and 16 x 5K Wheels only.   ▲On 16 x 5K Wheels only.

These pages of the Chevrolet Special Information Catalog show the Chevrolet commercial colors used from 1953-1959. Chevrolet Division

PAINT CHARTS (Cont.)   1956

| SOLID COLORS | TWO TONE COLORS | | | | Wheels |
| All Models Except 3124 | All Models Except 3106-3116-3124# | | 3124 | | |
	Upper	Lower	Upper	Lower	
Forest Green	Arabian Ivory	Forest Green	Cardinal Red*	Bombay Ivory*	
Cardinal Red	Arabian Ivory	Cardinal Red	Arabian Ivory	Cardinal Red	
Sand Beige	Jet Black	Golden Yellow	Jet Black	Golden Yellow	
Jet Black	Jet Black	Golden Yellow	Arabian Ivory	Regal Blue	
Omaha Orange	Arabian Ivory	Empire Blue	Arabian Ivory	Granite Gray	3000 Series
Granite Gray	Arabian Ivory	Yukon Yellow	Arabian Ivory	Ocean Green	Two-Tone Models
Empire Blue	Arabian Ivory	Ocean Green	Arabian Ivory	Crystal Blue	To Be
Golden Yellow	Arabian Ivory	Crystal Blue	Cardinal Red	Sand Beige	Upper Body Color;
Yukon Yellow	Arabian Ivory	Granite Gray			All Other Wheels
Ocean Green	Arabian Ivory	Omaha Orange			Black
Regal Blue	Cardinal Red	Sand Beige			
Crystal Blue	Arabian Ivory	Regal Blue			
Pure White					

*Regular Production Colors.
#Deluxe Equipment and Two Tone Options are not available for Models 3106-3116.

1957

| SOLID COLORS | TWO TONE COLORS | | | | Wheels° |
| All Models Except 3124 | All Models Except 3106-3116-3124# | | 3124 | | |
	Upper	Lower	Upper	Lower	
*Brewster Green	Ocean Green	Brewster Green	*Cardinal Red	*Bombay Ivory	
Ocean Green	Bombay Ivory	Ocean Green	Bombay Ivory	Sand Beige	
Alpine Blue	Alpine Blue	Royal Blue	Bombay Ivory	Cardinal Red	
Royal Blue	Bombay Ivory	Alpine Blue	Jet Black	Golden Yellow	
Sand Beige	Bombay Ivory	Sand Beige	Bombay Ivory	Indian Turquoise	
Cardinal Red	Bombay Ivory	Cardinal Red	Bombay Ivory	Granite Gray	3000 Series
Indian Turquoise	Bombay Ivory	Indian Turquoise	Bombay Ivory	Ocean Green	Two-Tone Models
Golden Yellow	Jet Black	Golden Yellow	Bombay Ivory	Alpine Blue	To Be
Granite Gray	Bombay Ivory	Granite Gray	Bombay Ivory	Sandstone Beige	Lower Body Color;
Jet Black	Bombay Ivory	Jet Black			All Other Wheels
Omaha Orange	Bombay Ivory	Omaha Orange			Black
Yukon Yellow	Bombay Ivory	Sandstone Beige			
Pure White	Bombay Ivory	Yukon Yellow			
Sandstone Beige					

*Regular Production Colors.
•When exterior colors are Bombay Ivory over Jet Black and Cardinal Red over Bombay Ivory the wheel colors will be Bombay Ivory and Cardinal Red respectively.
#Deluxe equipment and Two Tone option are not available for Models 3106-3116.

PAINT CHARTS (Cont.)

1958

SOLID COLORS		All Models Exc. Sub. Carryalls, Cameo Carrier, Fleetside			TWO TONE COLORS				
All Models Except 3124	Option No.	Upper	Lower	Option No.	Cameo Carrier		Option No.	Wheels	
					Upper	Lower			
Jet Black*	700	Cardinal Red	Black	728	Cardinal Red*	Bombay Ivory	701C	3000 Series	
Dawn Blue	707	Dawn Blue	Marine Blue	735	Golden Yellow	Jet Black	729C	Two-Tone Models	
Marine Blue	708	Marine Blue	Dawn Blue	736	Bombay Ivory	Cardinal Red	740C	To Be	
Pure White	721				Jet Black	Tartan Turquoise	727C	Lower Body Color	
Kodiak Brown	712	Bombay Ivory	Kodiak Brown	738	Kodiak Brown	Bombay Ivory	738C	All Other Wheels	
Granite Gray	723	Bombay Ivory	Granite Gray	746	Bombay Ivory	Granite Gray	746C	Are Black	
Glade Green	705	Glade Green	Polar Green	733	Glade Green	Polar Green	733C	Except Prod.	
Oriental Green	703	Bombay Ivory	Oriental Green	731	Marine Blue	Dawn Blue	736C	Cameo Carrier	
Polar Green	704	Glade Green	Polar Green	732	Dawn Blue	Marine Blue	735C	Which Are	
Omaha Orange	716	Bombay Ivory	Omaha Orange	742	Bombay Ivory	Oriental Green	731C	Cardinal Red.	
Cardinal Red	714	Bombay Ivory	Cardinal Red	740				Cast Spoke Wheels	
Tartan Turquoise	710	Jet Black	Tartan Turquoise	727				Are Gray	
Golden Yellow	718	Jet Black	Golden Yellow	729					
Yukon Yellow	719	Bombay Ivory	Yukon Yellow	744					

*Regular Production Colors.

1959

SOLID COLOR OR MAIN TWO-TONING COLOR*	OPTION NUMBER		Wheels
	Solid	Two Tone	
Frontier Beige	712	738	
Jet Black	700	728	
Baltic Blue	708	735	
Dawn Blue	707	736	3000 Series
Cadet Gray	723	746	Two-Tone
Galaway Green	703	731	Models to
Glade Green	705	732	Be Main
Sherwood Green	704	733	Body Color.
Omaha Orange	716	742	All Other
Cardinal Red	714	740	Wheels Are
Tartan Turquoise	710	727	Black
Pure White	721	—	
Golden Yellow	718	729	
Yukon Yellow	719**	744	

*Bombay Ivory is used as the secondary two-toning color in all combinations.
**On School Bus Chassis this is a two-tone combination with Jet Black.

category. Because of this, organizations such as the Antique Automobile Club of America stress the fact that options do not add judging points, but could lead to point deductions if they are deemed inappropriate. Nevertheless, collectors still enjoy adding extras for the same reasons the options were merchandised in the first place.

Even more fascinating than genuine factory accessories are the vocational options that truck buyers could order through the Chevrolet *Silver Books* I mentioned earlier. Since these books were supplied to Chevrolet dealers to enable them to sell complete trucks with special equipment, the question arises as to how a vocational model—such as a crew cab pickup produced by Proctor-Keefe Body Company of Detroit—would be judged in a show. Who can really say what was original equipment for such a model?

Certainly, this book is not going to settle such a question, but we do want to emphasize just how many variables there are when considering the topic of individual options for Chevrolet trucks. There was so much equipment available, especially in the sixties and seventies, that compiling a complete list of extra-cost equipment in a book of this size would be impossible.

In addition to the immensity of such an undertaking, there's also another item to consider: the fact that many of the individual options are of little or no interest to the collector, except as historical trivia. A certain rear axle ratio, oil bath air cleaner, radiator bug screen or oversize tires will usually not have any great effect on a truck's collector appeal or collector value. There are even some *big* options that seem to hurt a truck's collectibility. For example, four-wheel-drives are not very

---

Chevrolet truck exterior colors 1964-72

Color	Year(s)	Color	Year(s)
Acanthus Dark Blue	72	Light Green	64-69,72
Adonis Yellow	72	Light Sandalwood	70
Anniversary Gold Poly	68	Light Yellow	68
Balboa Blue	64	Madder Red	72
Black	67-72	Maroon Poly	65,69
Blue	72	Matte Black	72
Cameo White	64-67	Medium Blue	70-72
Cardinal Red	64	Medium Blue Poly	67-68,70
Clematis Light Blue	64-69	Medium Blue-Green Poly	70
Copper Poly	70-72	Medium Gold Poly	70,72
Dark Aqua Poly	66-67	Medium Green	70-72
Dark Argent	72	Medium Olive Poly	71-72
Dark Blue	65-72	Ochre	71-72
Dark Blue Poly	70	Omaha Orange	64-67
Dark Blue-Green Poly	70	Orange	68-72
Dark Bronze	72	Pure White	64-67
Dark Bronze Poly	70	Red	64-72
Dark Gold Poly	70	Red-Orange	70
Dark Green	67-72	Saddle Poly	66,68-69
Dark Green Poly	70,72	Silver	72
Dark Olive Poly	70-72	Silver Poly	66-69
Dark Sandalwood	70	Tangier Gold Poly	64
Dark Yellow	69,72	Turquoise Poly	64-66,69
Fawn	64-65	Vermilion Poly	67-68
Flame Red	70	Walnut Beige	72
Gold	72	Weldenia White	72
Gray Grecian Poly	64	White	67-72
Hugger Orange	70-72	Woodland Green	64-67
Ivory	67-68	Yellow	65,67,69-72
Light Blue	64-69	Yellow Green Poly	69-70
Light Gray	64-66	Yuma Yellow	64-67

The following chart is part of the Ditzler Index No. 18 showing a truck color list. Ditzler Automotive Finishes

sought after because they are more likely to have mechanical drivetrain problems, and Camper Specials are generally avoided because they are big, bulky and usually worn-out from years of lugging a heavier camper-back module around.

Because of such factors, it seems to make more sense to concern ourselves with those options that most significantly improve a pickup's appeal and value to collectors. In other words, I have tried to create some sort of guide to which options have a positive effect on trucks in the collector's market. They are grouped on the following lists according to the different eras, such as the Wurlitzer-style, Advance-Design, Task Force, V-8 and Custom Sport Truck.

The lists do not include all the technical options such as air cleaners, rear axle ratios, four-wheel drive, locking front hubs, heavy-duty generators and alternators, oversize tires and gasoline tanks, and so on. They also do not include camper options, snow plows, dual rear wheels and other such options offered mainly to increase working utility of the trucks. In some cases, the introductory dates of certain options are noted. Options for Corvair and El Camino pickups and Blazers are not included. Also deleted from these lists are the option packages and groups discussed earlier in this chapter.

Popular options
Wurlitzer era, 1944–1946
Bumper guards
Chrome bumpers
Chrome hubcaps
Deluxe chrome grille
Directional signals
Dual interior sunshades
Dual taillights
Dual windshield wipers
External sunshade
Foglights
Four-speed manual transmission with floor shift
Heater and defroster
Master grille guard with crossbar
Rear bumper, painted or chrome
Sidemount spare tire
Spotlight(s)
Step plates for running board
Wheel trim rings

Advance-Design era, 1947–1955
Accessory hood ornament
Bright gas filler cap
Bumper guards
Carpeting, introduced in 1954
Chrome front bumper

Chrome hubcaps
Deluxe brightmetal cab molding package
Deluxe chrome grille
Deluxe cloth seat trim, introduced in 1954
Directional signals
Dual interior sunshades
Dual taillights
Dual windshield wipers
Electric windshield wipers, introduced in 1954
Exterior sunshade and prism
Foglights
Four-speed manual transmission with floor shift
Front fender clearance marker lights, traffic light type
Heater and defroster
Hydra-matic drive, introduced in 1954
Master grille guard
Nu-Vue auxiliary windows, for rear corners of cab
Rear bumper, painted or chrome
Ride-Control seat, introduced in 1954
Sidemount spare tire, re-introduced in 1953
Spotlight(s)
Step plates for running boards
Tinted glass, 1953
Venta-Shades (chrome, for side windows)
Wheel trim rings

Task Force era, 1955–1959
Accessory hood ornament, bombsight type, 1957
Accessory hood ornament, jet-plane type, 1955
Air conditioning, Cool-Pack type; introduced in 1958
AM radio
Back-up lights
Bumper guards
Carpeting
Chrome front bumper
Chrome hubcaps
Custom Cab option, introduced in 1958
Deluxe Cab option, pre-1958
Deluxe chrome grille
Directional signals
Electric windshield wipers
Exterior sunshade and traffic light prism
Foglights
Four-speed manual transmission with floor shift
Glovebox lamp, introduced in 1957
Heater and defroster
Heavy-duty three-speed manual transmission
Hydra-matic drive
Illuminated cigar lighter
Locking gas cap
Nonglare rearview mirror, introduced in 1957
Overdrive transmission, 1955–1957
Panoramic rear window, also called Full-View and known as Big Window

Posi-traction rear axle, introduced in 1959
Power brakes
Power steering
Rear bumper, painted or chrome
Seatbelts
Sidemount spare tire
Super Turbo Fire 265 V-8 engine, introduced 1956
Tinted glass
Trademaster 265 V-8 engine, introduced 1955
Trademaster 283 V-8 engine, introduced 1957
Two-tone paint
White sidewall tires

V-8 era, 1960–1966
Air conditioning, Deluxe type
AM radio
Back-up lights
Chrome front bumper (included in some Custom Chrome options)
Custom Cab option
Custom side moldings
Deluxe chrome grille (included in Custom Chrome option)
Dual exhausts
Engines: 262 ci six; 292 ci six; 283 ci V-8; 327 ci V-8; 348 ci V-8
Four-speed manual transmission with floor shift
Full-depth foam seat
Full-View rear window
Gauge package
Heaters, Deluxe or Thrift-Air styles
Heavy-duty eleven-inch clutch
Heavy-duty four-speed manual transmission, Muncie
Heavy-duty radiator
Heavy-duty shock absorbers, front and rear
Heavy-duty springs, front and rear
Heavy-duty three-speed manual transmission, Warner T898 or Saginaw
Level-Ride seat
Long-Reach rearview mirrors, outside; right and/or left
Nonglare rearview mirror, inside
No-Spin rear axle
Padded instrument panel
Posi-traction rear axle
Power brakes
Powerglide transmission, 1961–1962 cast iron; 1963–1966 aluminum
Power steering
Rear bumper, painted or chrome
Seatbelts
Sidemount spare tire
Tachometer, introduced 1964
Tinted glass

Tu-Tone paint
White sidewall tires

Custom Sport Truck era, 1967–1972
Air conditioning, Deluxe type
AM push-button radio
AM/FM push-button radio, introduced in 1971
Back-up lights
Bucket seats
Body paint stripe, introduced 1969
Bodyside molding; belt molding, introduced 1969
Bodyside molding; upper feature-line, introduced 1969
Bodyside molding; wide lower feature-line, introduced 1969
Cargo compartment lamp, introduced 1971
Chrome front bumper
Chrome hubcaps
Cruise control, introduced 1968
Custom chrome option
Custom equipment package
Deluxe trim grille
Deluxe wheel covers, introduced 1972
Door-edge guards, introduced 1969
Dual exhausts
Engine-block heater, introduced 1969
Engines: 292 ci six, 327 ci V-8, 307 ci V-8, 350 ci V-8, 396 ci V-8
Four-speed manual transmission with floorshift
Front stabilizer bar, introduced 1969
Full-depth foam seats
Hazard light equipment
Heavy-duty close-ratio four-speed manual transmission
Heavy-duty clutch
Heavy-duty four-speed manual transmission, Muncie
Heavy-duty radiator
Heavy-duty shocks, front and/or rear
Heavy-duty springs, front and/or rear
Heavy-duty three-speed manual transmission, Saginaw
Leaf-spring rear suspension
Level-Ride seat
Locking gas cap
Long-Reach rearview mirrors, right and/or left
Nonglare rearview mirror
No-Spin rear axle
Padded instrument panel
Panoramic Cab, standard after 1967
Power brakes
Power steering
Rear bumper, painted or chrome
Roof marker lamps
Seatbelts, shoulder-harness type, introduced 1968
Seat, Custom bench
Sidemount spare tire carrier

Speed-warning indicator, introduced 1967
Tachometer
Transistor ignition, introduced 1967
Turbo Hydra-matic transmission
Two-tone paint
West Coast mirrors, Junior and Senior style
Wheel trim covers
White sidewall tires

Factory literature

Making reference to factory-issued literature about trucks is the best way to ensure that the vehicle is authentic or will be authentically restored. Such material generally breaks down into four general categories: sales literature, service manuals, owners manuals and miscellaneous other types.

Sales literature is usually thought of chiefly in terms of sales catalogs, brochures and folders that the manufacturer designed and printed to describe the features of the truck lines. These are often multipage product booklets with color artwork or photography showing different models and copy highlighting equipment features, interior appointments, technical data and, in some cases, options and color charts. There may also be flyers in color or black and white focusing on a single product offering.

Rarer types of sales literature would be product manuals that the manufacturer made available to dealership salesmen to familiarize them with truck features and allow them to show the customers various options—for example, color and interior catalogs with paint chips, carpet swatches and samples of upholstery fabrics.

Other types of sales aids were also produced by the sales department, including merchandising manuals, film strips, movies, salesman data books and postcards for salesmen to send to prospective customers.

In some cases, even the order forms that the salesmen used to order a truck from the factory may be found to include important information, such as a list of options and option codes. And, of course, the previously mentioned Chevrolet *Silver Books* are important to those who plan to research a truck that carries a vocational body.

The serious collector will want to obtain all possible sales literature about the vehicle he or she owns. Sales catalogs, brochures and folders are usually easiest to obtain and the most reasonable in price. Specialized items like color and interior catalogs are more expensive. Film strips and movies aren't essential and will require a projector. They're best suited for the owner who wants to know everything there is to know about a particular truck.

Service manuals will be of most interest to the restorer, although a factory shop manual is an essential item for every vintage truck owner. Even if you don't do your own maintenance, you will need a shop manual to tell your mechanic how to service or repair your particular vehicle. These books describe the various systems—engine, transmission, brakes, rear axle—of a truck, and provide step-by-step repair procedures. In the front you'll find a section explaining serial numbers and outlining how and when to do periodic maintenance. Electrical wiring diagrams are also included in most shop manuals.

If you are into a restoration, a master parts catalog is another useful bit of service literature to own. These manuals cover many years and show pictures of cars and trucks labeled with GM group numbers. By referring to the listing for a particular group number, you'll find a second list of part numbers for that group in a specific model year. Master parts catalogs also contain factory coding information, color and trim charts, certain specifications, parts price lists and exploded engineering drawings that illustrate how parts should be assembled.

A rare type of service literature that's very useful to restorers is a factory assembly manual. These were issued in limited numbers for workers to refer to while assembling vehicles on a production line. They are nearly impossible to obtain, but do turn up occasionally.

Factory service bulletins were also issued on light-duty trucks. These are essentially updates on information included in the shop manual. For example, if there was a mid-year change in parts that required a variation in original service procedures, the engineering department would issue a service bulletin covering the change. Most dealers kept these bulletins in looseleaf binders that Chevy issued for storage of bulletins, so it is not unusual to find complete sets at an old dealership or a flea market.

Sometimes General Motors branches would also issue separate service manuals for one part of a vehicle. For example, body manuals, Hydra-matic transmission manuals and convertible-top manuals were produced. While Chevy trucks didn't come with convertible tops until the Blazer was introduced, a Hydra-matic transmission manual might be something to look for.

The owners manual is the same kind of small user guide that you'll find in the glovebox of new trucks today, and it's not unusual to discover that the old truck you've purchased will also have one in the glovebox. If it's missing, you can get one from literature dealers by mail or at a flea market. They describe the correct way to operate a vehicle and give essential service information, light bulb charts, lubrication data, basic specification, tips on truck care and advice on how to store a vehicle.

Beginning in the 1960s, there were sometimes separate glovebox manuals covering tires, radio equipment, pollution devices, and so on. The more information you can obtain about your truck, the better care you'll be able to give it. So look for all of the glovebox manuals that you can find. Each one will reveal a little bit more about the vehicle's original equipment features and help you ensure that all equipment is of the type that the factory supplied.

The final category of factory literature is a catchall covering all types of "paper" that doesn't quite fit in the other categories. Magazine advertisements would fall into this group. These are readily available and low in cost, but can tell you much about your truck, including equipment features, colors and special trim packages. In some years, GM also issued stockholder reports that included photos and descriptions of trucks. Factory photographs are another miscellaneous type of automotive paper collectible. You might also be lucky enough to locate a factory press kit issued when your truck was introduced. These contain excellent descriptions of new features and standard or optional equipment.

Sometimes people entering the hobby are shocked at the prices being asked for literature items. In most cases these prices are fair, because the literature market is very competitive. It must be remembered, however, that vintage paper collectibles are as old and rare as the vehicles they cover and tend to increase in value over the years. Therefore, money spent purchasing literature at fair market prices will usually turn out to be an excellent investment in the long run. In other words, you'll be able to get more out of a literature collection than you have in it. And if you decide to sell your truck some day, the buyer will probably be willing to pay extra for the literature.

Before you start purchasing literature (especially truck literature, which hasn't been very much in demand until lately) there are a few places you can check to see if they have "any old books they want to get rid of." Start with your local gas station, car dealers in your hometown, Goodwill stores, rummage sales, used book shops and nearby wrecking yards. Such sources may produce a couple of truck literature items that you can get for free or for a "dime-on-a-dollar."

Tip: Don't pass up any free or bargain-priced literature because it doesn't apply to your vehicle. Take it anyway to use as trading stock. You may be interested only in the truck you own, but others may be collectors of general literature with many duplicates, and might trade you their duplicate of something you need for something else you discover while treasure hunting.

Once you've exhausted the above possibilities, it's time to start hitting flea markets and referring to hobby publications like *Old Cars Weekly* or truck-club newsletters. These publications will include ads from people selling literature by mail order. They will also contain listings of upcoming car and truck shows that have flea markets where vendors—either hobbyists or dealers—might be selling old literature.

Before you begin buying literature, you should have a general idea of the going prices in the market today. While the value of literature varies with supply and demand, it's possible to formulate a small price guide giving the highs and lows for different items.

Type of literature	High	Low	Average
Sales folder	$ 15	$ 3	$ 8
Sales catalog	25	7	15
Paint & upholstery manual	150	15	55
Film strip	40	8	20
Movie	75	45	50
Silver Book	100	15	35
Shop manual	65	15	30
Master parts manual	125	50	75
Factory service bulletins	10	3	5
Owners manual	20	8	12
Magazine ad	10	1	3.50
Factory photo	12	3	7
Postcard	30	5	15

One fascinating way to purchase automotive literature is through the mail-bid auctions that dealers such as Tom Gibson, of Anoka, Minnesota, schedule on a regular basis. These dealers purchase large quantities of literature at dealership liquidations or from other collectors. They then print a long listing of excess items. These listings describe the nature, size and condition of each item and show an estimated value. The list is then mailed to auction subscribers. Each bidder is free to offer whatever he or she can afford for a particular item and all items are sold to the highest bidder, whether or not he or she has bid up to or above the estimated value. In other words, if you have the only bid on an item estimated to be worth more than you bid, you still get it. Gibson also includes what he calls $2 items, which are pieces he obtains in large quantities and wants to move quickly. Thus, as he puts it, "A $2 bid gets the item as long as supplies last." (Some of the $2 bid items include Chevy truck literature, mostly from the sixties and seventies.)

As you can see, there are many types of literature to seek, and several different ways to obtain it at reasonable prices. In addition, where originals are hard to get there are companies that sell reprints of original literature or books that include a lot of the same information. See Information Department for advice on how to contact these companies and dealers.

Obtaining the proper factory literature is an important step in restoring or maintaining your truck's "factory factors" and making it a show-class vehicle.

Chapter 9

Custom trucks

Although collectors have long been interested in antique commercial vehicles, it's only lately that postwar light-duty models have been getting the "find and fix to original" attention that they deserve. The branch of the car hobby oriented toward "improving" original vehicles with mechanical, exterior and interior modifications has been fascinated with postwar pickups and vans that can be documented back to fifteen years ago.

This 1949 or 1950 customized Chevrolet half-ton pickup was spotted at St. Ignace, Michigan, auto show. It's been lowered all around, and sports modern wide-oval tires and chrome-plated competition-style wheels. Finish was in a wild lime green color with flames.

A good example of a resto-rod is this modified 1950 half-ton pickup, which looks mostly original on the outside. Rearview mirror and white-letter tires are of modern design, as are the styled wheels.

Establishing the history of the modified postwar truck sport is important, because it actually paved the way for the booming interest we see today in restoring these vehicles to stock condition. The reasons for this are basic; they have to do with the supplying of parts that are used by both rodders and restorers.

There are dozens of specialized companies involved in this business today. Many of these firms were formed years ago, when only rodders were working on postwar pickups. As a result, they were well-established by the time that restoration of original trucks started catching on.

A common difference between modified and stock restoration projects is the condition of the truck at the start of the process. The collector of stock vehicles generally looks for one that is operable and solid, with nearly all of its original parts. The enthusiast seeking to build a personalized pickup, however, needs only a halfway-decent cab and frame to get going. Many arti-

This 1954 Chevy half-ton owned by Ken Furbur features a 1969 Oldsmobile drivetrain with a 350 ci V-8, Turbo Hydra-matic 400 automatic transmission and 12-bolt posi rear end.

Homemade wood bed rails and white spoked wheels help give it a distinctive look. Ken Furbur

cles about modified trucks start with an introduction explaining how the owner purchased a $200 hulk and put a few thousand dollars into it to make his truck.

Most modified trucks have late-model V-8 engines, specially engineered suspensions, updated drivetrain components, modern tires and wheels, custom interiors and even home-built cargo boxes and load floors. The majority of rodders bring trucks back from the dead, rather than killing good ones. Maybe that's why there seems to be little friction between the stockers and rodders in the light-duty truck hobby.

Engine swapping

Engine swapping has traditionally been the heartbeat of the modified sport, and light-duty trucks are hardly an exception. In fact, over the years there have probably been more engine swaps involving pickups than any other type of vehicle. There are logical reasons for this.

First of all, most older pickups were originally sold with six-cylinder engines. Those carrying optional V-8s were generally equipped with smaller-displacement

blocks. This makes these vehicles natural candidates for the high-performance enhancements provided by big-block V-8s.

A second motivation for a V-8 engine swap is technical. With their large, roomy engine compartments, heavier suspension systems and big radiators, trucks make the job of switching to V-8 engines an easier one for home-builders. There's usually no need to cut, weld or shape metal for exhaust manifold clearance. And hood height is rarely a problem, either.

As with modified cars, the main reason for swapping is to gain more power, better acceleration and extra torque. These benefits are especially appealing to truck owners, who may want to haul heavy loads, pull a trailer or attach a big pickup-bed camping unit. The original engines used in old trucks won't handle the heavy-duty chores as well as a late-model V-8.

Two other advantages of truck engine swaps are smoother performance and—believe it or not—heavier weight. The V-8s make a truck easier to drive over long distances. In addition, the 100 or so more pounds of the V-8 sometimes reduces the ride harshness caused by those heavy-duty truck springs.

Full-house customizing treatment sets off this 1955 Cameo pickup. It's loaded with accessories, including factory-type sunshade, custom cruiser fender skirts, chromed bed rails, a flip-up and upholstered tonneau cover, and wire spoke wheels.

143

Most engine swaps used to begin with a trip to a wrecking yard well-stocked with late-model cars that became accident-prone early in their existence. Today, however, such vehicles are generally powered by fours or sixes. You'll have to look for big wagons, full-size luxury cars or other trucks as donor vehicles.

While almost any V-8 will be at home in a pickup, Chevy buffs are most likely to avoid Ford, Mercury or Lincoln powerplants out of a sense of brand loyalty. This is true to a lesser degree with Chrysler, but Chrysler V-8 engines are getting hard to find. The real preference is for engines from the GM family of cars, particularly Corvette or Cadillac. Both of these make for excellent swaps.

With trucks from the early 1950s, the Chevy owner has more problems than the Ford fan when it comes to swapping engines. Even though there's plenty of underhood room, the steering on the 1946–1954 Chevy pickups has to be moved to fit even a Chevy V-8. A neat way to do this is to adopt GM power-steering parts, fabricate a homemade drag link and move the steering to the left 1½ inches.

The front of the engine can be attached to the frame with universal motor mounts. A dropped tubular cross-member is used at the rear. The radiator is moved forward and the front shocks and mounts are swapped from one side to the other, giving them a rearward (instead of forward) angle.

Also remember that Chevy used a torque tube driveline through 1954. This is replaced with a late-model GM open drive shaft cut down to fit. In many cases, the front of a Chevrolet drive shaft is welded to the rear of a Pontiac shaft, which allows use of the beefier Pontiac rear axle.

GM Turbo Hydra-matic transmission is considered the way to go for a gearbox these days. In most cases, a Hurst dual-gate shifter is added for gear changing. This degree of alteration, however, will not be required for swapping engines in post-1955 models. These trucks were engineered for V-8s, and such a change is virtually a bolt-in operation.

The Cadillac engine with Turbo Hydra-matic is a neat, clean installation in the later 1967–1972 Chevy pickups. Cadillacs from the 1970s had big, powerful, long-lasting engines that outlived their rust-prone bodies. Here it might be best to scour the classified section of your local newspaper for a car that's still running well. They can usually be purchased cheap—for between

First year for factory four-wheel-drive trucks was 1957, but someone converted this 1956 Chevy half-ton into a 4x4.

Modern accessories and tires are used to set off the bright red paint. Tires are of the all-terrain type.

$200 and $400—and used as donors. Simply yank the engine, give it a good cleaning and tune-up, and drop it into your pickup after fabricating some engine mounts. Then hook up the linkage and you're about ready to go. Caddy-powered Chevy pickups really get out and scoot, and they have a great dual-exhaust sound to them.

Suspension

Suspension modifications aren't absolutely necessary, but many rodders prefer a low-to-the-ground look for their early postwar trucks. This is no longer accomplished by the use of lowering blocks or the simple removal of spring leaves, as was the practice years ago. Instead, the modern trend involves a total re-engineering of the frame and chassis components to provide independent front suspension.

Basically, the entire stub-frame from a unit-body donor vehicle like a Corvair, Mustang II or Nova-Firebird-Camaro, is mated to the old ladder-type chassis. The job begins by leveling the stock frame on jacks and taking accurate reference measurements. Then the front of the original frame is cut off at a point where the

Black Gold *is a 1965 Chevrolet pickup customized with 24-karat-gold plating on the body trim. Updated wheels and tires and a tufted bed cover are included in modifications to the professionally done show truck on display at the Rearview Mirror Museum, in Nags Head, North Carolina. Rearview Mirror Museum*

An unusual sight at the St. Ignace, Michigan, auto show was a six-cylinder-powered custom 1964 Chevy half-ton. Most modified pickups have V-8s installed. Nicknamed Fantasy Breaker, *the truck is pinstriped and fitted with wide white-letter tires, even the sidemount spare.*

145

properly prepared stub-frame can be "surgically" attached with a tack weld and lap joint. This is followed by a heating and hammering process, finish-welding and bracing or boxing. A grinder is used for cleanup.

Full-house hot-rodded Chevy V-8 under the hood of the Black Gold *show truck also has 24-karat-gold-plated valve covers and accessories. The engine looks as good as it runs and adds a lot to the overall look of professionalism on this custom.* Herb Etheridge, Rearview Mirror Museum

If the process sounds simple, don't be fooled into thinking that it is. It takes a lot of work, skill and craftsmanship. There are detailed articles that should be read before attempting this job. Even better, have it done by a shop that specializes in stub-frame work. The result will be greatly improved ride and handling characteristics, and you can even use a different type of stub-frame to add features like rack-and-pinion steering.

A simpler alternative for the home-builder is to retain the stock Chevy I-beam axle and steering with coil-overs from a later pickup to improve ride control. In this setup, lowering the front *can* be achieved by removing two leaf springs.

At the rear, the typical treatment is addition of a later axle (using a ten-bolt type with chrome quick-change cover) attached to the stock springs. Coil springs—cut down a bit—can be fitted if the low-rider look is desired. Some truck builders have even gone to the popular Jaguar independent rear suspension setup, with gobs of chrome plating.

Tires and wheels

With the drivetrain and chassis finished, the next modification is tires and wheels. Though some builders stick with stock rims and tires, most turn to their local speed shop for a set of fancy wheels and fat tires. Mag-style spoke wheels were the trick way to go in the

El Caminos are also popular with customizers. This one is basically a mint original, with fat white-letter tires and tur- *bine spoke wheels. Snap-on tonneau cover adds to the detailed image.*

early 1970s. The latest trends, however, indicate that many modified-truck builders opt for wire-spoke rims, cast-aluminum knock-offs or turbine-style wheels today.

Trucks with updated front or rear axles, or both represent no problem for the enthusiast who is able to buy a set of new aftermarket rims. He simply purchases the correct size, and bolts the new wheels in place. Mounting aftermarket wheels to older brake drums may require the use of adaptors to alter the bolt pattern. These may also be used to make a set of wheels purchased secondhand bolt up to the hubs used on the truck. The adapters can be purchased at any speed shop or auto supply store.

Nearly any size tires will work on most pickups without interfering with fender or frame clearance. There's usually plenty of room in those huge wheelwells on pickup trucks to fit extra-wide or larger-diameter tires. Most hobby truckers seem to prefer black sidewall tires or raised-white-letter styles. White sidewall designs are rarely used on trucks. The exception to this is a few of the trucks done in nostalgia rod style, where original-looking tires and rims are retained.

Body and paint

With the engine, chassis and running gear taken care of, bodywork and paint are the rodder's next con-siderations. Most modified pickups are the exposed-rear-fender style—or Stepside in Chevy lingo—and the most important sheet metal components are the cab, front fenders, hood and grille. These should be checked to ensure that the metal is straight, solid and basically rust-free. The condition of the running boards and the cargo box is secondary. These can be fabricated. For example, many good-looking rods consist of a restored cab and front-end sheet metal with custom-made wood running boards and cargo deck.

There seem to be two schools of thought among rodders on the final appearance of the cab and front of pickups. The first group prefers the clean, low look, with bumpers discarded and the front pan leaded-in. Usually, the grille will be Frenched, and the choice of chrome or painted finish for the grille is a matter of personal taste. Both look great, when properly done.

The second school may go with either stock or lowered riding height, but prefers using more plating and more chrome bolt-on parts. Trucks of this type are nearly always built with deluxe chrome grilles, chrome front and rear bumpers and, possibly, accessory driving lamps. Both groups, however, usually remove name-badges, ornaments, hood mascots and such unneces-sary "gingerbread." The mounting holes are then leaded-in and ground to a smooth finish.

This bright yellow 1969 Fleetside was lowered by cutting the springs. This is a popular technique with customizers, who like their trucks low to the ground. Stepside styling lends itself well to a sporty, fun-type appearance on these late-model haulers.

More radical body modifications may include a chopped top and custom fabricated grilles. The latter may be totally homemade items or adaptations from other cars or trucks. Chopping a cab entails cutting several inches from the window posts with a torch, and lowering the roof, with the windows and windshield cut down to fit. This is specialized work and must be carefully planned and executed. Entire articles and books are available on this technique.

Today's street rodders go for the integrated, detailed look, and trucks are no exception. An example would be electronically operated door controls without external handles. With components such as rearview mirrors, the goal is to hide all attaching hardware so that the finished vehicle has a total design appearance. In other words, nothing seen on the end product should leave the impression that it was an afterthought.

Some of these high-tech hot rods actually seem like the creation of highly paid professional stylists working in a Detroit design studio. The backyard builder image is out, except in the case of competition roadsters, which are purposely designed to look like early hot rods. Some prewar trucks may be done up this way, but the postwar models really don't fit into this category.

As mentioned earlier, many hot-rodded trucks start off in rough condition, and the running boards and cargo box may have to be discarded. Running boards can be fashioned out of oak boards or other hardwoods, sheet metal or diamond plate. Use the dimensions of the original panel (what's left of it) as a pattern for the replacement. When using wood, make sure it has been kiln-dried so no warping will occur. The boards can be fastened to the cab sill with sturdy angle iron braces. Use trim moldings on the edges for a neat, professional appearance. Running boards upholstered in tufted vinyl were once the rage, but the trend today is toward the clean, simple look. Woodgraining or diamond plate can be attractive.

The pride of most truck builders shows through in their cargo box treatments. Early postwar pickups had wood beds; many of these are redone with finished oak floors and chrome or stainless steel skid strips. The inner tailgate panel is often fixed up in a matching fashion, and carpeted inner sides are common. Sometimes a custom upholstered auxiliary seat may be installed behind the cab. Accessories like chrome bed rails and tonneau covers are virtually standard equipment on the well-detailed hot rod pickup.

Many modified trucks are completed in boxless form, with homemade wood platforms in back. Some builders go the stake-bed route, while others may construct a complete oak cargo box to replace the rusty or

Other than lowering, this '69 custom has only minor dechroming, with fender-side identification removed. The bow tie emblem was left on the hood, however. Personalization is *part of the customizing game, aimed at creating a distinctive look.*

dented metal original. Reproduction boxes in metal can even be purchased for some models.

Trick ways to go with rear-body treatments again favor the integrated look, with all seams between fenders, running boards and cargo boxes molded-in to give a single-unit appearance. This works the best when reproduction fiberglass parts are used.

Fiberglass and steel reproduction body parts are readily available for Chevrolet (and GMC) trucks at hot rod shops, flea markets or by mail order. For example, the Glassworks in Bolton, Ontario, has a thick 500-plus-page catalog with 5½ pages listing nearly 250 parts for Chevrolet and GMC pickup trucks. They include front and rear fenders, tailgate panels and skins, various patch panels, cab components, running boards, bed panels, door skins, hoods and box sides. Applications range from 1934 to 1980 models. About half of these parts are made from fiberglass, while the other half are steel. The firm also sells good used parts.

When it comes to custom paint jobs, the creativity of the modified crowd is unequaled and the degree of craftsmanship is superb. Multicoat hand-rubbed refinishing techniques have long been associated with the rod-and-custom industry, not to mention eye-catching body graphics ranging from far-out flames and scallops to subtle pin striping. Such treatments can be used quite effectively on older pickups because they have so many separate shapes to the fenders, hoods, cabs, cargo boxes, grilles and tailgates. Graphics can emphasize these distinctive shapes quite effectively.

For the home-builder, an important phase of body refinishing is prepping the vehicle's body panels prior to the application of paint. Removal of the original finish, metal straightening and filling, masking of the bright-metal trim and glass, and the application of primer coats are operations that are all well within the amateur's level of skills.

Even when the finish coats are applied professionally, the amateur restorer or builder can save himself lots of money by readying the truck for the paint shop. The main investment in this phase of the refinishing operation is time, since hours of labor are required to prepare a truck body for paint application. The home-builder will be hundreds of dollars ahead if he or she uses his or her own spare time for paint prepping, instead of paying the professional a high shop rate to do the same

Custom wheels are virtually mandatory on custom trucks. These were finished in yellow to match the body, with plated centers. Black sidewall radial tires looked great with yellow *paint and improved ride characteristics. The owner-builder was obviously after the clean look and succeeded in getting it.*

job. Not everyone can handle a spray gun, but nearly anyone can do a good job with sandpaper, masking tape and body primers.

An important part of prepping a truck for paint, if you want a truly first-class appearance, is the removal of as much brightmetal trim as possible. This takes many, many hours, as the parts must be carefully removed and sketched or photographed, then carefully stored in cartons, bags or envelopes. These steps ensure that the trim gets back on the truck correctly, but this operation requires lots of time and patience to accomplish.

Trim removal is definitely the best way to go, however, as even the best job of masking trim with tape will usually lead to areas where overspray from the paint gun gets on the edges of moldings and ornaments. The goal is to make the paint job look like factory finish, and telltale traces of paint on the brightmetal parts will detract from this image.

One of the best things about customizing a pickup is that you do not have to worry about selecting or sticking to original paint color schemes or patterns. You can pick up paint-chip books at a swap meet or use books that your local jobber has. Once you have found the color(s) you like best, the paint jobber can mix up a can for you according to the formulas given on the

samples in the paint-chip book. With older colors, a perfect match may prove impossible, but you can usually get very close with a modern approximation.

With a modified truck, acrylic enamels are the best type of paint to use. These provide a hard, shiny, long-lasting finish that will look just as good as, if not better than, the twenty hand-rubbed coats of lacquer that rodders preferred years ago. If your taste runs toward the exotic side, you may want to pick a wild metallic color or even a pearlescent finish. There is even a new type of paint called Moon-Glow that absorbs natural light and glows in the dark. If you're a night person who need lots of attention, it may be something you'd like to try on your truck.

If you happen to be a professional person with your own business, you might want to use your pickup as a rolling advertisement and letter a name and telephone number or sales slogan on the doors. At a recent show, one vintage truck made by a certain manufacturer in Dearborn, Michigan, carried the legend, A-Ford-Able Service, on the truck's side.

Years ago, at the old-car auctions, one auctioneer used to say that an old truck lettered this way could be used as an advertising tax write-off. Possibly this is no longer so under the new tax laws, but a lettered-up truck

Rear of this low-to-the-ground 1969 Custom features a tonneau cover on the bed and chrome dual exhaust extensions.

The sliding cab rear window was a factory extra, but the smoked glass is another touch of personalization.

often looks attractive and might even get you some extra business. And, if nothing else, it's a good way to display your imagination and sense of humor.

Interior

Once you have painted your truck and put all the parts back together, restoring or customizing the interior becomes the next step. Original seat upholstery kits, headliners, door panels, glovebox and interior paint colors for Chevy pickups through the late-fifties can be purchased from suppliers such as Jim Carter, Golden State Pickups, Obsolete Chevrolet Parts Company, Heavy Chevy Truck Parts and Roberts Motors Parts. Also available are custom-made floor mats and carpets, plus detailing items like windlace and door gaskets.

In many cases, the truck rodder may want to replace the stock bench seats with a set of bucket seats from a donor car or truck. This is basically a bolt-in operation, though it may be necessary to fabricate a base on the floor platform to get the seats to the proper

riding height. Most buckets are upholstered in vinyl, so redoing the door panels in matching material is virtually a must.

After the seat(s) question is dealt with, lay down the carpeting or floor mats. The available kits will give you a professional fit and appearance that's superior to carpets made from cut-down rugs. Years ago, shag-type carpets were the rage, but these don't look right in the high-tech modified trucks you see today.

Most kits come with complete, easy-to-understand instructions, but if you need additional help, let the supplier know. These companies will be glad to do all that they can to help you, because they place great importance on customer satisfaction.

Dressing up the interior and dashboard comes next. Depending on the design of door panels and dash, you may want to add woodgrain or engine-turned appliques, which are available in speed shops. As for bolt-on items, most sport truckers consider a gauge package with tachometer, a high-quality AM/FM stereo sound system and a CB radio to be standard equipment.

Mild customizing is illustrated by this 1971–1972 Fleetside. A horizontal bar grille has been purchased or hand-built, and the badges, emblems and other identification are removed from the front. Accessories include wide whitewalls, styled wheels, twin spotlights, vent-a-shades on side windows and chrome bed rails. Mild customs are a fine way to achieve personalization at modest cost.

151

A lot of accessories made for custom vans—like drink trays, consoles, and so on—can also be used on a pickup interior.

Some modifiers like to install power brakes, power steering, tilt steering or power seats in their trucks. The equipment can be scavenged from donor vehicles in a wrecking yard and adapted to the truck with a little extra work. Here, again, your best source of parts, advice and how-to-do-it books will be your local speed shop.

A final cab modification you may want to try is the installation of extra windows or a pop-up sunroof. Almost every major city has a body shop or van conversion business that specializes in this type of work. The parts you need, in a wide variety of sizes, shapes and styles, are easy to get because of the large aftermarket industry involved in customizing travel vans today.

Bolt-on accessories

At this point, your truck is virtually complete and ready to roll down the road again. But before you turn on the ignition and blast off, how about adding those shiny, final details, that may set your hot rod light-duty off from all the rest? We're talking about chrome bolt-on accessories for the exterior, interior and under the hood.

Exterior

Chrome bodyside and wheel-lip moldings designed for universal fit can be obtained at nearly any auto parts outlet. There are similar moldings available for door edges and roof gutter, too. Then add a pair of chrome or brass license plate frames. Foglights and spotlights are other shiny extras easy to install. Grille irons, designed for modern trucks, can be added to improve both looks and protection. For a competition look—especially popular on Stepsides—bolt a roll bar into the cargo box. Bed rails, cab clearance marker lights, chrome-housed taillights, a CB antenna, chrome security chains, chrome spare-wheel carriers, even a set of van-type air horns, can be used to brighten up the overall image.

One warning. Don't just bolt-on everything you find. Instead, consider the overall shape and design of your truck, the colors you have painted it and the image you are looking for. Then select the features that will help you best achieve your goals as a modified-truck builder.

Interior

Easy-to-install chrome pieces that you can use for interior trimming include bright rearview mirrors, chrome door-lock buttons, self-adhesive moldings, chrome gearshift handles, custom steering wheels with punched chrome spokes, gauges, consoles, chrome dashboard knobs, chrome radio speaker housings, toggle switches for accessories and brightmetal snap-fast upholstery buttons. Once again, caution should be used to avoid adding too much tinsel and making the interior look like a house of mirrors. Remember that you are designing a total interior package, and subtle chrome highlights will work far better than the gaudy approach.

Underhood

The crowning touch of the custom pickup is underhood detailing. In fact, if you're going to be guilty of using too many bolt-on chrome parts anywhere, this is the place to do it. Being overly showy with engine dress-up items is practically a prerequisite of being tagged with the hot rod label. This dates back to the early days of rodding, where the engine was far more important than the cut-down Model T pickup body it was supposed to pull around.

There are dozens of brightmetal parts available for Chevrolet (and other) V-8 engines. Chrome valve covers, oil filler caps, spark plug wire looms, distributor caps, alternators, coil covers, voltage regulator covers, air cleaners, generator housings, wire sheaths, carburetor horns, hose clamps, radiator caps, dipsticks and hardware are easy to find at any shop selling parts for cars and trucks. Of course, before you start adding such goodies, you'll want to paint the engine block a nice bright red, blue or orange (black looks great, too) and porcelainize those exhaust manifolds . . . if you haven't added chrome-plated header pipes, that is!

If modified trucks are your thing, this chapter can provide some direction for the efforts you'll make in changing that old pickup from a junker to a jewel. No, I haven't had the room to cover the whole nine yards when it gets down to spraying on a coat of paint or trimming up a door panel. What I have tried to do is emphasize the fact that you'll be the architect and general contractor for the project that you have in mind. You'll set down the general design parameters, contact suppliers for the needed parts, hire out the labor that you can't do at home and, finally, handle the final reassembly.

As you can see, that makes you a VIP—Very Important Person—in the overall creation of a very personalized form of light-duty transportation. That alone should be sufficient inspiration to get the project in gear as soon as you put down this book.

Chapter 10

Collecting and restoring

So you want to collect postwar Chevy pickups? Rule number one: Purchasing vintage pickups is a lot like buying used ones, except for two things. First, there are special places to look for them. Second, you might have to consider a truck that's in worse shape than you'd normally see on a car lot. In this case, restoration would be in order.

How to find vintage trucks

The first place to look for vintage trucks is everywhere: streets, driveways, alleys, body shops, junkyards. You may find the best bargain under your nose, but don't count on it. Noncollectors sometimes overvalue their old pickups. Every old vehicle is for sale if you're willing to pay enough. The trick is buying the right one at the right price, not bargain-hunting.

Chevy pickups underwent a role change during the postwar era. Until 1955, they were used mainly in rural areas for utilitarian purposes. There are still many of these models being used in small towns and on farms. After 1955, pickups gained favor as second cars for American families everywhere. Good sixties and seventies models often turn up on small used car lots.

You'll often find the best survivors in sunbelt states or on the west coast. Trucks used in the snowbelt—where roads are salted in winter—had higher scrappage rates. That's why the collector vehicle market is nationwide in scope. Many California trucks wind up in Wisconsin and Minnesota.

If you don't stumble upon the Chevy pickup you want in your area, the place to start looking is in the classified ads of special hobby publications. These range from club newsletters and regional shoppers to trader magazines published strictly for collectors. In addition to classified ads, these publications carry schedules of hobby events and display advertising for collector car dealers, shows and auctions. You'll find many vintage pickups for sale in these places. (See Information Department for a list of sources.)

Local newspapers, estate or farm auctions, even parades, are other places to keep your eyes open. Check those free bulletin boards at your favorite supermarket. Or put the shoe on the other foot and write an ad saying that you want to buy an old truck. This has worked great for some people.

How to buy vintage trucks

Unless you're looking for a specific rare model, it's best to skip trucks needing major restoration work. We all know that used car dealers don't waste their money fixing up really rough vehicles. They wholesale them quickly or just scrap them out. After a certain point, putting a vehicle back in shape costs more than buying a good one. In most cases, collectors are better off paying a slight premium for a pickup in used-car-lot condition.

There are many good books on buying used vehicles. Most libraries carry a few. They explain how to inspect and road test a vehicle, how to use a *Blue Book* to estimate value, and how to arrange financing and insurance. Instead of repeating their tips, let's concentrate on the differences in buying collector vehicles.

In the used car market, odometer readings are very important. There may be a $1,000 value difference between similar cars with 30,000 and 70,000 miles. Also, a 1982 pickup with 40,000 original miles might be advertised as a low-mileage cream puff.

Collectors place more emphasis on exceptionally low miles, but less on high readings. They know that thirty-five-year-old vehicles with under 1,000 miles showing have turned up, but that a 1952 Chevy pickup with 30,000 miles might be a rust-bucket. On the other hand, there's also the realization that a restored pickup with 300,000 miles could be as good as new. On the bottom line, collectors look at odometer readings differently than used car salespeople.

Rather than mileage, collectors rely on grading systems to rate a vehicle's condition. One such system is based on concours judging using a 100-point scale with points deducted for flaws. A ninety-eight-point truck would be near-perfect. A simpler system uses five or six numbered grades, with a number one being tops. A typical condition-code system, developed by *Old Cars Weekly*, looks like this:

1) EXCELLENT: restored to current maximum professional standards of quality in every area; or perfect original with all components operating and appearing as new.

2) FINE: well-restored; or a combination of superior restoration and excellent original; or an extremely well-maintained original showing very minimal wear.

3) VERY GOOD: completely operable original or older restoration showing wear; or amateur restoration; all presentable and serviceable inside and out. Also, combinations of well-done restoration and good operable components; or partially restored car with all parts necessary to complete/or valuable New Old Stock (NOS) parts.

4) GOOD: a driveable vehicle needing no or only minor work to be functional; or a deteriorated restoration; or a very poor amateur restoration. All components may need restoration to be EXCELLENT, but mostly useable "as is."

5) RESTORABLE: needs complete restoration of body, chassis and interior. May or may not run, but isn't weathered, wrecked or stripped to the point of being useful only for parts salvage.

Once you've inspected an old pickup and rated its condition, the next step in the buying process is arriving at a price mutually agreeable to buyer and seller. Collectors do not have a *Blue Book* to tell them the wholesale, retail and trade-in values of different models. Instead, they have price guides that help them estimate what vehicles in different conditions should sell for.

There are two types of price guide. The first records actual prices announced at collector car auctions. The second uses auction results as a basis to appraise every model that manufacturers built. At least thirteen different guides are available, and all are good tools for making wise buying decisions by providing an idea of whether a seller's or a buyer's expectations are realistic.

Contrary to what some people think, lenders—such as banks—*will* make loans for collector vehicles.

In most cases, this will require proving the vehicle's value, which is another instance where price guides come in handy. Most banks will not allow one collectible to be used as collateral for buying another one, however. Beyond this, the mechanics are about the same as making a personal loan.

As for insurance, many collectors take out special policies for antique vehicles. These give broad, low-cost coverage with certain restrictions on how and how often the vehicle can be used. If you plan to use your postwar Chevy pickup on an everyday basis, ask your regular insurance agent about arranging a stated value policy. Insurance companies will require price guide references to help establish what the truck is worth.

Car shows and auctions bring buyers and sellers together. Check listings in hobby magazines for dates, times, locations and admission fees. At shows you'll find older vehicles for sale in swap meets and flea markets, or special areas called car corrals. Most auctions are for vehicle sales only, although some auctions are intended to liquidate existing collections, while still others are consignment sales of privately owned vehicles.

Shows offer every type of old vehicle, in conditions from junkers to jewels. On the other hand, most auction vehicles are in good-to-excellent shape and operable. Take your price guides along to either type of event, and a note pad. The process is simple. Write down the good and bad features of each truck you're interested in. Grade them accordingly and write down this rating, too. Look up the price for the model in that condition given in a price guide. On the same page, note things like asking price, seller's name and contact information. Try to find the owner to discuss the truck.

At a show, your next step is making an offer. Let the seller know how to contact you. Many owners decide to sell at a better price a day or two later, after sorting out the offers they've had. That's when it pays to make sure they know how to reach you. If you buy the truck, make sure you get a proper bill of sale, receipt, title certificate and registration.

Auctions represent a fast-paced, high-pressure method of selling collector vehicles. They do offer some very good buys on excellent cars and trucks to wise buyers; the novice, however, should approach auctions with particular care. We have all seen spoofs where someone scratches his head during an auction and winds up buying the Brooklyn Bridge.

Those who do best at auctions are professional dealers and big collectors. If you go to an auction, try to make contact with such people and talk to them about the tricks of the trade. Attend a couple of sales before you do any buying. When you reach the purchasing point, check the trucks you like in advance, set maximum bid prices in your mind, write them down and bid accordingly.

From personal experience, I can tell you that you can get some good buys at auctions. The biggest complaint at such sales comes from people who travel long distances for a particular advertised vehicle that doesn't show up. Unfortunately, this can happen when a consignor sells his car or truck before the date and substitutes another vehicle in the slot he has purchased. This practice, though legal, is disappointing to the buyer who came to the auction for the truck that was advertised originally.

Two auction companies—Kruse International and Von Reese Auctioneers—regularly publish informative newsletters that give tips about buying and selling at auctions. Write them to get on the mailing list.

A final way to purchase an old pickup is from a collector car dealer. These professionals advertise in hobby publications. Most of them stress the investment angle and sell vehicles that are priced on the high end of the scale. My personal experience with dealers has been encouraging. I purchased a vehicle for the most I've spent on a collectible, but it's a very nice machine that could easily be resold for as much (or more) than the purchase price. The same couldn't be said for some of the bargains I bought years ago that turned out to need lots of restoration.

How to restore vintage trucks

Vehicle restoration is an expensive, time-consuming process. A complete restoration entails totally disassembling the vehicle, repairing or replacing all worn-out parts, painting and upholstering the truck, reassembling all the pieces, making all necessary final adjustments and taking care of finish details.

The cost of restoring a truck could be as much as two or three times its market value when finished! The only logical reason for a complete restoration is that you want to own a particular model truck and can't find a good original or restored example.

If you locate a pretty good truck with a totally rust-free body, a partial restoration is possible. In this case, mechanical repairs, body and paint work and replacement of brightmetal trim can be accomplished without complete disassembly. This means the cost of the work will be significantly less.

There are numerous other books covering restoration; a book of this size cannot hope to cover all the how-to information of things like engine rebuilding, sheet metal work, painting and detailing. Here I will discuss special information on restoring pickups instead of what grit of sandpaper to use or how much pressure a paint spraygun should be operated at. For example, the use of lead body filler rather than plastic filler will be recommended, but the fine points of working with lead will have to be learned through other books and, later, through hands-on experience.

When contemplating any restoration, the first things to think about are planning, record keeping, work space and expense. Think of yourself as a general contractor who is supervising the work, subcontracting certain jobs to other contractors, purchasing outside parts and services, shipping and receiving parts and supplies, controlling expenses and generally managing the project from start to finish. You will need a logbook to guide the project. Use it to record what's being done, who's doing it and what costs are involved. Some hobbyists estimate the cost of the total job and save up that amount before they start. This allows the work to move quickly. Others budget a weekly or monthly amount for their hobby and proceed accordingly, a step at a time. The main thing is to avoid getting in deeper than you can afford to be.

Generally speaking, a space large enough for two or three trucks is required for a complete restoration. One space will hold the chassis, the second is for the body parts, and the third is for storing the small parts removed and a work area. It's possible to get by in a two-car garage, if the small parts can be stored on shelves or if you are doing only a partial restoration.

Many books recommend photographing all parts that are removed, although few veteran restorers do this. Instead, you can color-code, label, tag or box up the parts you remove. Then, buy an original Chevrolet master parts catalog from a literature dealer. This includes assembly drawings showing all parts and how they go together. For 1947–1954 Chevy pickups, a company called Golden State Pickups sells reprints of the factory assembly manual that includes the same information. Chevy truck shop manuals for models through 1959 are also available in reprint form from most pickup parts suppliers. Similar books for newer models can be purchased from dealers who sell original literature.

Shop manuals will provide step-by-step disassembly instructions. Taking things apart is easy. First remove bumpers and trim, front-end sheet metal, rear fenders and the cargo box (on Stepside types). A hoist will be required to lift the cab (or cab and rear body on Fleetsides) from the frame. Mount the body securely on jack stands or sawhorses. Be sure these are placed on level ground or the body will set unevenly and may remain lopsided when remounted on the frame. The frame, front and rear suspensions, drivetrain and wheel parts make up a rolling chassis. This will be the last thing you uncover and the first you start restoring.

With the help of local businesses, you will be able to rebuild most of the mechanical chassis parts like the engine, brake system, electrical system and rear axle. Suspension kits are available from hobby suppliers who sell new-old-stock (unused original) or reproduction parts. Most likely, you'll have to order hard-to-get transmission, clutch and steering parts from these sources, too. The shop manual will again give step-by-step rebuilding instructions. Once the parts are obtained, you should have few problems reassembling things yourself or having this done at your local shop.

One snag that novices run into with shop manuals is the need for special tools called for to complete step-by-step procedures. Don't worry too much about this. Find an old-time mechanic who worked on these trucks years ago and he'll tell you how common modern tools can be used to do the same thing. In a few cases, you may have to rely on a machine shop to put things together. The special tools were often a short cut by which truck makers earned extra profits by selling hardware to their dealers.

Some hobbyists prefer farming out the work on all mechanical subassemblies to machine shops. The drawback to this is the additional labor expense, plus the fact that the machine shop will not spend the time to paint the parts and make them look new. Therefore, it will be up to you to refinish the parts before reassembling the vehicle, and many truck clubs have researched the proper colors parts should be painted. Also, you'll need special paints, available from hobby suppliers, to use on the engine, engine compartment and frame.

As an example of how truck clubs can help you accomplish a first-class, completely authentic restoration, the following information about Chevy truck engine colors was compiled by Bill Braamse, of the Light Commercial Vehicle Association:

The 1941-1949 235 ci truck engines with long side pans were painted dark gray with Loadmaster High Torque engine written in yellow script on the right side of the rocker cover. The 1950-1952 235 ci truck engines which had short side panels were also dark gray with Loadmaster written on the side of the rocker cover in yellow paint.

The 1954-1962 235 ci truck engines were painted dark gray with Loadmaster written on the rocker cover. The 1954-1959 261 ci truck engines were painted yellow with Jobmaster written on the rocker cover with yellow script paint. The 1960-1962 261 ci truck engines were painted green with no writing.

Some mechanical parts were left unpainted by the factory. These can be restored by sandblasting or by cleaning them with solvents that remove rust and grease. Perhaps the safest and easiest way to accomplish this is by taking them to a commercial stripper who can dip them in tanks filled with solvents.

Commercial strippers who specialize in restoration work have tanks large enough to handle a complete frame or truck body. You'll need a trailer to transport these large parts. If you don't own one, you may be able to borrow a trailer from a friend in the hobby or a member of the clubs you join. Stripping will reveal any evidence of early bodywork or hidden corrosion and rust. The caustic solutions used will also clean the metal and arrest further oxidation into solid metal.

The fine points of repairing sheet metal that has been damaged by impact or rust can best be learned from *Automobile Sheet Metal Repair,* a textbook by Robert L. Sargent. Most important to the restorer are sections of this book outlining the use of body repair tools, the fabrication of patch panels and the use of lead body filler.

Several companies sell body repair tools and lead body solder supplies (see Information Department). I have used the products of Eastwood Supply Company with excellent results. Thanks to the efforts of firms like Eastwood, these products and other specialty items are more readily available to restorers today, than they were eight to ten years ago. Having one of Eastwood's catalogs in your shop is highly recommended.

Fabricating patch panels is a good skill to know when restoring vehicles for which reproduction parts aren't readily available. But Chevrolet truck owners are especially lucky in that many modern duplicates of original factory parts have been stamped out by hobby suppliers. Sheet metal items advertised in American hobby magazines include cab corners, cowl panels, rocker panels, front bed panels, cab front floor and reinforcements, rear bed sills, angle strip covers, tailgates, inner fender shields, firewall covers and bed strips. In addition, a catalog published by Glassworks lists front and rear fender parts and patches, door skins, wheel arches—a total of ninety-five body parts in steel or fiberglass—for vintage Chevrolet pickups. This company also sells new and used body parts, and illustrations in the catalog indicate that virtually an entire truck could be built from their inventory!

Installing such parts requires cutting away bad metal, welding or riveting patches in place and using body filler to fill in the seams. Fiberglass patches and filler could also be used, but metal and lead are preferred for a first-class restoration. Of course, fiberglass repairs would be correct on the bed of the Cameo Carrier models.

When the body is patched and ready, it can be painted. We'll cover painting and refinishing operations a little later. You should paint the rest of the body parts—hood, fenders, cargo box, tailgate, running boards—at the same time to ensure you get the same paint mix. The parts usually needed to mount these parts back on the frame are available from companies like Heavy Chevy, The Truck Shop, Fiberglass & Wood Company, Golden State Pickups, Roberts Motor Parts, Chevy Duty, Obsolete Chevrolet Parts Company and Jim Carter. Order the catalogs they print and you'll know everything that's available.

With the sheet metal in place and the running gear done, your truck is starting to look like something. Now you'll be installing upholstery and door panels, a new wiring harness, chrome trim parts, accessory items and floor mats or carpeting, and rewooding the bed on early models. Parts or kits for these purposes are sold by the same suppliers listed above or by flea market vendors who sell new-old-stock Chevy items. The kits come with complete instructions, while the trim parts and accessories usually are simple bolt-on pieces.

The final stage of your restoration will be a set of new, authentic looking tires available from antique tire companies like Coker, Universal, Kelsey, Sears or Lucas Automotive.

I used to also advise adding reproduction factory decals, but due to some recent developments concerning the legality of copying old decals, these may no longer be available. If they are, the decals really add that like-new appearance to an engine compartment.

With the truck completely refinished and reassembled, your next step will be a series of final adjustments, such as greasing the chassis, tuning up the ignition, setting the carburetor and having the front wheels aligned so you don't wear out those expensive new tires. Go over all of the nuts and bolts (with a torque wrench where possible), and put in oil, coolant and gas. After washing the truck, you'll be ready to head off to your first car show.

Notes on paint

Painting will be one of the most important steps in restoring your pickup. Whether you farm out this operation or do it yourself, it pays to prep the vehicle in your home shop. The first stage in prepping the body is to remove all bolt-on items like bumpers, grille and bright-metal trim. On some trucks, the bumper and grille will be correctly finished with paint, but you'll still want to remove them and spray them separately. This is also a good practice when it comes to parts like the hood and fenders. For a partial restoration, it's possible to paint all these parts without disassembly, but the results will be better if each part is sprayed individually.

Application of a primer comes first. Prime coats help prepare the surface and give the paint solid adherence. Wash the body parts with water and treat them with a solvent that will remove all traces of wax, grease and road tar. Next, use newspaper and masking tape to protect the glass and any nonremovable trim. Automotive primer comes in different colors. A red primer will work best under dark earth colors. Dark gray primer is recommended for black paint. Light gray primer works well under whites and yellows.

Before priming use 80-grit coarse sandpaper to scuff up the body for better paint adhesion. Also apply a metal-prep product, then clean it off and apply a synthetic primer-sealer, then apply primer, working top to bottom. Primer should be applied with a quality airgun-air compressor outfit for best results. The sprayer should be able to maintain an even 30 psi. For safety purposes, wear a respirator.

After application of the primer, the body parts should be sanded with fine-grit #320 paper. Blow away sanding residue with the air compressor and apply a second primer coat. Resand with even finer #400 paper. When the primer is smooth and residue free, it will be time to think about the color coats and whether you want to do it yourself or leave things to a professional shop.

With the high standards evident in restoration work today, many hobbyists are having their vehicles painted by professionals who have the equipment and skills to do factory-quality refinishing. For those who own only one collector car or truck, this is probably the most economical way to go simply because of the cost of items such as spray booths. The skills required to paint a vehicle can be learned, but the investment in equipment and on-the-job education can be considerable. Many hobbyists feel that it pays for them to prep their own vehicles, but to hire the services of a professional to complete the job.

This is probably true. The car owner has more time to spend on minor preparation tasks—removal of trim or extra-careful masking of chrome and glass—and can be meticulous at these tasks. This will count in car show judging. Unlike the professional, the hobbyist does not have to worry about rolling the next job in. A body shop will, of course, usually do acceptable prepping, but show quality is one step beyond that, at least. That's why I recommend prepping the car yourself. This will mean borrowing or renting a compressor and spray gun to apply the prime coats. But the time and expense involved will be worth it in the end.

Unlike the laborious job of body preparation, the application of color coats moves quickly. At this stage, the professional's experience will weigh heavily. An amateur paint job will look like an amateur paint job (unless the amateur gets some expert training, that is).

Of course, there are many hobbyists who enjoy the feelings of pride and personal accomplishment that go along with painting their own trucks. If you fall into this category, there are many books available on how to paint automobiles. You will also need hands-on experience, however. Two excellent ways to attain a working knowledge are to practice with another, more experienced amateur restorer or to enroll in a continuing education course where bodywork and painting are taught.

Another alternative that has also been gaining popularity lately is the seminars on restoration taught at colleges, on weekends or at night, as a continuing education program.

The instructor at one such course, arranged by Marquette University, of Milwaukee, Wisconsin, was "Beaver" Culver, a well-known restorer of cars like Packards and Duesenbergs. Culver explained that paint manufacturers now market their products as complete refinishing systems and stressed that it pays to use the same brand of products. "There's enough of a problem choosing different enamels and lacquers," he noted. "Why use different brands?" Beaver advised using a brand other restorers have had good results with. "The idea of thirty coats of hand-rubbed lacquer is out," he said.

Improvements in paint technology have created refinishing products requiring only a few coats to give excellent results. Novices find lacquer easiest to spray, followed by acrylic, then enamel.

Mix the paint with the proper amount of thinner, following manufacturer's recommendations. Stir thoroughly. Select the correct spray gun head and adjust the spray so that it has a fan-out area about eight inches wide and twelve inches from the gun head. Make a few practice passes on a sheet of cardboard. Keep the gun parallel to the surface and swing horizontally back and forth, overlapping on each pass.

When paint is applied correctly, it will appear smooth and wet for a short time after application. Graininess indicates the paint is too thick or you're holding the gun too far away from the truck. If the paint runs, it's too thin or the gun is too close. Avoid spraying in one spot too long.

Spray just one panel—hood, fender, door—at a time and try to adopt a natural spraying technique, so the coatings are consistent in texture, thickness and color depth. Beginners sometimes do better making horizontal strokes across a panel first, followed directly by vertical strokes. Everyone has his own style of applying paint. When cars were hand-sprayed on the old assembly lines, operators were matched in technique, so both sides of the vehicle would have the same quality.

Techniques will vary somewhat according to the type of paint. Lacquer requires the least worry. With acrylic, the paint must "flash" or harden on its surface before a second coat is applied. Enamel dries slowly and can't be applied all at once. Enamel actually requires a tack coat, color coat and finish coat, and should be sprayed only in a moisture-free environment. The environment for all painting should be dust-free.

If runs develop, adjust the gun for lighter spray and, when the first color coat has been sprayed, dip a tiny brush in a can of thinner and use it to remove excess paint. Then simply "fog" that area lightly on the finish coat. Do not try moving the truck until the paint is completely dry.

After you have finished spraying the body, allow the paint to dry while keeping the truck indoors overnight. After three days, wash the pickup with clean water. Then color-sand the entire truck, by hand, with 600-grit sandpaper. Buff lightly with an electric buffer and suitable rubbing compound (ask your parts store clerk about which compound to use). Clean up the garage or shop and you're done.

Instructions like these make it sound like a snap to refinish a truck, but of course, it's not all that simple. There is no substitute for hands-on experience or good advice from a veteran hobbyist, professional body worker or paint retailer who knows his or her product line. You should practice on scrap pieces of metal before ever lifting a spray gun. And, of course, sign up for those night school classes, if they're available in your area.

Clubs and events

If you've gotten this far without joining a truck club, it's definitely time to sign on the dotted line. In some areas of the country, there are local clubs for truck collectors. More common are national clubs with local chapters or regions. Membership dues for the nationals usually run $15 to $25, and in most cases this gets you a membership card, window decal, club roster and one-year subscription to the club's magazine or newsletter.

These club publications vary in quality from photocopied sheets stapled together to professional magazines with color photos. The content is much more important than the appearance. You'll want to read lots of good information like history, technical tips, listings of upcoming events and stories written by other pickup owners that tell how they restored their vehicles.

When clubs operate both nationally and locally, it is usually required that you first join the national. Then you'll be qualified for membership in a chapter or region. These local groups have dues ranging from $10 to $15, and will help you contact other collectors who live nearby.

Clubs that offer the services of technical advisors can be a big help in a restoration. These people are experts in one brand of truck, or even one year or model. They provide advice through correspondence. If you have a question, you mail it to the technical advisor along with a self-addressed stamped envelope (SASE) for the answer. Other than the cost of the stamp, there is no charge for this service.

In addition to clubs aimed specifically at truck collectors, there are clubs that cover both cars and trucks. For example, the Classic Chevrolet Club, in Orlando, Florida, recognizes all vehicles—including commercial types—manufactured by Chevrolet from 1955 to 1957.

The first step in arranging membership in a club is to identify those organizations that seem best suited to your particular interests. Write to them to see if they have a flyer or brochure available (it may be a good idea to enclose an SASE). Enclose a questionnaire that will help determine if the group is geared to your particular needs and wants. For example, does the club provide a technical advisor service that will help me in restoring my truck? You'll also need information about membership fees and dues, the existence of local chapters in your area, and so on. In some cases, clubs will also have a parts store through which obsolete or reproduction parts can be ordered.

Some clubs will require another member to sponsor you. The person must sign a form or membership application that will attest to your interest and qualifications for club membership. The Antique Automobile Club of America is one that includes this prerequisite.

Hobby events

After you restore your Chevrolet pickup, chances are good that you'll want to use it to participate in hobby events such as shows, tours and parades. Such activities are regularly held in all parts of the country.

Almost every vintage car show now has at least one class—and possibly several—for commercial vehicles. In most cases these classes are structured according to model year. If your truck is of a certain type—a van or a military vehicle—there might be a separate class for it. Some shows also give awards for the best modified vehicles, the longest distance driven or trailered, best paint job and so on.

In addition to shows for both cars and trucks, the popularity of shows solely for trucks is growing. Also, most of the clubs listed below have annual conventions that include a show. If the club is for trucks only, the show will usually be organized accordingly.

The majority of shows provide trophies for the vehicles placing first, second and third in their classes. Sometimes vehicles are judged by experts. In other cases, the public is allowed to pick winners by voting.

Admission of vehicles may be free or require a modest fee. The fees are generally used for the purchase of trophies and awards, although they may be earmarked for a charity, too.

Tours require driving the vehicles, usually in convoy fashion. They may be set up as just a weekend excursion during which participants follow a specific route and stop at points of interest along the way. In other cases, the tour may be a type of rally. For example, the drivers may be given a set of instructions that tell them which way to turn as they reach certain landmarks or checkpoints.

Calendar listings of upcoming events are regularly listed in many club newsletters, as well as in national hobby publications like *Old Cars Weekly*. Many groups also send out flyers to members and other clubs.

At most shows, nearly all participants will receive a dash plaque in recognition of their appearance at a show. Often, the show promoters will also distribute goodie bags filled with gifts and premiums donated by local businesses or those who vend parts and services to hobbyists.

Another popular activity is individual or club participation in holiday parades, sporting events or shopping mall promotions. Some clubs even make members' trucks available for business promotions in exchange for a small fee, with proceeds benefiting the club treasury. Other hobbyists have rented their vintage vehicles to motion picture studios for use in movies or allowed photographers to use them for illustrating books, magazine articles and calendars. In short, there are many activities that car and truck collectors participate in for fun, recognition and worthy causes and, sometimes, the opportunity to make some money for their clubs or themselves.

Chapter 11

Truckomobilia

Memorabilia is defined as something worthy of remembrance. The business of making and selling trucks has led to the creation of many items, both large and small, that are related to the full-size vehicles. As this memorabilia grows older, it follows a pattern of increasing in historical significance and value.

Truck memorabilia—or truckomobilia—falls into two basic categories: special-interest and general. The first category includes items that fit into organized areas of collecting, such as models, toys, literature or license plates. In the second group are miscellaneous items that are mainly collected by vehicle owners wishing to gather anything and everything connected to the trucks that they have. The generalist may have key chains, ballpoint pens, showroom banners, penknives and paperweights that were used as promotional items to spur the sale of trucks.

Although a great deal of memorabilia were originally produced by the truck manufacturers, this isn't always the case. Toy makers, oil companies, auto parts suppliers, calendar producers, independent publishers and countless other sources have been known to develop various items for the consumer market or promotional use, and these items later became desirable to truckomobilia buffs.

When it comes to Chevrolet truckomobilia, there are probably thousands of individual items available to the hobbyist. The famous bow tie emblem has appeared on countless promotional premiums and official factory materials. In addition, toy makers have patterned many of their miniatures after the best-selling American trucks, and the automotive aftermarket has generated books, posters, license plate frames, drinking glasses—you name it—picturing Chevrolet models or insignias.

Some collectors are interested in purchasing any type of Chevrolet truckomobilia. Others target their purchases to a specific era, model or year. No matter how broad or narrow the interest may range, there's plenty of stuff to keep your eyes open for.

The best place to look for truckomobilia is at the same automotive flea markets where vehicles and parts are sold. Some vendors even specialize in the exclusive sale of such items, although the best buys—in terms of price—will often occur when a vendor has picked up memorabilia while cleaning out the inventory of an old dealership or shop. He will be happy to unload these miscellaneous items, since he is more interested in selling parts.

Sometimes, truckomobilia will turn up at garage sales, swap shops, general flea markets, antiques stores or classified advertisements in local newspapers. You may also be able to purchase the special-interest type at shows organized for other types of collectibles such as toys, literature, postcards, license plates and key fobs. In these larger and more organized areas, there are even separate trader publications such as *Antique Toy World* magazine, *Paper Collector's Marketplace* and *Book Mart*. Farm auctions are an excellent source of truck memorabilia, since light-duty trucks play such a major role in the operation of American farms.

A great way to build up a large collection of truckomobilia is to place your own advertisements in both the automotive and nonautomotive hobby publications. Classified ads usually run between seven and twenty cents a word, and a small ad for "memorabilia wanted" may reap dozens of items you'll want to add to your collection as it grows.

An advantage of collecting general items is that each individual piece might be quite inexpensive, although it will grow in value as part of a large collection. In other words, the value of the total collection is often greater than the sum of its parts. On the other hand, a specialty item collected by many people may have greater intrinsic value. Car dealer promotional models, for example, may be worth several hundred dollars, depending on rarity.

Some truck hobbyists pursue the gathering of memorabilia as serious collectors seeking to put together a large assortment that is as complete as possible. Other buffs focus on the nostalgia or decorative aspects. For instance, they may want to find the toy Chevy truck they owned as a kid or use the truckomobilia to decorate their house or garage. If size or completeness is not of primary importance, expenditures can be kept to a minimum. A major collection may require a major investment, however.

The important thing to remember is that almost anything that relates to your old truck can be considered memorabilia. If the big truck is your primary interest, you'll have the luxury of approaching the truckomobilia market as a pure hobbyist. That means that buying decisions will be guided primarily by your tastes and the quest for having fun. Therefore, the financial side of things will be secondary. You won't make many purchases based strictly on the concept of investment value, though you may want to splurge a bit if an outstanding buy comes along.

In this chapter, we're going to focus on a few popular types of truckomobilia: toys and models, dealer films and film strips, art and artifacts (like literature and postcards), and books that you'll enjoy having in your Chevy truck library.

Models and toys

Miniature versions of cars and trucks have been around since the earliest days of the motor vehicle industry. Models are scale miniatures of real vehicles and are often accurate in terms of colors and details. Toys are replicas made to approximate scale and are often less detailed than models.

For the postwar-Chevrolet-truck buff, the most important type of miniature is the dealer promotional model. These are exact-scale models (usually $\frac{1}{25}$ the size of the real truck) that Chevrolet dealers used to illustrate the appearance of new vehicles to their customers. They were supplied through the company's parts department.

The first Chevrolet promos were made of diecast aluminum and were introduced in 1947. They were made by Product Miniatures Company. Four years later, the switch to plastic construction for promos was made. These Chevrolet sales tools were fully-assembled miniatures and sold for about ninety-eight cents when new. Some examples are worth several hundred dollars today.

Ron Pittman, a collector who has over 3,000 Chevrolet promos, told the editors of *Friends* magazine why prices are high. "Collectors place the highest value on the promo because they offer the closest link to the real thing," he explained. "Like advertisements and sales literature, they have nostalgic value."

Due to the quality of plastics used in the early postwar years, some of the 1950s promos are susceptible to warpage. This became less of a problem later on, although any plastic promotional will be damaged by sunlight, heat or other environmental effects.

In some cases, the companies that produced promos also released kit versions of the same miniature for the consumer's market, as well as wind-up or friction-motor editions with tin chassis substituted for the detailed plastic chassis. The same firms also built models for special purposes.

An example of a special model Chevrolet truck was a promotional item made by JoHan plastic company for B. F. Goodrich tire dealers. A total of 15,000 of these Chevrolet service trucks were produced during 1958. They had the cab styling of the 1947–1953 Chevrolet Advance-Design trucks, but with dual headlamps. On the back was a swiveling tow truck-wrecker boom. These models were finished in a two-tone combination of tan and blue with B. F. Goodrich lettering hot-stamped on them. The tires were especially well detailed, with B. F. Goodrich lettering. These service trucks were slightly small than $\frac{1}{25}$ the scale and are extremely rare today, often priced in the $150 to $200 range.

The pioneer maker of plastic promotionals was AMT (also known as SMP) which began production around 1948 and continued to 1972. Other leading manufacturers were Hubley, JoHan (1955–1979), Master Caster, MPC (1965–1980) and National Products, Incorporated. As previously mentioned, the early Chevy truck promos were done by Product Miniatures, which also produced International Harvester truck models. Production dates for this company are 1948 to 1960.

Some of the handsomest promos patterned after Chevrolet half-ton pickups were the Fleetside versions of the late 1950s. These were usually two-toned, in color combinations that make them particularly attractive to own. Also highly desirable to collectors are the models of early 1959 and 1960 El Camino pickups, which came complete with chrome full-wheel covers and whitewall tires.

While the rarest promotional models can cost up to $300 or more, many can be found for prices between $50 and $100, or less for newer trucks.

In many instances, the climbing values are driving full-size truck owners away from the promos and toward the purchase of vintage kits. Kits of 1950s and 1960s pickups can be found in the $10–$25 range, although even the prices on these are climbing rapidly. When properly assembled, the kits will give the hobbyist a replica of his full-size truck at lower cost.

Another type of model is the metal diecast version, which range in price from under $10 to as much as $150. These are generally made in smaller scales and are often highly detailed.

In addition to models, there are hundreds of different toy trucks that have been produced in the postwar era made from steel, tin, wood or plastic. I am not aware of any specific toy replicas of 1947–1972 Chevrolet pickups, although there are certainly dozens of them that have been produced in this twenty-five-year period.

Antique Toy World magazine is a lavish monthly periodical that serves serious toy collectors. It includes articles and research on old toys, auction results, display ads from manufacturers and dealers and classified ads placed by other hobbyists. The magazine also sells an extensive line of books focusing on specialized areas of interest. There are other publications that are popular with toy enthusiasts as well (see Information Department).

Dealer films and film strips

Motor vehicle makers such as Chevrolet have active photographic sections that are charged with making publicity photos, films and film strips. Such visual aids have been used for a number of purposes, including product promotion, sales and service training, and general publicity. The product films are particularly informative as to descriptions of the vehicles and their features, while the training films designed to help mechanics make repairs are valuable to restorers.

In the early prewar period, film strips were common. Later, Chevrolet developed an item called the Mini-Theatre, which projected cassette-type film cartridges on a display unit that resembled a television set. These Mini-Theatres sell for about $200 today when found at a flea market. That typically includes the film cartridges, many of which focus on Chevrolet pickups.

Over the past several years, these audiovisual aids from extinct car dealers have turned into hot collectibles. Many of the people who specialize in films and film strips advertise regularly in hobby publications such as *Old Cars Weekly* and *Hemmings Motor News*. Most film strips sell for $10–$20, and some dealers have started reproducing films on video cassettes, which can be played on your VCR.

If you are interested in old film strips or films, an excellent place to start looking for them is at a Chevrolet dealership that was around when your truck was new. Many dealers may have such material in their storerooms, and they will probably be happy to part with them for a reasonable price. Usually, this will be somewhat lower than you'd have to pay for the same items at an automotive flea market.

Another collectible originally produced by the GM Photographic Department is the publicity still or factory photo. The best known of these are 8x10-inch black and white pictures of trucks (sometimes showing many different views) that were distributed to the media individually or in press kits. Also available are color transparencies that were used for the same purposes.

These factory photos are a good visual aid for the restorer, as they illustrate how Chevrolet pickups looked when they were new and often show trucks that have many desirable options and accessories. They can be used to authenticate features that judges may question on a vehicle being judged at a show.

One of the leading suppliers of factory photographs is Applegate & Applegate, which sells photos of vintage vehicles both individually and in packaged sets.

Art and artifacts

Many truckomobilia items can be broadly classified as art and artifacts related to the full-size trucks. This category is broad in breadth and difficult to define. Perhaps the best way to cover it is to tell the story of Jay Katelle, a salesman for Plains Chevrolet in Amarillo, Texas. In addition to selling new Chevrolet cars and trucks, Katelle has one of the largest collections of Chevy nostalgia items.

According to an article in *Friends* magazine, the Katelle collection includes examples of the following items: Corvair cuff links, Chevy poker chips, tokens, sales catalogs and brochures, promo models, calendars, auto show programs, plant tour booklets, old racing programs, ball-point pens, tie tacks, ashtrays, ink blotters, key chains, pencils, cigarette lighters, playing cards, banks, rulers and—a personal specialty— advertising postcards.

Katelle began selling cars twenty-eight years ago and selling new Chevys in 1964; it was in 1972 that he became a serious collector of art and artifacts. Since then, he has amassed an assortment of thousands of items, most of which relate to Chevrolet cars and trucks. Katelle's hobby has even expanded into a sideline business with an extensive computerized inventory and mail-order catalog.

Twice each year, Katelle puts together a publication called the *Automobile Literature and Collectibles Wishbook*, which is mailed to more than 1,500 hobbyists in all fifty states and over a dozen foreign countries.

The 1985 edition, which Jerry Heasley wrote about, contained more than 5,000 different art and artifact items in a listing that ran fifty-six pages. Many of the entries are truckomobilia pieces.

According to the *Friends* article, customers ordering material from the *Wishbook* have to telephone Katelle, since the supply of collectibles is limited. Some are one-of-a-kind items. "Jay accepts calls until midnight," the article noted. "And he recently received more than 100 long-distance rings in one day."

To get in touch with Katelle, send a self-addressed stamped envelope to Jay Katelle, 3721 Farwell, Amarillo, Texas 79109.

Building a Chevy truck library

Another form of truckomobilia that most hobbyists are interested in is books about the truck(s) they own. In some cases, these are publications that were produced in the period in which the truck was made. This category would include owners manuals, service manuals, parts manuals, service bulletins, assembly manuals, sales literature and so on. But to build a good library about older Chevrolet pickups, you'll also want to find both current and out-of-print books on this topic, as well as other books covering the history of trucks. The basic items that you'll want to have in your own library are various types of sales brochures, an owners manual, a shop manual and a Chevrolet master parts catalog.

In most cases, sales literature can be obtained only from dealers in *original* literature. When it comes to owners manuals and technical literature for Chevrolet pickups, reproductions of original materials for postwar models are readily available. These will generally be somewhat less expensive than originals and can be ordered from mail-order suppliers, which will save you money, effort and time.

In Information Department you'll find listings for a number of businesses that sell original factory literature. There are many vendors dealing in the literature market, with several vendors stocking a good supply of Chevrolet material. Many sell their books and manuals at car shows and flea markets.

Pickup truck and commercial car specifications

Wurlitzer-style models

Type	Job number	Delivery price	Shipping weight
1944–1945 Prefix: BK Series: 3100 (½-ton) GVW: 4,600 lb. W.B.: 115″			
Pickup	831	$ 757	2,870 lb.
1946 Interim Prefix: CK Series: 3100 (½-ton) GVW: 4,600 lb. W.B.: 115″			
Chassis		$ 664	2,235 lb.
Chassis & cab		679	2,235
Chassis, cowl & w/s		754	2,630
Pickup	831	784	2,870
Suburban (doors)	017	1,014	3,320
Suburban (gate)	023	1,014	3,330
Canopy	013	904	3,085
Panel	009	869	3,090
1946 2nd series Prefix: DP Series: 3100 (½-ton) GVW: 4,600 lb. W.B.: 115″			
Chassis		$ 796	2,300 lb.
Chassis & cab		922	2,680
Chassis, cowl & w/s		817	2,350
Pickup	854	963	2,925
Suburban (doors)	075	1,283	3,370
Suburban (gate)	077	1,281	3,385
Canopy	073	1,126	3,135
Panel	071	1,077	3,145
1946 2nd series Prefix: DR Series: 3600 (¾-ton) GVW: 5,800 lb. W.B.: 125¼″			
Chassis		$ 891	2,495 lb.
Chassis & cab		1,016	2,890
Chassis, cowl & w/s		911	2,545
Pickup	852	1,069	3,215
Panel	079	1,212	3,450
Platform	106	1,101	3,300
Stake	885	1,127	3,450

1947 models

Type	Job number	Delivery price	Shipping weight
Prefix: EP	Series: 3100 (½-ton)	Max. GVW: 4,600 lb.	W.B.: 116″
Chassis		$ 843	2,420 lb.
Chassis & cab		1,030	2,915
Chassis, cowl & w/s		863	2,470
Pickup	083	1,087	3,205
Panel	071	1,238	3,415
Canopy express	075	1,289	3,415
Suburban (gate)	077	1,474	3,515
Prefix: EP	Series: 3600 (¾-ton)	Max. GVW: 5,800 lb.	W.B.: 125¼″
Chassis		$ 941	2,660 lb.
Chassis & cab		1,128	3,180
Chassis, cowl & w/s		962	2,710
Pickup	085	1,201	3,440
Platform	088	1,211	3,560
Stake	098	1,258	3,720

1948 models

Type	Job number	Delivery price	Shipping weight
Prefix: FP	Series: 3100 (½-ton)	Max. GVW: 4,600 lb.	W.B.: 116″
Chassis		$ 890	2,430 lb.
Chassis & cab		1,113	2,960
Chassis, cowl & w/s		910	2,555
Pickup	083	1,180	3,215
Panel	813	1,377	3,425
Canopy express	811	1,429	3,415
Suburban (gate)	814	1,627	3,515
Prefix: FR	Series: 3600 (¾-ton)	Max. GVW: 5,800 lb.	W.B.: 125¼″
Chassis		$1,004	2,660 lb.
Chassis & cab		1,227	3,180
Chassis, cowl & w/s		1,025	2,860
Pickup	085	1,315	3,460
Platform	088	1,320	3,655
Stake	098	1,378	3,740

1949 models

Type	Job number	Delivery price	Shipping weight
Prefix: GP	Series: 3100 (½-ton)	Max. GVW: 4,600 lb.	W.B.: 116″
Chassis		$ 961	2,430 lb.
Chassis & cab		1,185	2,920
Chassis, cowl & w/s		982	2,525
Pickup	160 (3104)	1,253	3,185
Panel	427 (3105)	1,450	3,425
Canopy express	429 (3107)	1,502	3,385
Suburban (gate)	435 (3116)	1,700	3,710

Prefix: GR	Series: 3600 (¾-ton)	Max. GVW: 5,800 lb.	W.B.: 125¼"
Chassis		$1,060	2,750 lb.
Chassis & cab		1,284	3,170
Chassis, cowl & w/s		1,081	2,845
Pickup	106 (3604)	1,372	3,520
Platform	518 (3608)	1,378	3,550
Stake rack	098 (3608)	1,435	3,725

Note: The number in parenthesis after the job number in the second column is the Fisher body style number.

1950 models

Type	Job number	Delivery price	Shipping weight
Prefix: HP	Series: 3100 (½-ton)	Max. GVW: 4,600 lb.	W.B.: 116"
Chassis & cowl		$ 951	2,440 lb.
Chassis, cowl & w/s		972	2,540
Chassis & cab		1,175	2,910
Pickup	160 (3104)	1,243	3,175
Panel	733 (3105)	1,440	3,375
Canopy express	735 (3107)	1,492	3,315
Suburban (doors)	879 (3106)	1,690	3,670
Suburban (gate)	875 (3116)	1,690	3,675
Prefix: HR	Series: 3600 (¾-ton)	Max. GVW: 5,800 lb.	W.B.: 125¼"
Chassis & cowl		$1,050	2,700 lb.
Chassis, cowl & w/s		1,071	2,810
Chassis & cab		1,274	3,125
Pickup	106 (3604)	1,362	3,515
Platform	844 (3608)	1,368	3,540
Stake	098 (3608)	1,425	3,700

1951 models

Type	Job number	Delivery price	Shipping weight
Prefix: JP	Series: 3100 (½-ton)	Max. GVW: 4,800 lb.	W.B.: 116"
Chassis & cowl	(3102)	$1,035	2,435 lb.
Chassis & cab	(3103)	1,282	2,880
Chassis, cowl & w/s	(3112)	1,057	2,420
Pickup	026 (3104)	1,353	3,120
Panel	833 (3105)	1,556	3,350
Canopy express	835 (3107)	1,610	3,325
Suburban (doors)	841 (3106)	1,818	3,630
Suburban (gate)	851 (3116)	1,818	3,635
Prefix: JR	Series: 3600 (¾-ton)	Max. GVW: 5,800 lb.	W.B.: 125¼"
Chassis & cowl	(3602)	$1,170	2,655 lb.
Chassis & cab	(3603)	1,417	3,095
Chassis, cowl & w/s	(3612)	1,190	2,635
Pickup	028 (3604)	1,508	3,470
Platform	915 (3608)	1,514	3,510
Stake rack	947 (3608)	1,578	3,690

1952 models

Type	Job number	Delivery price	Shipping weight
Prefix: KP	Series: 3100 (½-ton)	Max. GVW: 4,800 lb.	W.B.: 116″
Chassis & cowl	(3102)	$1,076.23	2,435 lb.
Chassis & cab	(3103)	1,334.25	2,880
Chassis, cowl & w/s	(3112)	1,098.92	2,420
Pickup	026 (3104)	1,407.46	3,120
Canopy express	291 (3107)	1,675.72	3,325
Panel	287 (3105)	1,619.62	3,350
Suburban (doors)	289 (3106)	1,933.00	3,640
Suburban (gate)	293 (3116)	1,933.00	3,635
Prefix: KR	Series: 3600 (¾-ton)	Max. GVW: 5,800 lb.	W.B.: 125¼″
Chassis & cowl	(3602)	$1,215.99	2,655 lb.
Chassis & cab	(3603)	1,474.00	3,095
Chassis, cowl & w/s	(3612)	1,237.67	2,635
Pickup	028 (3604)	1,568.79	3,470
Platform	397 (3608)	1,575.17	3,510
Stake rack	947 (3608)	1,642.00	3,690

1953 models

Type	Job number	Delivery price	Shipping weight
Prefix: H53	Series: 3100 (½-ton)	Max. GVW: 4,800 lb.	W.B.: 116″
Chassis & cowl	(3102)	$1,076.23	2,440 lb.
Chassis & cab	(3103)	1,334.25	2,855
Chassis, cowl & w/s	(3112)	1,098.92	2,515
Pickup	794 (3104)	1,407.46	3,100
Panel	523 (3105)	1,619.62	3,335
Canopy express	773 (3107)	1,675.72	3,305
Suburban (doors)	709 (3106)	1,946.53	3,625
Suburban (gate)	781 (3116)	1,946.53	3,635
Prefix: J53	Series: 3600 (¾-ton)	Max. GVW: 5,800 lb.	W.B.: 125¼″
Chassis & cowl	(3602)	$1,215.99	2,675 lb.
Chassis & cab	(3603)	1,474.00	3,110
Chassis, cowl & w/s	(3612)	1,237.67	2,780
Pickup	796 (3604)	1,568.79	3,480
Platform	397 (3608)	1,575.17	3,515
Stake rack	947 (3608)	1,642.00	3,700

1954-1955 models

Type	Job number	Delivery price	Shipping weight
Prefix: H54/H55	Series: 3100 (½-ton)	Max. GVW: 4,800 lb.	W.B.: 116″
Chassis & cowl	(3102)	$1,087/1,098	2,430/2,455 lb.
Chassis & cab	(3103)	1,346/1,357	2,870/2,845
Chassis, cowl & w/s	(3112)	1,109/1,120	2,525/2,550
Pickup	794 (3104)	1,419/1,430	3,145/3,125

Panel	523 (3105)	1,631/1,642	3,375/3,340
Canopy express	773 (3107)	1,688/1,699	3,325/3,300
Suburban (doors)	709 (3106)	1,958/1,968	3,655/3,630
Suburban (gate)	781 (3116)	1,958/1,968	3,660/3,630

Prefix: J54/J55	Series: 3600 (¾-ton)	Max. GVW: 5,800 lb.	W.B.: 125¼"
Chassis & cowl	(3602)	$1,227/1,238	2,685/2,685 lb.
Chassis & cab	(3603)	1,486/1,497	3,120/3,135
Chassis, cowl & w/s	(3612)	1,249/1,260	2,780/2,780
Pickup	796 (3604)	1,582/1,593	3,485/3,525
Platform	397 (3608)	1,587/1,598	3,540/3,550
Stake rack	947 (3608)	1,654/1,665	3,700/3,725

Note: Prices and weights to left of slash are for 1954; prices and weights to right of slash are for 1955 first series.

1955 second series models

Type	Job number	Delivery price	Shipping weight
Prefix: H255	Series: 3100 (½-ton)	Max. GVW: 6,300 lb.	W.B.: 114"
Chassis & cowl	(3102)	$1,156	2,335 lb.
Chassis & cab	(3103)	1,423	2,850
Chassis, cowl & w/s	(3112)	1,193	2,460
Pickup	707 (3104)	1,519	3,210
Panel	079 (3105)	1,801	3,440
Suburban (doors)	081 (3106)	2,150	3,715
Suburban (gate)	083 (3116)	2,150	3,725
Suburban pickup	117 (3124)	1,981	3,355
Prefix: M255	Series: 3200 (½-ton)	Max. GVW: 6,703 lb.	W.B.: 123¼"
Long-box pickup	711 (3204)	$1,540	3,305 lb.
Prefix: J255	Series: 3600 (¾-ton)	Max. GVW: 7,700 lb.	W.B.: 123¼"
Chassis & cowl	(3602)	$1,316	2,730 lb.
Chassis & cab	(3603)	1,583	3,205
Chassis, cowl & w/s	(3612)	1,353	2,815
Pickup	(3604)	1,690	3,625
Platform	(3609)	1,711	3,630
Stake rack	(3609)	1,780	3,815

1956 models

Type	Job number	Delivery price	Shipping weight
Prefix: 3A	Series: 3100 (½-ton)	Max. GVW: 6,300 lb.	W.B.: 114"
Chassis & cowl	(3102)	$1,303	2,374 lb.
Chassis & cab	(3103)	1,567	2,872
Chassis, cowl & w/s	(3112)	1,341	2,505
Pickup	506 (3104)	1,670	3,217
Panel	175 (3105)	1,966	3,457
Suburban (doors)	177 (3106)	2,300	3,736
Suburban (gate)	179 (3116)	2,300	3,752
Cameo	117 (3124)	2,144	3,373

Prefix: 3B	Series: 3200 (½-ton)	Max. GVW: 6,703 lb.	W.B.: 123¼″
Long-box pickup	508 (3204)	$1,692	3,323 lb.

Prefix: 3E	Series: 3600 (¾-ton)	Max. GVW: 7,700 lb.	W.B.: 123¼″
Chassis & cowl	(3602)	$1,481	2,736 lb.
Chassis & cab	(3603)	1,745	3,252
Chassis, cowl & w/s	(3612)	1,519	2,870
Pickup	508 (3604)	1,858	3,633
Platform & stake	335 (3609)	1,950	3,834

1957 models

Type	Job number	Delivery price	Shipping weight
Prefix: 3A	Series: 3100 (½-ton)	Max. GVW: 6,300 lb.	W.B.: 114″
Chassis & cowl	(3102)	$1,433	2,374 lb.
Chassis & cab	(3103)	1,697	2,871
Chassis, cowl & w/s	(3112)	1,471	2,514
Pickup	506 (3104)	1,800	3,217
Panel	761 (3105)	2,101	3,458
Suburban (doors)	769 (3106)	2,435	3,738
Suburban (gate)	099 (3116)	2,435	3,752
Cameo carrier	117 (3124)	2,273	3,373

Prefix: 3B	Series: 3200 (½-ton)	Max. GVW: 6,703 lb.	W.B.: 123¼″
Long-box pickup	844 (3204)	$1,838	3,322 lb.

Prefix: 3E	Series: 3600 (¾-ton)	Max. GVW: 7,700 lb.	W.B.: 123¼″
Chassis & cowl	(3602)	$1,616	2,741 lb.
Chassis & cab	(3603)	1,880	3,252
Chassis, cowl & w/s	(3612)	1,654	2,881
Pickup	844 (3604)	1,993	3,632
Platform & stake	335 (3609)	2,055	3,876

1958 models

Type	Job number	Delivery price	Shipping weight
Prefix: 3A	Series: 31/3100 (½-ton)	Max. GVW: 5,000 lb.	W.B.: 114″
Chassis	(3102)	$1,517	2,401 lb.
Chassis & cab	(3103)	1,770	2,910
Stepside	045 (3104)	1,884	3,273
Panel	619 (3105)	2,185	3,495
Suburban (doors)	623 (3106)	2,518	3,794
Suburban (gate)	625 (3116)	2,518	3,799
Cameo Carrier	117 (3124)	2,231	3,423
Fleetside	(3134)	1,900	NA

Prefix: 3B	Series: 32/3200 (½-ton)	Max. GVW: 5,000 lb.	W.B.: 123¼″
Chassis & cab	(3203)	$1,808	3,102 lb.
Long-box Stepside	048 (3204)	1,922	3,342
Long-box Fleetside	(3234)	1,938	NA

Prefix: 3C	Series: 36/3600 (¾-ton)	Max. GVW: 6,900 lb.	W.B.: 123¼"
Chassis	(3602)	$1,689	2,751 lb.
Chassis & cab	(3603)	1,953	3,270
Stepside	048 (3604)	2,066	3,674
Fleetside	(3634)	2,082	NA
Stakebed	335 (3609)	2,158	3,894

1959 models

Type	Body style number	Delivery price	Shipping weight
Series: 1100/1200	(½-ton)	Max. GVW: 4,900 lb.	W.B.: 119"
El Camino	1170	$2,363	3,590 lb.
Series: 31/3100	(½-ton)	Max. GVW: 5,000 lb.	W.B.: 114"
Chassis	3102	$1,580	2,421 lb.
Chassis & cab	3103	1,834	2,909
Stepside	3104	1,948	3,260
Panel	3105	2,249	3,490
Suburban (doors)	3106	2,583	3,778
Suburban (gate)	3116	2,616	3,796
Fleetside	3134	1,964	3,304
Series: 32/3200	(½-ton)	Max. GVW: 5,000 lb.	W.B.: 123¼"
Chassis & cab	3203	$1,872	2,988 lb.
Stepside	3204	1,986	3,386
Fleetside	3234	2,002	3,381
Series: 36/3600	(¾-ton)	Max. GVW: 6,900 lb.	W.B.: 123¼"
Chassis	3602	$1,753	2,780 lb.
Chassis & cab	3603	2,018	3,275
Stepside	3604	2,132	3,669
Fleetside	3634	2,148	3,664
Stake	3609	2,223	3,844

1960 models

Type	Body style number	Delivery price	Shipping weight
Series: 1100/1200	(½-ton)	Max. GVW: 4,900 lb.	W.B.: 119"
El Camino (6-cyl.)	1180	$2,366	3,545 lb.
El Camino (V-8)	1280	2,473	3,550
Prefix: C-14	(½-ton)	Max. GVW: 5,200 lb.	W.B.: 115"
Chassis	1402	$1,623	2,505 lb.
Chassis & cab	1403	1,877/2,640	3,035/3,460
Stepside	1404	1,991/2,754	3,395/3,820
Fleetside	1434	2,007/2,770	3,425/3,850
Panel	1405	2,308/3,071	3,615/4,040
Suburban (doors)	1406	2,690/3,453	3,960/4,365
Suburban (gate)	1416	2,723/3,486	3,975/4,380

Prefix: C-15	(½-ton)	Max. GVW: 5,200 lb.	W.B.: 127″
Chassis & cab	1503	$1,914	3,090 lb.
Stepside	1504	2,028	3,505
Fleetside	1534	2,044	3,565

Prefix: C-25	(¾-ton)	Max. GVW: 7,500 lb.	W.B.: 127″
Chassis	2502	$1,795	2,785 lb.
Chassis & cab	2503	2,069/2,849	3,370/3,810
Stepside	2504	2,173/2,693	3,790/4,230
Fleetside	2534	2,189/2,979	3,845/4,285
Stake	2509	2,264	4,000

Note: Where two prices and weights appear, the figures to the right of the slash are for K series four-wheel-drive models.

1961 models

Type	Body style number	Delivery price	Shipping weight
Prefix: R	Series: 95 (½-ton)	Max. GVW: 4,600 lb.	W.B.: 95″
(Corvair)			
Greenbrier station wagon	1206	$2,650	2,895 lb.
Corvan panel	1205	2,290	2,890
Rampside pickup	1244	2,080	2,730
Loadside pickup	1254	2,135	2,770

Prefix: C-10	Series: 1400 (½-ton)	Max. GVW: 5,400 lb.	W.B.: 115″
Chassis	1402	$1,623	2,520 lb.
Chassis & cab	1403	1,875/2,555	3,170/3,700
Stepside	1404	1,990/2,670	3,530/3,960
Fleetside	1434	2,005/2,685	3,570/4,100
Suburban (doors)	1406	2,670/3,345	4,130/4,690
Suburban (gate)	1416	2,704	4,160
Panel	1405	2,310/2,986	3,820/4,350

Prefix: C-15	Series: 1500 (½-ton)	Max. GVW: 5,600 lb.	W.B.: 127″
Chassis & cab	C1503	$1,915/2,590	3,230/3,680 lb.
Stepside	C1504	2,030/2,705	3,650/4,150
Fleetside	C1534	2,045/2,720	3,700/4,220

Prefix: C-20	Series: 2500 (¾-ton)	Max. GVW: 7,500 lb.	W.B.: 127″
Chassis & cab	C2503	2,060/2,765	3,580/3,960 lb.
Stepside	C2504	2,175/2,875	3,990/4,420
Fleetside	C2534	2,190/2,875	4,030/4,420
Stake rack	C2509	2,265	4,200

Note: Where two prices and weights appear, the figures to the right of the slash are for K series four-wheel-drive models.

1962 models

Type	Body style number	Delivery price	Shipping weight
Prefix: R series 95	(½-ton)	Max. GVW: 4,600 lb.	W.B.: 95″
(Corvair)			
Greenbrier sport wagon	R1206	$2,655	2,990 lb.

Panel	R1205	2,295	2,930
Rampside pickup	R1244	2,085	2,700
Loadside pickup	R1254	2,140	2,720

Prefix: C series 10	(½-ton)	Max. GVW: 5,200 lb.	W.B.: 115″
Chassis & cab	C1403	$1,895	3,170 lb.
Stepside	C1404	2,010	3,530
Fleetside	C1434	2,025	3,570
Panel	C1405	2,330	3,820
Suburban (doors)	C1406	2,625	4,110
Suburban (gate)	C1416	2,655	4,140

Prefix: K series 10	(½-ton)	Max. GVW: 5,600 lb.	W.B.: 115″
Chassis & cab	K1403	$2,550	3,660 lb.
Stepside	K1404	2,660	4,030
Fleetside	K1434	2,680	3,990
Panel	K1405	2,980	4,130
Carryall (doors)	K1406	3,275	4,670
Carryall (gate)	K1416	3,305	4,670

Prefix: C series 15	(½-ton)	Max. GVW: 5,200 lb.	W.B.: 127″
Chassis & cab	C1503	$1,935	3,230 lb.
Stepside	C1504	2,050	3,690
Fleetside	C1534	2,065	3,750

Prefix: K series 15	(½-ton)	Max. GVW: 5,600 lb.	W.B.: 127″
Chassis & cab	K1503	$2,585	3,660 lb.
Stepside	K1504	2,700	4,080
Fleetside	K1534	2,715	4,130

Prefix: C series 20	(¾-ton)	Max. GVW: 7,500 lb.	W.B.: 127″
Chassis & cab	C2503	$2,080	3,560 lb.
Stepside	C2504	2,196	3,990
Fleetside	C2534	2,210	4,030
Stake	C2509	2,285	4,200

Prefix: K series 20	(¾-ton)	Max. GVW: 7,600 lb.	W.B.: 127″
Chassis & cab	K2503	$2,755	3,910 lb.
Stepside	K2504	2,870	4,370
Fleetside	K2534	2,885	4,430

Note: K prefix indicates four-wheel-drive models.

1963 models

Type	Body style number	Delivery price	Shipping weight
Prefix: R series 1200	(½-ton)	Max. GVW: 4,600 lb.	W.B.: 95″
(Corvair)			
Greenbrier sport wagon	R1206	$2,655	2,990 lb.
Panel	R1205	2,212	2,910
Loadside pickup	R1254	2,136	2,785

172

Prefix: C series 10	(½-ton)	Max. GVW: 5,000 lb.	W.B.: 115″
Chassis & cab	C1403	$1,895	2,955 lb.
Stepside	C1404	2,009	3,325
Fleetside	C1434	2,025	3,370
Panel	C1405	2,326	3,585
Suburban (doors)	C1406	2,620	3,865
Suburban (gate)	C1416	2,653	3,880

Prefix: K series 10	(½-ton)	Max. GVW: 5,600 lb.	W.B.: 115″
Chassis & cab	K1403	$2,546	3,655 lb.
Stepside	K1404	2,660	4,030
Fleetside	K1434	2,676	4,080
Panel	K1405	2,977	4,320
Carryall (doors)	K1406	3,271	4,655
Carryall (gate)	K1416	3,304	4,655

Prefix: C series 15	(½-ton)	Max. GVW: 5,000 lb.	W.B.: 127″
Chassis & cab	C1503	$1,933	2,985 lb.
Stepside	C1504	2,046	3,415
Fleetside	C1534	2,062	3,460

Prefix: K series 15	(½-ton)	Max. GVW: 5,600 lb.	W.B.: 127″
Chassis & cab	K1503	$2,584	3,675 lb.
Stepside	K1504	2,697	4,130
Fleetside	K1534	2,713	4,200

Prefix: C series 20	(¾-ton)	Max. GVW: 7,500 lb.	W.B.: 127″
Chassis & cab	C2503	$2,079	3,455 lb.
Stepside	C2504	2,193	3,885
Fleetside	C2534	2,209	3,930
Stake	C2509	2,284	4,065

Prefix: K series 20	(¾-ton)	Max. GVW: 7,600 lb.	W.B.: 127″
Chassis & cab	K2503	$2,757	3,900 lb.
Stepside	K2504	2,869	4,370
Fleetside	K2534	2,885	4,430

Note: K prefix indicates four-wheel-drive models.

1964 models

Type	Body style number	Delivery price	Shipping weight
El Camino	Series: 5000 (½-ton)	Max. GVW: 4,300 lb.	W.B.: 115″
Sedan pickup	5380	$2,271	2,935 lb.
Custom sedan pickup	5580	2,352	2,935
Prefix: G series 1200	(½-ton)	Max. GVW: 5,000 lb.	W.B.: 90″
Chevyvan panel	G1205	$2,067	2,735 lb.
Prefix: R series 1200	(½-ton)	Max. GVW: 4,600 lb.	W.B.: 95″
Corvan panel	R1205	$2,212	2,800 lb.

Type	Body style number	Delivery price	Shipping weight	Production
Rampside pickup	R1254		2,136	2,665
Greenbrier sport wagon	R1206		2,666	2,990

Prefix: C series 10	(½-ton)	Max. GVW: 5,000 lb.		W.B.: 115″
Chassis & cab	C1403	$1,893	2,940 lb.	
Stepside	C1404	2,007	3,300	
Fleetside	C1434	2,023	3,330	
Panel	C1405	2,324	3,550	
Carryall (doors)	C1406	2,629	3,840	
Carryall (gate)	C1416	2,662	3,850	

Prefix: K series 10	(½-ton)	Max. GVW: 5,600 lb.		W.B.: 115″
Chassis & cab	K1403	$2,544	3,295 lb.	
Stepside	K1404	2,658	3,660	
Fleetside	K1434	2,674	3,690	
Panel	K1405	2,975	3,945	
Carryall (doors)	K1406	3,280	4,225	
Carryall (gate)	K1416	3,313	4,235	

Prefix: C series 10	(½-ton)	Max. GVW: 5,000 lb.		W.B.: 127″
Chassis & cab	C1503	$1,931	2,955 lb.	
Stepside	C1504	2,044	3,390	
Fleetside	C1534	2,060	3,435	

Prefix: K series 10	(½-ton)	Max. GVW: 5,600 lb.		W.B.: 127″
Chassis & cab	K1503	$2,582	3,370 lb.	
Stepside	K1504	2,695	3,805	
Fleetside	K1534	2,711	3,855	

Prefix: C series 20	(¾-ton)	Max. GVW: 7,500 lb.		W.B.: 127″
Chassis & cab	C2503	$2,078	3,400 lb.	
Stepside	C2504	2,192	3,830	
Fleetside	C2534	2,208	3,875	
Stake	C2509	2,283	4,020	

Prefix: K series 20	(¾-ton)	Max. GVW: 7,600 lb.		W.B.: 127″
Chassis & cab	K2503	$2,757	3,685 lb.	
Stepside	K2504	2,869	4,120	
Fleetside	K2534	2,885	4,170	

Note: K prefix indicates four-wheel-drive models.

1965 models

Type	Body style number	Delivery price	Shipping weight	Production
El Camino	Series: 13000 (½-ton)	GVW: 4,300 lb.		W.B.: 115″
Sport pickup	13380	$2,270	3,105 lb.	NA
Custom sport pickup	13580	2,355	3,105	NA
Prefix: R series 1200	(½-ton)	GVW: 4,600 lb.		W.B.: 95″
Greenbrier wagon	R1206	$2,609	2,990 lb.	NA

Prefix: G series 1200		(½-ton)	GVW: 5,000 lb.		W.B.: 90"
Chevy Van panel	G1205	$2,105	2,610 lb.	35,270
Sportvan	G1206	2,355	2,870	3,835
Custom Sportvan	G1226	2,490	2,970	1,969
Sport deluxe van	G1236	2,715	NA	1,925

Prefix: C-10 series 1400		(½-ton)	GVW: 5,000 lb.		W.B.: 115"
Chassis & cab	C1403	$1,895	2,940 lb.	4,944
Stepside	C1404	2,005	3,300	52,899
Fleetside	C1434	2,025	3,330	55,300
Panel	C1405	2,325	3,550	8,228
Carryall (doors)	C1406	2,630	3,840	4,685
Carryall (gate)	C1416	2,665	3,850	4,834

Prefix: K-10 series 1400		(½-ton)	GVW: 5,600 lb.		W.B.: 115"
Chassis & cab	K1403	$2,545	3,925 lb.	48
Stepside	K1404	2,660	3,660	1,127
Fleetside	K1434	2,675	3,690	633
Panel	K1405	2,975	3,945	103
Carryall (doors)	K1406	3,280	4,225	444
Carryall (gate)	K1416	3,315	4,235	433

Prefix: C-10 series 1500		(½-ton)	GVW: 5,000 lb.		W.B.: 127"
Chassis & cab	C1503	$1,930	2,955 lb.	1,283
Stepside	C1504	2,045	3,390	27,432
Fleetside	C1534	2,060	3,435	157,746

Prefix: K-10 series 1500		(½-ton)	GVW: 5,600 lb.		W.B.: 127"
Chassis & cab	K1503	$2,580	3,370 lb.	52
Stepside	K1504	2,695	3,805	513
Fleetside	K1534	2,710	3,855	1,459

Prefix: C-20 series 2500		(¾-ton)	GVW: 7,500 lb.		W.B.: 127"
Chassis & cab	C2503	$2,080	3,400 lb.	6,267
Stepside	C2504	2,190	3,830	9,872
Fleetside	C2534	2,210	3,875	46,608
Stake	C2509	2,285	4,020	1,505

Prefix: K-20 series 2500		(¾-ton)	GVW: 7,600 lb.		W.B.: 127"
Chassis & cab	K2503	$2,755	3,685 lb.	308
Stepside	K2504	2,870	4,170	889
Fleetside	K2534	2,885	4,120	1,364

Note: K prefix indicates four-wheel-drive trucks.

1966 models

Type	Body style number	Delivery price	Shipping weight	Production
El Camino	Series: 13000 (½-ton)	GVW: 4,300 lb.		W.B.: 115"
Sedan pickup	13380	$2,318	2,930 lb.	NA
Custom sedan pickup	13580	2,396	2,930	NA

Prefix: G series 1200		(½-ton)	GVW: 5,000 lb.		W.B.: 90″
Chevy Van panel	G1205	$2,141	2,755 lb.		28,180
Sportvan	G1206	2,388	2,965		4,209
Custom Sportvan	G1226	2,521	3,065		2,673
Sport deluxe van	G1236	2,747	3,125		2,341

Prefix: C-10 series 1400		(½-ton)	GVW: 5,000 lb.		W.B.: 115″
Chassis & cab	C1403	$1,927	2,835 lb.		3,030
Stepside	C1404	2,050	3,195		59,947
Fleetside	C1434	2,066	3,220		57,386
Panel	C1405	2,361	3,420		8,344
Carryall (doors)	C1406	2,598	3,710		6,717
Carryall (gate)	C1416	2,629	3,725		5,334

Prefix: K-10 series 1400		(½-ton)	GVW: 5,600 lb.		W.B.: 115″
Chassis & cab	K1403	$2,579	NA		40
Stepside	K1404	2,702	NA		1,123
Fleetside	K1434	2,718	NA		678
Panel	K1405	2,993	NA		170
Carryall (doors)	K1406	3,250	NA		530
Carryall (gate)	K1416	3,281	NA		418

Prefix: C-10 series 1500		(½-ton)	GVW: 5,000 lb.		W.B.: 127″
Chassis & cab	C1503	NA	NA		1,155
Stepside	C1504	$2,087	3,290 lb.		26,456
Fleetside	C1534	2,104	3,225		178,752

Prefix: K-10 series 1500		(½-ton)	GVW: 5,600 lb.		W.B.: 127″
Chassis & cab	K1503	NA	NA		30
Stepside	K1504	$2,739	NA		457
Fleetside	K1534	2,756	NA		1,976

Prefix: C-20 series 2500		(¾-ton)	GVW: 7,500 lb.		W.B.: 127″
Chassis & cab	C2503	$2,112	3,265 lb.		6,520
Stepside	C2504	2,236	3,700		9,905
Fleetside	C2534	2,252	3,700		55,855
Stake	C2509	2,358	3,890		1,499

Prefix: K-20 series 2500		(¾-ton)	GVW: 7,600 lb.		W.B.: 127″
Chassis & cab	K2503	$2,789	3,570 lb.		431
Stepside	K2504	2,913	4,005		924
Fleetside	K2534	2,929	4,005		1,796

Note: K prefix indicates four-wheel-drive trucks.

Model-year production includes all trucks built in US factories for domestic and export sale through August 8, 1966.

1967 models

Type	Body style number	Delivery price	Shipping weight	Production	(4x4s)
El Camino	Series: 13000 (½-ton)		GVW: 4,300 lb.		W.B.: 115″
Sedan pickup (V-8)	13480	$2,497	3,100 lb.	NA	
Custom sedan pickup V-8	13680	2,575	3,100	NA	
Prefix: G-10 series 11000		(½-ton)	GVW: 5,000 lb.		W.B.: 90″
Panel van	GE11005	$2,396	2,955 lb.	18,923	
Sportvan	GE11006	2,574	3,145	2,398	
Custom Sportvan	GE11026	2,709	3,245	777	
Deluxe Sportvan	GE11036	2,898	3,280	258	
Prefix: G-10 series 11000		(½-ton)	GVW: 5,000 lb.		W.B.: 108″
Panel van	GE11305	NA	NA	13,684	
Sportvan	GE11306	NA	NA	2,568	
Custom Sportvan	GE11326	NA	NA	1,608	
Deluxe Sportvan	GE11336	NA	NA	1,665	
Prefix: G-20 series 21000		(¾-ton)	GVW: 6,000 lb.		W.B.: 108″
Panel van	GE21305	$2,660	3,195 lb.	6,013	
Sportvan	GE21306	2,852	3,335	930	
Custom Sportvan	GE21326	2,987	3,440	501	
Deluxe Sportvan	GE21336	3,176	3,485	588	
Prefix: C-10 series 10700		(½-ton)	GVW: 5,000 lb.		W.B.: 115″
Chassis & cab	CE10703	$2,175	2,985 lb.	2,790	(39)
Stepside (6½ ft.)	CE10704	2,301	3,325	45,606	(1,229)
Fleetside (6½ ft.)	CE10734	2,339	3,395	43,940	(1,046)
Prefix: C-10 series 10900		(½-ton)	GVW: 5,000 lb.		W.B.: 127″
Stepside (8 ft.)	CE10904	$2,339	3,405 lb.	19,969	(500)
Fleetside (8 ft.)	CE10934	2,377	3,495	165,973	(2,715)
Panel (8 ft.)	CE10905	2,757	3,502	3,827	(30)
Suburban (8 ft.)	CE10906	2,988	3,670	5,206	(509)

Note: Add $651 and 325 pounds for K-10 four-wheel-drive models.

Type	Body style number	Delivery price	Shipping weight	Production	(4x4s)
Prefix: C-20 series 20900		(¾-ton)	GVW: 7,500 lb.		W.B.: 127″
Chassis & cab	CE20903	$2,352	3,420 lb.	6,320	(498)
Stepside (8 ft.)	CE20904	2,352	3,420	7,859	(872)
Fleetside (8 ft.)	CE20934	2,516	3,910	5,013	(2,773)
Stake (8 ft.)	CE20909	2,568	4,050	1,415	(——)
Panel	CE20905	2,897	3,917	940	(8)
Suburban	CE20906	3,124	4,093	709	(120)

Note: Add $676 and 230 pounds for K-20 four-wheel-drive models.

Note: The above figures are cumulative 1967 model-year production totals through July 31, 1967, and include all sixes and V-8s made in US plants, plus trucks imported from Canada for the US market. They do not include cowl-less-windshield configuration. Figures in parentheses at far right-hand side are additional totals for four-wheel-drive truck production.

1968 models

Type	Body style number	Delivery price	Shipping weight	Production	(4x4s)
El Camino	Series: 13000 (½-ton)		GVW: 4,300 lb.		W.B.: 115″
Sedan pickup	13480	$2,613	3,193 lb.	NA	
Custom sedan pickup	13680	2,694	3,210	NA	
Prefix: G-10 series 11000		(½-ton)	GVW: 3,900 lb.		W.B.: 90″
Panel	GE11005	$2,458	3,005 lb.	18,617	
Sportvan	GE11006	2,634	3,191	2,153	
Custom Sportvan	GE11026	2,758	3,295	685	
Deluxe Sportvan	GE11036	2,945	3,331	403	
Prefix: G-10 series 11300		(½-ton)	GVW: 5,000 lb.		W.B.: 108″
Panel	GE11305	NA	NA	17,569	
Sportvan	GE11306	NA	NA	2,961	
Custom Sportvan	GE11326	NA	NA	2,158	
Deluxe Sportvan	GE11336	NA	NA	1,881	
Prefix: G-20 series 21300		(¾-ton)	GVW: 6,200 lb.		W.B.: 108″
Panel	GE21305	$2,737	3,262 lb.	5,504	
Sportvan	GE21306	2,904	3,390	715	
Custom Sportvan	GE21326	3,028	3,514	325	
Deluxe Sportvan	GE21336	3,215	3,558	383	
Prefix: C-10 series 10700		(½-ton)	GVW: 4,400 lb.		W.B.: 115″
Chassis & cab	CE10703	$2,320	3,048 lb.	2,735	(43)
Stepside	CE10704	2,430	3,389	46,322	(1,706)
Fleetside	CE10734	2,468	3,467	46,483	(1,449)
Prefix: C-10 series 10900		(½-ton)	GVW: 5,400 lb.		W.B.: 127″
Stepside	CE10904	$2,468	3,477 lb.	18,632	(552)
Fleetside	CE10934	2,506	3,572	204,236	(3,625)
Panel	CE10905	2,839	3,641	4,801	(59)
Suburban	CE10906	3,081	3,809	11,004	(1,143)
Prefix: C-20 series 20900		(¾-ton)	GVW: 7,500 lb.		W.B.: 127″
Chassis & cab	CE20903	$2,499	3,458 lb.	6,636	(498)
Stepside	CE20904	2,610	3,865	7,666	(1,047)
Fleetside	CE20934	2,647	3,960	60,646	(4,705)
Stake	CE20909	2,702	4,085	1,103	
Panel	CE20905	2,981	4,035	1,572	(68)
Suburban	CE20906	3,264	4,217	1,573	(299)
Prefix: C-20 series 21000		(¾-ton)	GVW: 7,500 lb.		W.B.: 133″
Fleetside	CE21034	$2,711	NA	1,902	

Note: The production figures listed above are model-year totals through Aug. 1, 1968, and include all Chevrolet trucks built in US factories (including export units). Totals in parentheses at far right are for four-wheel-drive trucks.

1969 models

Type	Body style number	Delivery price	Shipping weight	Production	(4x4s)
El Camino	Series: 13000 (½-ton)		GVW: 4,300 lb.		W.B.: 116″
Pickup (6-cyl.)	13380	$2,550	3,192 lb.	NA	
Custom pickup (6-cyl.)	13580	2,630	3,219	NA	
Pickup (V-8)	13480	2,640	3,320	NA	
Custom pickup (V-8)	13680	2,725	3,352	NA	
Prefix: G-10 series GS11000		(½-ton)	GVW: 3,900 lb.		W.B.: 90″
Standard van	GS11006	$2,680	3,208 lb.	1,730	
Custom van	GS11026	2,805	3,311	526	
Deluxe van	GS11036	3,000	3,347	270	
Chevy Van	GS11005	2,410	3,021	18,456	
Prefix: G-10 series GS11300		(½-ton)	GVW: 5,000 lb.		W.B.: 108″
Standard van	GS11306	$2,810	3,316 lb.	3,065	
Custom van	GS11326	2,935	3,439	2,598	
Deluxe van	GS11336	3,125	3,483	1,758	
Chevy Van	GS11305	2,595	3,189	20,730	
Prefix: G-20 series GS21300		(¾-ton)	GVW: 6,200 lb.		W.B.: 108″
Standard van	GS21306	$2,930	3,414 lb.	625	
Custom van	GS21326	3,055	3,538	382	
Deluxe van	GS21336	3,245	3,582	306	
Chevy Van	GS21305	2,670	3,281	6,030	
Prefix: K-5 Blazer	Series 10500 (½-ton)		GVW: 5,000 lb.		W.B.: 104″
Utility pickup (4x4)	KS10514	$2,850	3,708 lb.	NA	(4,935)
Prefix: C-10 series CS10700		(½-ton)	GVW: 4,400 lb.		W.B.: 115″
Chassis & cab	CS10703	$2,285	3,076 lb.	2,343	(58)
Stepside	CS10704	2,400	3,417	49,147	(1,698)
Fleetside	CS10734	2,435	3,495	54,211	(1,849)
Prefix: C-10 series CS10900		(½-ton)	GVW: 5,000 lb.		W.B.: 127″
Chassis & cab	CS10903	$2,325	3,097 lb.	1,230	(35)
Stepside	CS10904	2,435	3,507	18,179	(521)
Fleetside	CS10934	2,475	3,602	268,233	(4,937)
Panel	CS10905	2,865	3,672	5,492	
Suburban (doors)	CS10906	3,100	3,844	7,263	(697)
Suburban (gate)	CS10916	3,131	3,847	6,793	(730)

Note: Add $650 for K-10 four-wheel-drive trucks in half-ton series above.

Type	Body style number	Delivery price	Shipping weight	Production	(4x4s)
Prefix: C-20 series CS20900		(¾-ton)	GVW: 7,500 lb.		W.B.: 127″
Chassis & cab	CS20903	$2,520	3,508 lb.	8,440	(556)
Stepside	CS20904	2,625	3,915	8,090	(1,071)
Fleetside	CS20934	2,665	4,010	74,894	(6,124)
Panel	CS20905	3,075	4,091	1,779	
Suburban (doors)	CS20906	3,350	4,267	1,649	(289)

Type	Body style number	Delivery price	Shipping weight	Production	(4x4s)
Suburban (gate)	CS20916	3,385	4,271	1,087	(256)

Note: Add $680 for K-20 four-wheel-drive trucks in three-quarter-ton series above

Prefix: C-20 series CS21000		(¾-ton)	GVW: 7,500 lb.		W.B.: 133″
Fleetside	CS21034	$2,736	4,037 lb.	8,797	

Note: Totals above are for model-year 1969 through December 31, 1969, and include all trucks made in US plants, plus imports from Canada. Production totals in parentheses at far right-hand column are for four-wheel-drive models.

1970 models

Type	Body style number	Delivery price	Shipping weight	Production	(4x4s)
El Camino	Series: 13000 (½-ton)		GVW: 4,100 lb.		W.B.: 116″
Pickup (6-cyl.)	13380	$2,675	3,302 lb.	NA	
Custom pickup (6-cyl.)	13580	2,760	3,384	NA	
Pickup (V-8)	13480	2,770	3,418	NA	
Custom pickup (V-8)	13680	2,850	3,442	NA	
Prefix: G-10 series GS11000		(½-ton)	GVW: 3,900 lb.		W.B.: 90″
Sportvan	GS11006	$2,725	3,255 lb.	277	
Custom Sportvan	GS11026	2,850	3,362	57	
Deluxe Sportvan	GS11036	3,035	3,400	42	
Chevy Van	GS11005	2,490	3,059	3,933	
Prefix: G-10 series GS11300		(½-ton)	GVW: 5,000 lb.		W.B.: 108″
Sportvan	GS11306	$2,850	3,350 lb.	422	
Custom Sportvan	GS11326	2,975	3,480	303	
Deluxe Sportvan	GS11336	3,100	3,425	158	
Chevy Van	GS11305	2,675	3,210	3,069	
Prefix: G-20 series GS21300		(¾-ton)	GVW: 6,200 lb.		W.B.: 108″
Sportvan	GS21306	$2,970	3,414 lb.	134	
Custom Sportvan	GS21326	3,095	3,538	61	
Deluxe Sportvan	GS21336	3,280	3,582	45	
Chevy Van	GS21305	2,745	3,281	1,195	
Prefix: C-5 Blazer	Series 10500 (½-ton)		GVW: 5,000 lb.		W.B.: 104″
Utility (4x2)	CS10514	$2,385	3,375 lb.	985	
Prefix: K-5 Blazer	Series 10500 (½-ton)		GVW: 5,000 lb.		W.B.: 104″
Utility (4x4)	KS10514	$2,955	3,677 lb.	NA	(11,527)
Prefix: C-10 series 10700		(½-ton)	GVW: 4,400 lb.		W.B.: 115″
Chassis & cab	CS10703	$2,405	3,090 lb.	2,084	(64)
Stepside	CS10704	2,520	3,426	31,353	(1,629)
Fleetside	CS10734	2,560	3,506	40,754	(2,554)
Prefix: C-10 series 10900		(½-ton)	GVW: 5,000 lb.		W.B.: 127″
Chassis & cab	CS10903	$2,445	3,107 lb.	913	(26)
Stepside	CS10904	2,560	3,510	11,857	(464)

Type	Body style number	Delivery price	Shipping weight	Production	(4x4s)
Fleetside	CS10934	2,595	3,605	234,904	(7,348)
Panel	CS10905	3,040	3,730	3,965	
Suburban (doors)	CS10906	3,250	3,862	5,927	(926)
Suburban (gate)	CS10916	3,280	3,870	5,405	(951)

Note: Add $570 for K-10 four-wheel-drive trucks on 115" or 127" wheelbase

Prefix: C-20 series 20900		(¾-ton)	GVW: 7,500 lb.		W.B.: 127"
Chassis & cab	CS20903	$2,650	3,496 lb.	7,277	(582)
Stepside	CS20904	2,750	3,896	5,856	(953)
Fleetside	CS20934	2,790	3,991	70,880	(8,355)
Panel	CS20905	3,270	4,123	1,032	
Suburban (doors)	CS20906	3,440	4,245	1,344	(287)
Suburban (gate)	CS20916	3,475	4,253	880	(254)

Note: Add $705 for K-20 four-wheel-drive trucks; 127" wheelbase only

Prefix: C-20 series CS21000		(¾-ton)	GVW: 7,500 lb.		W.B.: 133"
Longhorn	CS21034	$2,951	4,034 lb.	5,281	

Note: Production figures are for model-year 1970, through August 31, 1970, and include total units built in US factories, plus imports from Canada. Far right-hand column shows four-wheel-drive truck production in parentheses for models available with this option.

1971 models

Type	Body style number	Delivery price	Shipping weight	Production	(4x4s)
Vega Panel Express	Series: 14100 (½-ton)		GVW: 3,500 lb.		W.B.: 97"
Panel express (4-cyl.)	K14105	$2,286	2,152 lb.	58,800	
El Camino	Series: 13000 (½-ton)		GVW: 3,500 lb.		W.B.: 116"
Pickup (6-cyl.)	13380	$2,886	3,302 lb.	NA	
Pickup (V-8)	13480	2,983	3,418	NA	
Custom pickup (V-8)	13680	3,069	3,442	NA	
Blazer C-5 series C10500		(½-ton)	GVW: 4,000 lb.		W.B.: 104"
Utility (4x2)	CS10514	$2,659	3,375 lb.	1,277	
Blazer K-5 series G10500		(½-ton)	GVW: 5,000 lb.		W.B.: 104"
Utility (4x4)	KS10514	$3,234	3,677 lb.	NA	(1,846)
Prefix: G-10 series 11300		(½-ton)	GVW: 5,100 lb.		W.B.: 110"
Sportvan	GS11006	$3,304	3,694 lb.	1,846	
Chevy Van	GS11005	2,881	3,460	15,012	
Beauville (V-8)	GE11036	3,738	3,936	481	
Prefix: G-10 series G11300		(½-ton)	GVW: 5,100 lb.		W.B.: 125"
Sportvan	GS11306	$3,552	3,995 lb.	2,011	
Chevy Van	GS11305	3,010	3,615	15,013	
Beauville (V-8)	GE11336	3,865	4,136	1,146	
Prefix: G-20 series GS21100		(¾-ton)	GVW: 5,200 lb.		W.B.: 110"
Sportvan	GS21006	$3,350	3,761 lb.	1,774	

181

Type	Body style number	Delivery price	Shipping weight	Production	(4x4s)
Chevy Van	GS21005	2,976	3,489	5,901	
Beauville (V-8)	GE21036	3,817	4,094	345	
Prefix: G-20 series G21300	(¾-ton)		GVW: 6,100 lb.		W.B.: 125″
Sportvan	GS21306	$3,477	3,929 lb.	2,796	
Chevy Van	GS21305	3,105	3,653	14,027	
Beauville (V-8)	GE21336	3,943	4,296	3,568	
Prefix: C-10 series 10700	(½-ton)		GVW: 4,400 lb.		W.B.: 115″
Chassis & cab	CS10703	$2,656	3,090 lb.	1,476	
Stepside	CS10704	2,816	3,426	19,041	(1,438)
Fleetside	CS10734	2,816	3,506	32,865	(3,068)
Prefix: C-10 series 10900	(½-ton)		GVW: 5,800 lb.		W.B.: 127″
Chassis & cab	CS10903	$2,689	3,107 lb.	588	
Stepside	CS10904	2,854	3,510	7,269	(364)
Fleetside	CS10934	2,854	3,605	206,313	(9,417)
Suburban (doors)	CS10906	3,599	3,862	4,550	(631)
Suburban (gate)	CS10916	3,631	3,870	5,395	(994)

Note: Add $570 for K-10 four-wheel-drives on 115″ or 127″ wheelbase

Type	Body style number	Delivery price	Shipping weight	Production	(4x4s)
Prefix: C-20 series 20900	(¾-ton)		GVW: 6,200 lb.		W.B.: 127″
Chassis & cab	CS10903	$2,897	3,496 lb.	4,523	(509)
Stepside	CS20904	3,058	3,896	3,523	(674)
Fleetside	CS20934	3,058	3,991	62,465	(10,006)
Suburban (doors)	CS20906	3,760	4,245	1,343	(256)
Suburban (gate)	CS20916	3,791	4,253	1,203	(353)

Note: Add $680 for K-20 four-wheel-drives on 127″ wheelbase

Type	Body style number	Delivery price	Shipping weight	Production	(4x4s)
Prefix: C-20 series 21000	(¾-ton)		GVW: 6,700 lb.		W.B.: 133″
Fleetside	CS21034	$3,236	4,090 lb.	3,331	

Note: Production figures are for model-year 1971, through August 31, 1971, and include total units built in US factories, plus imports from Canada. Far right-hand column shows four-wheel-drive truck production in parentheses for models available with this option.

1972 models

Type	Body style number	Delivery price	Shipping weight	Production	(4x4s)
LUV mini-pickup series 82	(½-ton)		GVW: 3,950 lb.		W.B.: 102.4″
Pickup	82	$2,196	2,360 lb.	21,098	
Vega Panel Express series 14100	(½-ton)		GVW: 3,290 lb.		W.B.: 97″
Panel express	15150	$2,080	2,152 lb.	4,114	
El Camino series 13000	(½-ton)		GVW: 4,690 lb.		W.B.: 116″
Sedan pickup (6-cyl.)	13380	$2,790	3,302 lb.	NA	
Sedan pickup (V-8)	13480	2,880	3,418	NA	
Custom sedan pickup (V-8)	13680	2,960	3,442	NA	

Blazer C-5 series 10514		(½-ton)	GVW: 4,400 lb.		W.B.: 104″
Utility (6-cyl)	10514	$2,585	3,375 lb.	487	
Utility (V-8)	10514	2,700	3,506	2,870	
Blazer K-5 series 10514		(½-ton)	GVW: 5,000 lb.		W.B.: 104″
Utility (6-cyl.)	10514	$3,145	3,677 lb.	NA	(1,071)
Utility (V-8)	10514	3,260	3,807	NA	(43,195)
Prefix G, series 11000		(½-ton)	GVW: 4,100 lb.		W.B.: 110″
Chevy Van	GS11005	$2,775	3,460 lb.	12,205	
Sportvan	GS11006	3,285	3,694	1,346	
Beauville (V-8)	GE11036	3,685	3,936	433	
Prefix G, series 11300		(½-ton)	GVW: 5,100 lb.		W.B.: 125″
Chevy Van	GS11305	$2,910	3,615 lb.	14,044	
Sportvan	GS11306	3,410	3,856	1,593	
Beauville (V-8)	GE11336	3,805	4,136	997	
Prefix G, series 21000		(¾-ton)	GVW: 5,200 lb.		W.B.: 110″
Chevy Van	GS21005	$2,890	3,489 lb.	4,618	
Sportvan	GS21006	3,335	3,761	605	
Beauville (V-8)	GE21036	3,760	4,094	345	
Prefix G, series 21300		(¾-ton)	GVW: 6,100 lb.		W.B.: 125″
Chevy Van	GS21305	$3,020	3,653 lb.	16,084	
Sportvan	GS21306	3,460	3,929	3,310	
Beauville (V-8)	GE21336	3,880	4,296	5,581	
Prefix C, series 10700		(½-ton)	GVW: 4,400 lb.		W.B.: 115″
Chassis & cab	CS10703	$2,530	3,090 lb.	1,640	
Stepside	CS10704	2,680	3,426	22,042	(1,736)
Fleetside	CS10734	2,680	3,506	39,730	(6,069)
Prefix C, series 10900		(½-ton)	GVW: 7,000 lb.		W.B.: 127″
Chassis & cab	CS10903	$2,560	3,107 lb.	717	
Stepside	CS10904	2,715	3,510	7,538	(407)
Fleetside	CS10934	2,715	3,605	273,249	(18,431)
Suburban (doors)	CS10906	3,495	3,862	6,748	(991)
Suburban (gate)	CS10916	3,525	3,870	10,757	(2,145)

Note: Add $575 for K-10 four-wheel-drives on 115″ or 127″ wheelbase

Prefix C, series 20900		(¾-ton)	GVW: 7,500 lb.		W.B.: 127″
Chassis & cab	CS20903	$2,760	3,496 lb.	5,974	(676)
Stepside	CS20904	2,915	3,896	3,973	(755)
Fleetside	CS20934	2,915	3,991	94,458	(19,648)
Suburban (doors)	CS20906	3,650	4,245	2,136	(503)
Suburban (gate)	CS20916	3,680	4,253	3,141	(879)
Prefix C, series 21000		(¾-ton)	GVW: 7,600 lb.		W.B.: 133″
Longhorn pickup (V-8)	CE21034	$3,088	3,950 lb.	3,328	

Note: Add $660 for K-20 four-wheel-drive on 127″ wheelbase only

Information department

As a collector of pickups or other types of light-duty Chevy trucks, you'll need parts for your vehicles, special restoration tools and sources of hobby information. You may also want to join a club.

Listed here are some 100 suppliers of parts, services and literature, a number of tool companies, hobby magazines and books. Where appropriate, the listing contains the company name and address. Most also indicate the firms' area of specialization in relation to what they sell or what types of trucks they cover.

Some of these companies market their wares primarily at flea markets or swap meets. Others have walk-in counter stores or sell via mail-order catalogs.

When contacting these sources initially, it is always a good idea to include a self-addressed stamped envelope (SASE), which they can use to reply to you. In some cases, the cost of purchasing a catalog will be refunded the first time you place an order.

Although more than 100 businesses are listed here, there are dozens of others you may be dealing with later. Therefore, it's a good idea to keep your own notebook in which you can add additional sources to this list as time goes by. A handy way to do this is to purchase a business card book, which is a looseleaf with plastic pages containing pockets designed to hold the business cards that you may pick up at shows.

Parts

Arizona
Grumpy's Truck Parts
Box 4721
New River Stage
Phoenix, AZ 85029
  General parts

Jeff's Customs
5432 Royal Palm
Tucson, AZ 85705
  Reproduction sun visors for 1955–59
Chevy trucks

Arkansas
B & T Truck Parts
P.O. Box 799
Siloam Springs, AR 72761
  General parts, new, used and reproduction; catalog

Heavy Chevy Truck Parts
P.O. Box 650
Siloam Springs, AR 72761
  General parts and books; catalog

David Stewman Company
Rt. 4, #2 Steven Ln.
Mena, AR 71953
  General parts 1947–54 Chevy trucks;
free catalog

Williamson's Speedometer
Rt. 1, Box 18, Highway 282
Chester, AR 72934
  Speedometer and clock repairs

California
Automotive Obsolete
1023 E. 4th St.
Santa Ana, CA 92701
  General parts, 1946–1964 models;
catalog

Bob's Trucks
11033 Woodside
Santee, CA 92071
  Hubcaps; parts list

Egge Machine Company
8403 Allport Ave.
Santa Fe Springs, CA 90670
  General mechanical parts; wiring harnesses; engine rebuilding

Faxon's Auto Literature
13955 E. Sixth St.
Corona, CA 91719
  Truck sales literature and service manuals

The Filling Station
6929 Power Inn Rd.
Sacramento, CA 95828
  Reproduction rubber, interior, brake & suspension parts; catalog

Golden State Pickup Parts
618 E. Gutierrez St.
Santa Barbara, CA 93103
  General parts, books, rubber parts; catalogs and guides

Bob Johnson GMC, Inc.
2699 Atlantic Ave.
Long Beach, CA 90806
  Parts and Service

Just Dashes, Inc.
5945 Hazeltine Ave.
Van Nuys, CA 91401
  Vinyl dashboard restoration

Lucas Automotive
2850 Temple Ave.
Long Beach, CA 90806
  Antique truck tires

A. Petrik
1006½ Tujunga Canyon
Tujunga, CA 91042
  Huck brake parts; 1946-1950 Chevy trucks

Professional Steering Wheel Service
1137 E. Mission
Fallbrook, CA 92028
  Steering wheel restoration

Redi Strip
9910 Jordon Cir.
P.O. Box 2745
Santa Fe Springs, CA 90670
  Nationwide paint stripping services

Y n Z's Yesterdays Parts
1615 W. Fern Ave.
Redlands, CA 92373
  Reproduction wiring harnesses 1946-1954 Chevy trucks

Colorado
Cruise-in Style Vintage Trucks
P.O. Box 29716
Thornton, CO 80229
  General parts

Bruce Whitt
2940 Rondalee
Grand Junction, CO 81503
  Used body parts for 1955-1959 Chevy trucks

Connecticut
Auto Body Specialties, Inc.
Rt. 66, Box 455
Middlefield, CT 06455
  Body parts for 1967-1972 Chevy trucks; catalog

Glasco
85 James St.
East Hartford, CT 06108
  Flat window glass for 1940s to 1950s models

PRO Antique Auto Parts
50 King Spring Rd.
Windsor Locks, CT 06096
  General parts

Florida
Banter's Chevrolet Parts
5904 Trouble Creek Rd.
New Port Richey, FL 33552
  Trim parts and floor mats 1947-1966 models

Georgia
Classic Chevy Truck Parts
6363 Pineview Ter.
Riverdale, GA 30296
  NOS body and trim parts; dash pads for 1967-1972 models

Fiberglass & Wood Company
Rt. 3, Box 800
Nashville, GA 31639
  General parts; catalog

Obsolete Chevrolet Parts Company
524 Hazel Ave., P.O. Box 68
Nashville, GA 31639
  NOS and reproduction mechanical parts; 1946-1972 models

Don Sumner/The Truck Shop
P.O. Box 5035
102½ W. Marion Ave.
Nashville, GA 31639
  General parts and books; catalog

Illinois
Bruce Falk
1105 Nicholson
Joliet, IL 60435
  General parts 1949-1954 models

Willies Antique Tires
5257 W. Diversey Ave.
Chicago, IL 60639
  Antique truck tires

Indiana
Agape Auto Parts
2825 Selzer
Evansville, IN 47712
  Fender skirts 1946-1972 trucks

Iowa
Iowa Glass Depot
P.O. Box 122
Cedar Rapids, IA 52406
  Obsolete window glass

Kansas
Chevy Parts
Box 936
Greensburg, KS 67054
  NOS and used chassis, frame, running gear parts and cabs for 1946-1954 trucks

Junior's
122 W. 6th
Quinter, KS 67752
  Used body parts

Kent Zook
121 W. Grant St.
Greensburg, KS 67054
  Used parts 1946-1959 models

Kentucky
O. B. Smith
P.O. Box 11703
Lexington, KY 40577
  Reprinted factory manuals

Massachusetts
Antique Auto Parts Cellar
P.O. Box 3
South Weymouth, MA 02190
  Fuel pump parts and repair kits

Auto Book Center, Inc.
48 Appleton
Auburn, MA 01501
  Original and reproduction factory manuals for trucks

Clark's Corvair Parts
Shelburne Falls, MA 01370
  Corvair parts and parts for Corvan and Greenbrier models

Roberts Motor Parts
17 Prospect St.
West Newbury, MA 01985
    General parts for trucks 1946–1970;
catalog

Michigan
Burchill Antique Auto Parts
4150 24th Ave. (M25 N.)
Port Huron, MI 48060
    General parts 1947–1954 models

Gary's Plastic Chrome Plating
39312 Dillingham
Westland, MI 48185
    Plastic parts plating service

Lawrence Auto Body
306 W. Grand River
Brighton, MI 48116
    Reproduction fiberglass fenders

Northwestern Auto Supply
1101 S. Division Ave.
Grand Rapids, MI 49507
    Mechanical parts

Radios & Wheel Covers
2718 Koper Dr.
Sterling Heights, MI 48310
    Original wheel covers; radio rebuilding service

Sherman & Associates
27940 Groesbeck Hwy.
Roseville, MI 48066
    Reproduction body panels

Douglas Vogel
1100 Shady Oaks
Ann Arbor, MI 48103
    Original sales literature

Minnesota
John Dragich Discount Auto Literature
1500 93rd Ln. N.E.
Minneapolis, MN 55434
    Original and reproduction literature

Bruce Horkey Cabinetry
R.R. 4, Box 188
Windom, MN 56101
    Bed strips and bolt sets 1947–1972
models; catalog

Metro Molded Parts, Inc.
11650 Jay St.
P.O. Box 33130
Minneapolis, MN 55433
    Reproduction rubber parts

Missouri
The Carburetor Shop
Rt. 1, Box 230-A
Eldon, MO 65026
    Carburetors

Jim Carter
1500 E. Alton
Independence, MO 64055
    General parts; 74¢ stamp for catalog

Chevy Duty Pickup Parts
4600 N.W. 52nd St.
Kansas City, MO 64151
    General parts, rubber, interior,
mechanical parts, books, trim, catalog

Kelsey Tire, Inc.
Box 564
Camdenton, MO 65020
    Antique truck tires

New Jersey
Stan Coleman, Inc.
Box 1235
Morristown, NJ 07960
    Rust prevention supplies

Bill Hirsch
396 Littleton Ave.
Newark, NJ 07103
    Paint; engine paint

Kanter Auto Products
76 Monroe St.
Boonton, NJ 07005
    Suspension kits; truck carpets

Harold Lauritano
584 Otterhole Rd.
West Milford, NJ 07480
    Cameo pickup parts; list for SASE

RS Auto Parts
P.O. Box 101
Mendham, NJ 07945
    NOS and rechromed bumpers

Stallion Auto Trim
509 Hurffville Rd.
Turnersville, NJ 08012
    Reconditioned body parts 1948–1953 models

New York
David Ficken
Box 11
Babylon, NY 11702
    Trico windshield wiper parts and
tune-up kits

Walter A. Miller
6710 Brooklawn
Syracuse, NY 13211
    Original sales and service literature

The Restoration Station
990 Westbury Rd.
Westbury, NY 11590
    Carpeting for 1953–1972 models;
free catalog

North Carolina
Dixie Truck Works
9233 Sandburg Ave.
Charlotte, NC 28213
    Emblems; catalog

The Oldie Goldie Shop
Rt. 1, Box 124
Elm City, NC 27822
    General parts for 1947–1959 models

Gerald Phillips
5101 Mockingbird Rd.
Greensboro, NC 27406
    Fender skirts for 1960–1972 models

Lynn H. Steele
1601 Hwy. 150E
Denver, NC 28037
    Reproduction rubber parts

Ohio
Seckman's Antique Radio
5340 Sandra Dr.
Ravenna, OH 44266
    Rebuilt radios

Oklahoma
Bill Cooper
4921 S. Birch
Broken Arrow, OK 74011
    General parts 1947–1954; send
SASE for list

Steve Davis
3909 Cashion Pl.
Oklahoma City, OK 73112
   Monthly newsletter for 1967–1972 trucks; NOS and used body and trim parts

Mar-K Specialized Manufacturing Co.
8022 N. Wilshire Court
Oklahoma City, OK 73132
   Reproduction bed panels, sides and sills

Tom Meyers
525 15th Pl. S.W.
Miami, OK 74354
   NOS and used body parts

Reynolds Head & Block Repair
2632 E. 13th Pl.
Tulsa, OK 74104
   Casting repairs

Oregon
Dan's Classic
40 S.E. 28th
Portland, OR 97214
   NOS parts for 1955–1959 trucks

High Country Classic Parts
P.O. Box 5792
Bend, OR 97708
   General parts for 1947-1966 trucks; catalog

Springfield Auto Recyclers
P.O. Box 127
Springfield, OR 97477
   Axle repair kits for pickups

Pennsylvania
Applegate & Applegate
Box 1
Annville, PA 17003
   Literature and factory photos

Crank 'N Hope Publications
450 E. Maple
Blairesville, PA 15717
   Books and reproduction literature

Newcastle Battery Co.
P.O. Box 5040
New Castle, PA 16105
   Reproductions of authentic-type batteries

Restoration Specialties and Supply, Inc.
P.O. Box 328
Windber, PA 15963
   Restoration hardware and fasteners

Universal Tire Company
987 Stony Battery Rd.
Lancaster, PA 17601
   Antique truck tires

South Carolina
All Chevrolet Parts
1981 South Lake Dr.
Lexington, SC 29072
   NOS tailgates for 1954–1972 pickups

Radiator Works
1981 South Lake Dr.
Lexington, SC 29072
   Radiators for 1946–1972 Chevy trucks

Tennessee
Coker Tire Company
1317 Chestnut St.
Chattanoga, TN 37407
   Antique truck tires

The Truck Shop
604 West Ave. N.
Crossville, TN 38555
   New and used parts for 1967–1972 trucks

B.J. Wilkinson
3161 Dothan
Memphis, TN 38118
   NOS parts for Chevy pickups

Texas
Jay Katelle
3721 Farwell
Amarillo, TX 79109
   Sales literature and postcards

Mooney's Antique Parts
Star Route Box 645C
Goodrich, TX 77335
   Body parts for 1947–1954 trucks; free catalog

Mr. G's Rechromed Plastic
5613 Elliott Reader Rd.
Ft. Worth, TX 76117
   Rechroming plastic parts

Old Chevy Trucks
3014 Dedman
Pasadena, TX 77503
   NOS, new, used and reproduction parts 1947–1966 models

Terrill Machine Inc.
Rt. 2, Box 61
DeLeon, TX 76444
   Mechanical parts for Chevys, including pickups

Virginia
Chewning's Auto Literature Ltd.
Box 727
Broadway, VA 22815
   Original literature

Glenn Pace
1495 Oakland
Richmond, VA 23231
   NOS parts 1941–1960 models

Washington
Chevys of the '40s
18409 N.E. 28th St.
Vancouver, WA 98662
   Mechanical and exhaust system parts; catalog

Jim Ellis
4143 Gunderson Rd. N.E.
Poulsbo, WA 98370
   Steering wheel restoration

Northwest Modern Classics
Box 5486
Kent, WA 98064
   Interior parts, rubber mats and carpets for 1947-1972 Chevy trucks

RB's Obsolete Automotive
7130 Bickford Ave.
Snohomish, WA 98290
   General parts; catalog

Vintage Auto Parts
24300 Hwy. 9
Woodinville, WA 98072
   NOS parts; catalog

Wisconsin
Instrument Services, Inc.
433 S. Arch St.
Janesville, WI 53545
   Authorized clock repair

Canada
Glassworks
P.O. Box 700, Hwy. 50 S.
Boulton, Ontario, Canada L0P 1A0
   New, used and reproduction steel and fiberglass body parts

Special tools

Whether you are completely restoring your Chevrolet light-duty truck by yourself or having it professionally restored, you will want to have a set of high-quality mechanic's tools such as those readily available from companies such as Sears Craftsman brand, Snap-On Tool Corporation or Proto Tool Company. These tools will come in handy for both disassembly and reassembly work, as well as for regular servicing and maintenance that the finished vehicle will require.

In addition to these standard tools, if you are handling some or all of the restoration work yourself, you may want to invest in a number of special tools custom-manufactured for restorers. These range from special body-shaping tools and lead body-filler supplies to stainless steel restoration kits and sandblasting equipment.

Listed below are the addresses and phone numbers of four companies that supply such tools. They will be happy to send product brochures or catalogs covering the items that they sell for vintage vehicle restorers.

C & D Products Co.
Rt. 8, Box 93
Piedmont, SC 29673
   Stainless steel buffing and restoration supplies and tools

The Eastwood Company
147 Pennsylvania Ave.
Box 296
Malvern, PA 19355
   Specialized restoration tools; catalog

Hoosier Distributing Company
3009 W. Sample St.
South Bend, IN 46619
   Pneumatic power tools and body tools

TIP Sandblasting Equipment Co.
7075 Rt. 446, P.O. Box 649
Canfield, OH 44406
   Body refinishing tools and sandblasting equipment

Literature

There are dozens of very informative hobby magazines available to old car and truck hobbyists. The following are some of the publications that regularly publish articles about older light-duty trucks and carry classified and display advertising that old truck enthusiasts will find helpful.

Antique Toy World
4419 Irving Park Rd.
Chicago, IL 60641
  Toy collecting

Car Exchange
P.O. Box 7050
Lakeland, FL 33807
  Concentrates on postwar models; mainly articles

Car Review
P.O. Box 7157
Lakeland, FL 33807
  Stories on 1960s and 1970s trucks and cars

Cars & Parts
P.O. Box 482
Sidney, OH 45367
  Carries articles and advertising for old cars and trucks

Collectible Automobile
3841 Oakton St.
Skokie, IL 60076
  Carries a regular column on collectible commercial vehicles

Collector Marketplace
Sharpe Publications
1550 Territorial Rd.
Benton Harbor, MI 49022
  Toy collecting

Hemmings Motor News
Box 100
Bennington, VT 05201
  A monthly magazine containing 100% advertising for old vehicles and parts for them

McElwee's Small Motor News
40 Fornof Ln.
Pittsburgh, PA 15212
  Toy collecting

New England Model & Toy Collector Catalog
30A Pilgrim Dr.
Northhampton, MA 01060
  Toy collecting

Old Cars Price Guide
700 E. State St.
Iola, WI 54990
  A bimonthly magazine containing "ballpark prices" for 80,000 vintage cars and trucks in five different graded conditions

Old Cars Weekly
700 E. State St.
Iola, WI 54990
  A weekly tabloid newspaper containing stories and ads for old vehicles and parts; 75% advertising; write for free sample copy

Special Interest Autos
Box 196
Bennington, VT 05201
  Bimonthly magazine; usually has an article on old trucks

Super Chevy
12301 Wilshire Blvd.
Los Angeles, CA 90025
  A monthly magazine with information for Chevy buffs

Truckin'
2145 W. LaPalma Ave.
Anaheim, CA 92801-1785
  A monthly magazine on all kinds of trucks, stock and modified

Trucks
20 Waterside Plaza
New York, NY 10010-2615
  A monthly magazine mainly for truck drivers; includes some material on vintage light-duty trucks

Here are some books that I highly recommend including in your Chevrolet pickup truck library:

75 Years of Chevrolet by George Dammann

The Standard Catalog of American Light-Duty Trucks by John Gunnell

Chevy Spotter's Guide 1920–1980 by Tad Burness

Automobile Sheet Metal Repair by Robert L. Sargent

El Camino: A Source Book by Edward A. Lehwald

Pickup & Van Spotter's Guide 1945–1982 by Tad Burness

American Truck & Bus Spotter's Guide 1920–1985 by Tad Burness

Auction companies

Bay Cities Collector Car Auction
29900 Auction Way
Hayward, CA 94544

Rick Cole Auctioneers
10701 Riverside Dr.
No. Hollywood, CA 91602

Kruse International
P.O. Box 190
Auburn, IN 46706

McLeod Auction
213 Lake St. S.
Kirkland, WA 98033

Spectrum Vehicle Auctions
18000 Devonshire St.
Northridge, CA 91325

Von Reece Auctioneers
6605 Live Oak Dr.
Austin, TX 78746

Charleston Auctioneers
5936 E. State Blvd.
Ft. Wayne, IN 46815

Brooks Motors Co.
186 E. Nacogdoches St.
New Braunfels, TX 78130

Hudson & Marshall
717 North Ave.
Macon, GA 31298

Clubs

Chevy truck clubs

Northeast Chevy/GMC Trucking Club
P.O. Box 155
Millers Falls, MA 10349

General truck clubs

American Truck Historical Society
Saunders Building
P.O. Box 59200
Birmingham, AL 35259

Antique Truck Club of America
P.O. Box 291
Hershey, PA 17033

Light Commercial Vehicle Association
Rt. 14, Box 468
Jonesboro, TN 37659

National Panel Delivery Club
4002½ Hermitage Rd.
Richmond, VA 23227

Antique Truck Club of New England
280 W. First St.
South Boston, MA 02062

South Hill Independent Truckers
15908 79th Ave.
East Puyallup, WA 98373

California Association of 4WD Clubs
5831 Rosebud Ln., Unit M-1
Sacramento, CA 95841

Chevy clubs (cars and trucks)

Classic Chevy Club International
(1955-1957)
P.O. Box 17188
Orlando, FL 32860

Vintage Chevrolet Club of America
P.O. Box 5387
Orange, CA 92667

Late Great Chevy Club (1958-1964)
P.O. Box 17824
Orlando, Fl 32860

Corvair Society of America (Corvans)
2506 Gross Point Rd.
Evanston, IL 60201

National Chevelle Owners Association
(El Camino)
P.O. Box 5014
Greensboro, NC 27435

Ultra Van Club (Corvair Motorhome)
1199 Dunsyre
Lafayette, CA 94549

General car and truck clubs

Antique Automobile Club of America
501 West Governor Rd.
Hershey, PA 17033

Contemporary Historical Vehicle
Association
P.O. Box 40
Antioch, TN 37013

Horseless Carriage Club of America
P.O. Box 1050
Temple City, CA 91780

Veteran Motor Car Club of America
18840 Pearl Rd.
P.O. Box 36788
Strongsville, OH 44136